JUDICIOUS CHOICES

The New Politics of Supreme Court Confirmations

SECOND EDITION

MARK SILVERSTEIN

W. W. Norton & Company · New York · London

W. W. Norton & Company has been independent since its founding in 1923, when William Warder Norton and Mary D. Herter Norton first published lectures delivered at the People's Institute, the adult education division of New York City's Cooper Union. The Nortons soon expanded their program beyond the Institute, publishing books by celebrated academics from America and abroad. By mid-century, the two major pillars of Norton's publishing program—trade books and college texts—were firmly established. In the 1950s, the Norton family transferred control of the company to its employees, and today—with a staff of four hundred and a comparable number of trade, college, and professional titles published each year—W. W. Norton & Company stands as the largest and oldest publishing house owned wholly by its employees.

Printed in the United States of America.

The text of this book is composed in Palatino.

Composition by Matrix.

Book design by Roy Tedoff.

Manufacturing by R. R. Donnelley & Sons—Haddon Division.

Production manager: Benjamin Reynolds.

ISBN 978-0-393-93044-3

W. W. Norton & Company, Inc., 500 Fifth Avenue, New York, N.Y. 10110-0017

www.wwnorton.com

W. W. Norton & Company Ltd., Castle House, 75/76 Wells Street, London W1T 3QT

1 2 3 4 5 6 7 8 9 0

To Aline, as always

CONTENTS

PREFACE TO THE SECOND EDITION   vii

INTRODUCTION: A NEW POLITICS
OF JUDICIAL CONFIRMATIONS   1

Chapter 1
THE AGONY OF ABE FORTAS   9

The Best Lawyer in America   9
Fortas on Trial   17
Abe Fortas and the New Politics of Judicial Confirmations   28

Chapter 2
THE JUDICIARY: THE CHANGING
NATURE OF JUDICIAL POWER   33

The Crisis of the Old Order   34
The New Deal and a New Judicial Liberalism   41
The Warren Court   49
The Burger Court   65

Chapter 3
THE DEMOCRATS: THE COMING
OF THE NEW PROGRESSIVES   85

The Demise of the New Deal Coalition   85

The New Progressives and the Judiciary   96
The New Progressives in the Republican Era   101
A Democrat in the White House   110

Chapter 4
THE REPUBLICANS: THE ASCENDANCY
OF THE NEW RIGHT   126

The Rise of the New Republican Majority   127
Capitalists and Fundamentalists   135
Republican Armageddon   152

Chapter 5
THE SENATE: FROM MEN'S CLUB
TO PUBLICITY MACHINE   159

The Senate at Midcentury   160
The Modern Senate   173
The Modern Politics of Judicial Confirmation   182

Chapter 6
THE SECOND BUSH PRESIDENCY:
IDEOLOGY AND CONFRONTATION   194

The War on Terror   195
The Senate on the Brink   200
A New Supreme Court   211

CONCLUSION: THE DEMOCRATIZATION
OF THE CONFIRMATION PROCESS   220

INDEX   231

PREFACE TO
THE SECOND EDITION

The first edition of *Judicious Choices* appeared in 1994 and coincided with the appointments of Justices Ginsburg and Breyer. In the ensuing years I often considered the possibility of a second edition but thought it prudent to await the next appointment to the Court. It turned out to be a very long wait. Although the membership on the Court remained stable for the next eleven years, the political forces that I tried to explain in the first edition continued to shape confirmation politics into the twenty-first century. They found immediate expression, however, in the appointment of Court of Appeals judges. In the first edition I considered the very occasional flap over a Court of Appeals appointment to be simply an aberration that nonetheless served to underscore how appointments to the federal judiciary had assumed significance to a far greater range of interests than ever before in modern American history. In retrospect, I probably underestimated the depth and breadth of the political changes chronicled in the first edition. In 1994 it was simply unthinkable that appointments to the lower federal courts could bring the U.S. Senate to the brink of implosion. By 2006, of course, the unthinkable had become almost commonplace. Thus, even in the absence of a defining and riveting Supreme Court confirmation battle, the politics of appointment and confirmation continued to evolve. When Justice O'Connor announced her retirement in 2005, it seemed that the appropriate moment to revisit the new politics of Supreme Court confirmations had arrived.

The focus of the second edition remains the same as that of the first; this is not a history of contemporary confirmation battles, but instead, an effort to understand the broader politics of judicial appointment and confirmation. In addition to generally updating material from the first edition and including a new chapter on the administration of George W. Bush, I have also expanded on some themes that I touched on in the first edition, but which now, with the aid of perfect hindsight, I feel deserve more attention. For example, in the first edition, my discussion of the Warren Court was principally directed at how that Court's willingness to entertain novel claims brought by a wide range of litigants had the unintended consequence of altering the process of appointing and confirming federal judges. I have now come to appreciate the extent to which the Warren Court has evolved into an icon of the 1960s and, as such, provides both the political left and right with a convenient symbol in the continual struggle to form the debate over the nature of judicial power and rally the faithful for the next confirmation battle. Hence I have reworked my discussion of the Warren Court to reflect this additional understanding.

On a personal note, I had not anticipated the extent to which revisiting one's prior work forces an author to face up to the misstatements and misinterpretations that were so confidently set on paper decades earlier. I hope I have corrected most, or at least the worst, of my errors of fact and judgment. However, the process of confronting my own blunders has not in any way altered my conviction that the study of how we choose our most important judges is significant beyond the worthy goal of learning more about the American judiciary. It provides a fascinating snapshot of the American political system at work, and I hope this new edition remains faithful to both of these endeavors.

Judicious Choices

INTRODUCTION: A NEW POLITICS OF JUDICIAL CONFIRMATIONS

In January of 1932, Justice Oliver Wendell Holmes, at the age of ninety-two, announced his retirement from the Supreme Court, after thirty years of distinguished service. Among the names quickly surfacing as a possible replacement for the legendary Holmes was Benjamin Cardozo, a Democrat and the respected chief judge of the New York Court of Appeals. During his years on New York's highest state court, Cardozo had established a national reputation as a progressive jurist and as author of the classic *The Nature of the Judicial Process*.[1] The nomination of Cardozo, however, presented President Herbert Hoover with several difficulties. The president was facing the prospect of a tough reelection battle, and the choice of a Democrat was certain to anger many in Hoover's Republican party. Cardozo's appointment, moreover, would bring a third New Yorker and a second Jew to the Court. One did not have to be an anti-Semite to maintain that the president might rightfully seek greater diversity on the Court. Finally, Cardozo's reputation as a progressive was firmly established, and there was little doubt that he would join with Brandeis and Stone on the "liberal" wing of the Court. In

---

1. One measure of Cardozo's influence may lie in the fact that *The Nature of the Judicial Process*, first published in 1921, sold over 170,000 copies through 1989 and continues to be found on the reading list in undergraduate and law school classes studying the process of judicial decision making.

sum, there was precious little political gain for Hoover in a Cardozo appointment.

Politics aside, however, there was much to recommend Cardozo. The stature of the nominee was of paramount importance. Cardozo was a highly distinguished jurist, and Hoover was conscious of the potential ignominy in being remembered by history as the president who filled the Holmes seat on the Court with an unknown. Although a Republican, Hoover was inclined to name a Democrat, if only to be faithful to his personal belief that appointments to the Court must be nonpartisan. Prior to making a final decision, Hoover received a visit from Senator William Borah, the powerful Republican senator from Idaho. Borah championed Cardozo as the best candidate regardless of residence, religion, or party affiliation and strongly hinted to Hoover that the Senate would resist unknown candidates on the grounds of "obscurity." Cardozo's nomination followed almost immediately, and he cleared the Senate without dissent or discussion. A few days later Hoover wrote a prominent Republican that the choice of Cardozo "was a difficult matter from many points of view. It contains more political liabilities than assets but I felt that I must disregard such questions."[2]

To the modern student of American politics, the story of Cardozo's appointment to the Court must appear as a wondrous fable of a land far away and a time long ago. It is difficult, if not impossible, to imagine prominent members of one political party today championing the nomination of a member of the opposition to the Supreme Court, and the notion that a president might be constrained to seek only nominees of stature and prominence is simply too fanciful to be seriously entertained. That a Democratic nominee with the long public career and the controversial publications of Cardozo could be nominated by a Republican

---

2. Quoted in Andrew Kaufman, *Cardozo* (Cambridge, MA: Harvard Univ. Press, 1998), 467. Much of the material concerning the Cardozo appointment is drawn from Professor Kaufman's book.

president and confirmed by a voice vote of a Republican-controlled Senate, all within a period of ten days, is itself beyond modern comprehension.

Equally startling, perhaps, is the fact that from the turn of the century through 1967, only one nominee—John J. Parker in 1930—out of a total of forty-three failed to gain Senate approval. The defeat of Parker, in spite of Republican control of both the White House and the Senate, came as a surprise and in a sense was a product of the same forces that produced the famous Court-packing controversy seven years later. Liberal Democrats and progressive Republicans, frustrated with a conservative Supreme Court that often denied the elected branches the constitutional authority to regulate capital, joined forces with labor and the NAACP to deny Parker confirmation.[3] Fourteen years earlier, in 1916, the nomination of Louis Brandeis had produced a bitter and far more divisive confirmation battle. The business community, united against the famous "people's attorney," mounted a furious four-month campaign to deny confirmation, based in large measure on Brandeis's "radical" beliefs on the distribution of wealth in America. Seven former presidents of the American Bar Association signed a public statement proclaiming Brandeis "unfit" to sit on the Supreme Court. Beneath the surface of the debate over political and judicial philosophy lay a virulent strain of anti-Semitism. Nonetheless, despite this most determined opposition, Brandeis was eventually confirmed by a rather comfortable margin.

The defeat of Parker and the bitter battle over Brandeis represented the extraordinary; for almost seventy years the confirmation process was distinguished by a strong presumption in

---

3. Three months earlier, Charles Evans Hughes had been confirmed as chief justice with a surprising amount of opposition because of his links with Wall Street. Parker was a far weaker candidate for the Court, and his civil rights record galvanized the opposition of the NAACP. For an interesting study asserting that the defeat of Parker was an important stage in the development of the NAACP, see Kenneth Goings, *The NAACP Comes of Age: The Defeat of Judge John J. Parker* (Bloomington: Indiana Univ. Press, 1990).

favor of deference to presidential prerogative to fill vacancies on the Supreme Court.[4] A president could be expected to seek counsel from diverse sources both in and out of government, and part of the process might at times require behind-the-scenes deals to guarantee the necessary support of key Senate elders. As long, however, as the nominee exhibited a basic level of competence and his political views fit within the narrow confines of acceptable American political discourse (which is why interests seeking to deny confirmation to nominees as different as Louis Brandeis and Robert Bork inevitably characterize the nominee as "radical"), the president's choice was typically confirmed by a voice vote, with no opposition on record. From 1945 through 1967 not one nominee excited the opposition of even one-fifth of the Senate, and, when a recorded vote was taken, the opposition was token, averaging a mere twelve votes.

In 1968 the politics of judicial confirmations underwent an abrupt transformation, and the presumption respecting presidential control was honored more in the breach than in the observance. The failure of the Senate to confirm Abe Fortas in 1968 as chief justice was quickly followed by the defeats of Clement Haynsworth and G. Harrold Carswell. In 1987 the controversial Robert Bork was denied confirmation in proceedings that captured wide public attention. Before the Bork defeat President Reagan had elevated William Rehnquist to the chief justiceship, but only after factious hearings and even though the new chief justice received more negative votes than any other successful nominee in the twentieth century. Rehnquist held this dubious record for a mere five years, when it was shattered by the confirmation of Clarence Thomas in proceedings that stunned a nation. In 2005,

---

4. This presumption did not exist in the nineteenth century, when one out of every three nominees to the Court was rejected by the Senate. With senators appointed by state legislatures—the Seventeenth Amendment was ratified in 1913—powerful state party leaders were often sent to the Senate to funnel patronage back to the party organization. In an age of relatively strong party politics, simple partisan political considerations undercut any notion of deference to presidential appointments to the Court.

President George W. Bush's nomination of Harriet Miers was undone by potent opposition within his own party, and the eventual nominee, Samuel Alito, received forty-two negative votes.

The principal genre for the study of judicial confirmations has been the case study. The selection of a Supreme Court justice often gives rise to weighty political drama and has generated, particularly in recent years, a fair share of insider accounts.[5] This micro-analysis of the confirmation process reveals a wealth of valuable detail about a single nomination and, perhaps more significantly, enables the student of American government to gain important insight into the strategy and tactics of key actors in the process. At the same time, the case study may focus the reader's attention too narrowly, resulting in an unfortunate failure to appreciate the wonders of the forest while concentrating attention on a single, albeit dazzling, tree. The tension of the battle over Robert Bork, for example, or the wretched spectacle of the Clarence Thomas hearings focused our attention, but perhaps at the expense of the larger picture. The Bork and Thomas battles, I believe, cannot be considered as simply grotesque abnormalities in the traditional, business-as-usual model of judicial confirmations but instead must be examined in context as vivid examples of the evolution in the way we select and confirm

---

5. Consider the following, hardly exhaustive, sample of studies of the Bork confirmation battle, including a notation on the author's relationship to the proceedings: Paul Simon (senator and member of the Judiciary Committee), *Advice and Consent: Clarence Thomas, Robert Bork and the Intriguing History of the Supreme Court's Nomination Battles* (Washington, DC: National Press Books, 1992); Mark Gitenstein (the former chief counsel to the Judiciary Committee), *Matters of Principle: An Insider's Account of America's Rejection of Robert Bork's Nomination to the Supreme Court* (New York: Simon & Schuster, 1992); Patrick McGuigan and Dawn Weyrich (New Right activists supporting the nomination), *Ninth Justice: The Fight for Bork* (Washington, DC: Free Congress, 1990); Robert Bork (the nominee), *The Tempting of America: The Political Seduction of the Law* (New York: Simon & Schuster, 1990); Michael Pertschuk and Wendy Schaetzel (liberal activists opposing the nomination), *The People Rising: The Campaign against the Bork Nomination* (New York: Thunder's Mouth Press, 1989); Ethan Bronner (reporter covering the Supreme Court for the *Boston Globe*), *Battle for Justice: How the Bork Nomination Shook America* (New York: Norton, 1989).

Supreme Court justices. Hence the intent of this book is to provide the reader with an appreciation of the evolving political and legal contexts in which the transition from the politics of acquiescence to the politics of confrontation has taken place.

The current process is disorderly, contentious, and unpredictable. In short, it is now a thoroughly democratic process, and the increased public participation in the selection of federal judges and Supreme Court justices is a consequence of profound changes in American politics and institutions. The most important development is the heightened activism of the modern federal judiciary.[6] Whether one welcomes or laments the "imperial judiciary," scholars are in rare accord in their assessment that in the last forty years the federal courts have exercised greater control over the affairs of the citizenry than previously and that the modern Supreme Court is distinguished by its readiness to strike down the acts of elected bodies.[7] Even quantifying the increasing will-

6. When scholars speak of the "modern" judiciary, particularly the Supreme Court, they are typically referring to the Court from the New Deal to the present. I prefer a more narrow definition. In my view the "modern" era of the Supreme Court and the rest of the federal judiciary begins in 1962, with the retirement of Justice Felix Frankfurter and the decision in *Baker* v. *Carr*, 369 U.S. 186 (1962). See chapter 2 for the logic underlying this conclusion.

7. The phrase "imperial judiciary" comes from the title of Nathan Glazer's oft-quoted critique of judicial activism. See Glazer, "Towards an Imperial Judiciary?" *Public Interest* (Fall 1975): 104. For a more sympathetic treatment see Abram Chayes, "The Role of the Judge in Public Law Litigation," *Harvard Law Review* 89 (1976): 1281. "Since 1960, the Supreme Court has been striking down laws passed by Congress and the president at an average of two a year, more than double the rate of the earlier part of this century and four times the rate since 1790. The work of state and local lawmakers has fallen at a much faster rate: The Court has invalidated an average of seventeen state and local laws each year since 1960, more than four times the rate during all of the Court's previous history." David Adamany, "The Supreme Court," in John Gates and Charles Johnson, eds., *The American Courts: A Critical Assessment* (Washington, DC: CQ Press, 1991), 23. See also David O'Brien, *Storm Center: The Supreme Court in American Politics*, 2d ed. (New York: Norton, 1990), 60–61; Gregory Caldeira and Donald McCrone, "Of Time and Judicial Activism: A Study of the U.S. Supreme Court, 1800–1973," in Stephen Halpern and Charles Lamb, eds., *Supreme Court Activism and Restraint* (Lexington, MA: Lexington Books, 1982). Consider also Thomas M. Keck, *The Most Activist Supreme Court in History: The Road to Modern Judicial Conservatism* (Chicago: Univ. of Chicago Press, 2004).

ingness to exercise the power of judicial review fails to capture fully the extent of the changing judicial role. Since the early 1960s the federal courts have dramatically relaxed the strict rules that made access difficult and often precluded classes of issues from being raised in a federal judicial forum. Problems that only a generation or two ago would have been considered unfit for judicial resolution are now frequent subjects of litigation. Hand in hand with the disposition to entertain novel claims made by a wide range of litigants, the modern judiciary has fashioned a multitude of innovative forms of judicial relief designed to ensure compliance with court decrees by recalcitrant governmental officials. Over the last thirty years the federal judiciary has evolved to the point where it can provide litigants with relief previously available only through the executive or legislative branches.

The nature of judicial power was transformed at a time when the coalitions governing America were in a state of flux. In chapter 3, I attempt to show how the demise of the New Deal coalition increased the importance of the federal judiciary to powerful elements in the Democratic party. Chapter 4, in turn, details how promises to recast the Supreme Court through the appointment process were a critical factor in the resurgence of the Republican party at the national level. Without a stable governing coalition, policymaking by the judiciary becomes a more pronounced feature of American politics, producing substantial conflict over the staffing of the federal courts. The impact of these developments is further magnified by changes taking place in the U.S. Senate. The "advice and consent" of the Senate is, of course, the deciding event in the confirmation of a federal judge, and chapter 5 describes the transformation of that body from a hierarchical, inner-directed chamber into a more responsive and effective institution for the articulation of group interests.

The reader is forewarned that this is not a history of contemporary confirmations to the Supreme Court. Although chapter 1 introduces the modern confirmation process by briefly relating the tale of Abe Fortas, extended discussion of the battle over Abe Fortas or even the more recent, startling proceedings on the nominations of Robert Bork and Clarence Thomas is best left to case studies or general histories of appointments to the Supreme Court. The aim of this volume is to develop a greater understanding of the political and legal forces that shape the selection of nominees to the Court and the process of their confirmation.

Chapter 1

THE AGONY OF ABE FORTAS

The defeat of Robert Bork's nomination to the Supreme Court in 1987 was a bitter pill for conservatives to swallow. Possessor of perhaps the most impressive résumé of any nominee since Felix Frankfurter in 1939, Bork was an outspoken critic of modern judicial activism, and his appointment, it was thought, would mark the crowning achievement in the Republican effort to transform the Supreme Court. In the months following the failed appointment, Bork toured the country. Speaking before various conservative and business groups, he asserted that his defeat was the result of the "first all-out political campaign" directed at a nominee to the Supreme Court. Conservative columnists expressed similar sentiments in the editorial pages of the nation. The Right added a new word to our political lexicon to express its displeasure: To be "Borked" was to have one's writings and opinions wrenched out of context in a well-organized campaign by opposing interests. Conservatives were unanimous in their conclusion that Bork was the first nominee in modern history denied a seat on the Court for ideological reasons. They were quite wrong in this assertion. Less than twenty years earlier, in 1968, another extraordinarily qualified nominee had fallen victim to the modern ordeal of confirmation.

THE BEST LAWYER IN AMERICA

An Extraordinary Year

In the year 1968, the world appeared to turn upside down. The anguish of the Robert Kennedy and Martin Luther King assassinations merged with the searing images of the terror of the Tet offensive, the conflagration of America's urban ghettos, the drama of the Prague Spring, the turmoil of the May events in France, and the police riot at the Chicago Democratic National Convention to produce an overwhelming sensation that the center could not possibly hold. The chasm between black and white, young and old, hawk and dove, simply appeared too great. In the same year that Dr. Benjamin Spock, the author of the best-selling *The Common Sense Book of Baby and Child Care*, was convicted of conspiring to counsel evasion of the draft, Richard Nixon arose from the dustbin of political history to become the president of the United States. Campuses from Columbia University in New York to Nihon University in Tokyo were in open revolt. Even the once tranquil world of amateur sport could not escape the politics of confrontation; the most enduring portrait of the times remains that of a defiantly clenched fist raised in a black-power salute above an Olympic awards podium.

During a time of cataclysmic events, the merely extraordinary ones often escape attention. In June of 1968, as the nation buried another Kennedy, Chief Justice Earl Warren informed President Lyndon Johnson of his plan to retire after fourteen years on the Supreme Court. Johnson quickly formulated a strategy to elevate his friend and confidant Associate Justice Abe Fortas to the chief justiceship. The president would fail in this endeavor. Johnson's fabled mastery and control of the legislative process evaporated in an astonishing series of events, culminating in the Senate's refusal to end debate on the Fortas confirmation and in the president's subsequent withdrawal of the nomination. Within weeks of the Fortas disaster, Richard Nixon made the Warren Court a central issue in his campaign for the presidency, castigating the justices for "weakening the peace forces against the criminal forces" in American society and promising upon election to bring to the Court "strict constructionists" who would presumably redress the imbalance in constitutional decision making. The theme resonated throughout the Nixon campaign; in effect, the Republican candidate for the presidency ran against both his Democratic opponent and the U.S. Supreme Court.

The summer and fall of 1968 thus marked a pivotal moment in the history not only of the nation but of the Supreme Court as well. The Senate's failure to confirm Fortas was itself a remarkable event. Only once before in the twentieth century had the Senate blocked a nominee to the high court, and, although Johnson was a lame-duck president, there was little to suggest that the master of congressional relations would be thwarted in his attempt to name a new chief justice. Nor was Fortas an unknown outsider; only three years earlier, in a simple voice vote, the Senate had confirmed him as associate justice. The tawdry financial dealings that led to his resignation from the Court the following year were still, for the most part, hidden from public view. To even the most skeptical observer of the American political scene, the nomination of Fortas must have appeared a sure thing. To the astute observer, however, the Senate's failure to confirm signaled an important shift not only in the process of appointing Supreme Court justices but in the very nature of American politics.

"Get Me Abe Fortas"

In 1939 Lyndon Johnson arrived in the House of Representatives with his eyes on the real prize, the U.S. Senate. He first sought a Senate seat in 1941 when he challenged Texas Governor Pappy ("Pass the Biscuits") O'Daniel for the Democratic nomination. With 96 percent of the primary vote counted, Johnson held a substantial lead. When the final vote was tallied, however, Pappy had miraculously received in a few rural counties enough votes to secure the nomination.[1] Seven years later O'Daniel decided not

---

1. In 1941 the South and Texas were still solidly Democratic; a triumph in the Democratic primary thereby assured the successful candidate victory in the following general election. Two excellent, recent biographies of Abe Fortas are now available. See Laura Kalman, *Abe Fortas: A Biography* (New Haven: Yale Univ. Press, 1990); Bruce Murphy, *Fortas: The Rise and Ruin of a Supreme Court Justice* (New York: Morrow, 1988). Together with Robert Shogan's *A Question of Judgment: The Fortas Case and the Struggle for the Supreme Court* (Indianapolis: Bobbs-Merrill, 1972), they provide the factual basis for much of this chapter.

to seek reelection, and Johnson squared off against the current governor, Coke Stevenson, for the nomination. As the vote was counted, it appeared that Stevenson was the victor by a razor-thin margin of 114 votes. But in yet another Texas electoral miracle, 202 previously uncounted votes were found in a single ballot box in Jim Wells County. That all the newly discovered votes were for Johnson and in the same handwriting and ink raised some eyebrows, but the fact was that Johnson now had the nomination by 87 votes.

Alleging fraud, Coke Stevenson turned to the federal district court to secure an injunction preventing Johnson's name from appearing on the November ballot. Johnson turned to Abe Fortas. They had first met in 1939, Johnson a young congressman with a vision of providing his constituents electricity and flood control by means of a series of dams on the Colorado River and Fortas the brilliant general counsel to the Public Works Administration. In the following years they had become fast friends, each in effect recognizing the extraordinary talent that the other brought to his chosen career. In this moment of crisis, as Lyndon Johnson saw his dream of entering the Senate being snatched away, he called on Fortas. And Fortas did not disappoint his old friend. Working under intense time pressure, Fortas maneuvered the case before Supreme Court Justice Hugo Black, who, in his capacity as circuit justice for the Fifth Circuit, vacated the stay, thus enabling Johnson to run as the Democratic candidate in the general election. From that moment on, Johnson regarded Fortas, in the words of one of his biographers, as "the best lawyer he had ever known."[2]

Others shared that opinion. Editor in chief of the *Yale Law Review*, Fortas was offered a teaching position at Yale Law School upon graduation in 1933 and for six years commuted between New Haven and Washington, D.C., where he held several posi-

---

2. Kalman, *Abe Fortas*, 202. From that moment on, in honor of his victory over Stevenson, Johnson was to be known in Texas as Landslide Lyndon.

tions as one of Roosevelt's most devoted New Deal lawyers. In 1938 he resigned from Yale to work full-time with his mentor William O. Douglas at the Securities and Exchange Commission. When Douglas was nominated to the Supreme Court in 1939, Fortas went over to the Department of Interior to work with Secretary Harold Ickes, eventually rising to the position of undersecretary. Following Roosevelt's death in 1945, Fortas left the public service to establish with his friend Thurman Arnold the law firm of Arnold & Fortas. The firm quickly became the model Washington law firm and Fortas the quintessential Washington lawyer. The general assessment in the legal community was that Fortas ranked among the most talented lawyers of his generation. He did not use that talent solely in the service of the rich and powerful. His commitment to public-interest law was legendary; during the 1950s his firm waged a continuing legal battle against McCarthyism, and in the 1960s Fortas's pro bono representation of Clarence Earl Gideon before the U.S. Supreme Court produced one of the Warren Court's most acclaimed decisions.[3] And through it all, he remained friend, confidant, and adviser to Lyndon B. Johnson.

Mr. Justice Fortas

When Lyndon Johnson took the oath of office following the assassination of John F. Kennedy in November 1963, the life of Abe Fortas underwent an abrupt transformation. During LBJ's unhappy stint as vice president, Fortas remained his personal lawyer but had little to do with matters of high policy at the White House. In the initial months of the Johnson presidency, however, Fortas was in daily contact with the new president. Although he continued in private law practice, Fortas was Johnson's most trusted adviser, directly consulted and involved in every major political

---

3. *Gideon v. Wainwright*, 372 U.S. 335 (1963), establishing a right to counsel for indigent defendants in felony cases. See also Anthony Lewis, *Gideon's Trumpet* (New York: Vintage, 1964).

decision.[4] Johnson planned to make his friend a part of the administration; when Attorney General Robert Kennedy resigned during the summer of 1964 to run for a U.S. Senate seat, Johnson pressured Fortas to head the Justice Department. Fortas declined, asserting among other things that accepting an official position in the cabinet would limit the reach of services he could provide the president. Lyndon Johnson, however, was not a man who was easily denied. During the summer of 1965, when news reached the president that United Nations Ambassador Adlai Stevenson had died, Johnson persuaded Justice Arthur Goldberg to leave the Court and assume the post. To replace Goldberg, Johnson thought only of his friend Abe Fortas.

Johnson's initial task was to talk Fortas into taking the job. In 1965 Abe Fortas was at the top of his profession. His law firm—Arnold, Fortas, and Porter—was flourishing, and his income (when combined with that of his wife, Carolyn Agger, a partner in the firm) was over $300,000, a spectacular sum in 1965. His lifestyle was grand, and, as a private citizen, he could serve the president while maintaining his professional independence. A seat on the Supreme Court was a temptation, but Fortas, at least outwardly, resisted and initially turned the offer down. Later Johnson enjoyed recounting how he subsequently invited Fortas to the White House to be present for an important announcement concerning troop buildups in Vietnam. On the way to the press conference, the president told Fortas he also was about to announce his nomination to the Court. Johnson conceded that Fortas was, of course, free to refuse to attend the conference, but if thousands of young men could sacrifice for their country in

---

4. "There seemed to be no subject beyond Fortas's competence. He spoke about foreign policy with Ambassador W. Averell Harriman, disagreed with the Treasury Department over a plan to have banks pay interest on government deposits, suggested a way to present a planned Defense Department cost-consciousness program to the press, and drafted a six-point memo filled with mathematical calculations on how to reduce the funds required for foreign aid appropriations by subsidizing loans from the Export-Import Bank." Murphy, *Fortas*, 126.

Vietnam, Fortas could do so by leaving private practice and taking the position on the Court. Fortas could hardly refuse. When Herblock, the famed *Washington Post* political cartoonist, turned his attention to the Fortas nomination, he chose to depict the new justice with his arm being twisted.[5]

The confirmation proceedings went like clockwork, a reminder of how confirmations had once worked. Lyndon Johnson's Great Society appeared to have revived the New Deal coalition, and, with liberalism the order of the day, neither Democrat nor Republican perceived any electoral gain from a serious challenge to the nominee. The activism of the Warren Court had not yet reached its zenith, and the impact of expanding the reach of judicial power was still unclear. The desegregation decisions notwithstanding, appointments to the Court, for all their importance, were not matters of political life and death to a host of powerful group interests. The Senate, though in the midst of change, still functioned in its post–World War II mode, and, when the leadership accepted Abe Fortas without objection, the nomination was, for all intents and purposes, a done deal. At the Judiciary Committee hearings Fortas minimized his relationship with LBJ (there were a few grumbles about the president's appointing one of his "cronies"), and when some witnesses contended that Fortas had been too sympathetic to Communism in the 1930s, even the more conservative members of the committee rose in his defense.[6] A unanimous committee vote of approval came after less than three hours of hearings. Within two weeks of the formal nomination, the full Senate confirmed the new justice with a simple voice vote. From the perspective of the 1990s, a truly remarkable event had taken place: Abe Fortas, a friend of the president, a lifelong liberal and advocate of progressive politics, a

5. See Kalman, *Abe Fortas*, 240–48. As Professor Kalman notes, this version of the nomination, recounted by both Fortas and Johnson, makes for a classic political tale. In reality, the appointment was not only expected but also welcomed, although Fortas did have some qualms about the timing.

6. See Shogan, *Question of Judgment*, 113–17.

champion of civil rights, a controversial defender of the weak and unpopular during the McCarthy era, had been confirmed justice of the Senate Court without a single dissenting vote.

He would remain on the Court for a mere four years. During this brief tenure his was a consistent vote to safeguard the rights of the accused and to support the cause of the weak and downtrodden. In Fortas's view the judiciary was charged with the primary task of protecting individual rights, and he resolutely defended civil liberties. Justice Fortas, however, was not easily typecast as a "Warren Court liberal." He often, for instance, joined with the conservative members of the Court in defending business interests, narrowly interpreting the power of government to regulate and chiding his liberal colleagues for failing to appreciate the "real world" of business and finance. In short, Justice Fortas was in the unusual position of being at times the darling of both the American Civil Liberties Union and the *Wall Street Journal*.

After his rise to the high court, Fortas continued to serve the needs of two clients. One was Pablo Casals. Fortas had represented the famous cellist since the mid-1950s, negotiating among other things Casals's historic concert at the Kennedy White House. Casals was over ninety years of age when Fortas came to the Supreme Court, and Fortas made it quite clear that he was not inclined to attempt to explain to the aged musician that he could no longer act as his attorney.[7] His other client was the president of the United States. Lyndon Johnson simply could not do without his most trusted adviser, and as the Vietnam War and its political fallout ravaged both his domestic programs and his foreign policies, he continually sought Fortas's advice. Justice Fortas's involvement with the Johnson administration was far-reaching, ranging from active participation in the management of the Vietnam War to service as presidential speechwriter. Although both Johnson and Fortas sought to hide this arrange-

7. Ibid., 293.

ment from public scrutiny, throughout the latter years of the Johnson presidency Washington was buzzing with rumors of the dual role played by Fortas. The rumors actually understated the reality; from the moment of his appointment to the Court, Fortas was an official member of the judicial branch and an unofficial, but terribly significant, member of the executive branch.[8]

On March 31, 1968, Johnson announced that he would not seek another term as president. The war in Vietnam and the war at home had destroyed his presidency. Two weeks before Johnson's announcement, Earl Warren celebrated his seventy-seventh birthday; though in good health, he had spent over fifty years in the public service and now understandably might have anticipated retirement and leisure time away from the pressures of public life. But his decision to retire in the summer of 1968 was also the product of careful political calculation. Johnson's decision not to seek another term, combined with the general disarray of the Democratic party, virtually guaranteed a Republican victory in the fall. By announcing his retirement during the remaining months of the Johnson presidency, Warren believed he had made certain that LBJ, and not Richard Nixon, would name the new chief justice. The fact that Warren anticipated that Johnson would choose Abe Fortas for the post made the decision to retire that much easier.[9]

FORTAS ON TRIAL

A Few Whales and Many Minnows

No one understood the Senate quite as well as Lyndon Johnson did. In the brief span of his two terms in office, the senator from Texas had made a lasting mark on the institution, and his instinc-

8. The extent of Justice Fortas's connection with the Johnson administration is amply documented by his biographers. See ibid., chap. 14; Murphy, *Fortas*, chap. 10.

9. G. Edward White, *Earl Warren: A Public Life* (New York: Oxford Univ. Press, 1982), 306–13, describes Warren's thinking with respect to his retirement.

tive feel for the legislative process and the human side of the Senate became the stuff of legends.[10] The move to the vice presidency
and then to the White House did not diminish his legislative
genius; Johnson's parliamentary skills, as well as the sheer force
of his personality in one-on-one confrontations, were augmented
by the aura of the presidency. During his years as president, Johnson's mastery of the legislative process dazzled even his most
jaded critics. The legislative record of the Johnson presidency was
remarkable: The Civil Rights Act of 1964, the Voting Rights Act
of 1965, the Economic Opportunity Act, Medicare, comprehensive federal aid to education, and a host of redevelopment programs for economically ailing areas formed merely the tip of the
Johnson legislative iceberg. The period of achievement was brief,
but for several years in the mid-1960s Lyndon Johnson could lay
claim to being the most effective president in modern American
history. And no small measure of that success was owing to his
understanding of the Senate.

Thus in June of 1968, when Johnson learned of Earl Warren's
decision to retire as chief justice, he immediately plotted a strategy to elevate Abe Fortas to the post. In formulating a plan of
action, Johnson relied on his extensive knowledge of the ways of
the Senate. In his view, the Senate consisted of a few "whales"
and many "minnows." The conventional wisdom held that in any
battle in the Senate (particularly in securing its advice and consent on appointments), the president had to negotiate only with
the appropriate whales. Once the consent of the powerful had
been secured, the remainder of the Senate would fall into line. In
the case of Fortas, there were two crucial whales. To guarantee

10. Senator J. William Fulbright: "When Lyndon was majority leader he was a
master at managing the Senate and at reconciling people with diametrically opposed
views. Nobody could match him. He knew every personal interest of every member
of the Senate just like he knew the palm of his hand. He knew how to bring people
together, because he could appeal to their different interests. If he asked Harry Byrd
to do something, he always knew what it was that Harry wanted in return." Quoted
in Merle Miller, *Lyndon: An Oral Biography* (New York: Putnam, 1980), 175.

success and to control sufficient votes to end a possible filibuster, Johnson felt he needed the support of either the Dixiecrats—the conservative bloc of southern Democrats who often balked at Johnson's Great Society legislative program—or several Republicans. He courted Richard Russell, the senior senator from Georgia, to secure the Dixiecrat vote. To balance the unpredictability of these southern Democrats, Johnson also sought Republican support from the minority leader, Everett Dirksen of Illinois.

During his years as majority leader, Johnson had often worked closely with Dirksen, and, when LBJ became president, Dirksen had provided needed Republican votes to break a southern filibuster and secure passage of the Civil Rights Act of 1964. Dirksen's aid never came cheap; for his backing of Fortas, Dirksen demanded continued support of the Subversive Activities Control Board.[11] When that deal was in place, Dirksen began his effort to provide a Republican cushion to the Fortas nomination. Several young Republican senators, led by freshman Robert Griffin of Michigan, had formed a group with the professed goal of blocking the nomination. Dirksen strove to undercut the upstarts, announcing that he would vote to break any filibuster and that a majority of Republicans was prepared to back Fortas. Because an insurgent group of young minnows was contrary to his understanding of the workings of the Senate, Johnson underestimated the potential of these Republicans to disrupt the orderly confirmation of Fortas. Nevertheless, the White House quietly

11. The SACB had been created in the early 1950s to identify Communists and Communist-controlled groups. The attorney general would bring cases before the SACB, and on the basis of these cases the SACB would publicize the list of supposed dangerous individuals and organizations. By the late 1960s the board was not only a vestige of the McCarthy era but also a haven for political patronage. Dirksen, however, used his support of the SACB to solidify his standing among old-line conservatives and backed its continued funding. The Senate had agreed to fund the board only if the attorney general brought a case to the SACB by June 20, 1968 (no case had been brought in over two and one-half years). Ramsey Clark, the attorney general, believed the SACB a threat to civil liberties and was reluctant to give it continued life. Dirksen's payment in return for his support of Fortas was the president's promise to insist that the attorney general forward cases to the SACB. The story is detailed in Murphy, *Fortas*, 294–97.

responded by communicating with business interests in the states of the recalcitrant Republicans to put pressure on any senator considering bucking both the minority leader and the White House.[12] These efforts put the young Republicans on the defensive; the power of the executive to influence important constituents, plus statements by the Republican leadership that the insurgents were alone in opposing Fortas, set the minnows adrift in uncharted and dangerous waters. One of Dirksen's aides captured the prevailing mood: "Young guys just don't filibuster around here. If they are foolish enough to try it, they'll find that it doesn't work. And if, by some fluke, it should work, they'll pay for it."[13]

The courting of Russell was another matter. Russell had represented Georgia in the U.S. Senate since 1932. His seniority in the Senate made him the chair of the powerful Armed Services Committee and the de facto head of the Appropriations Committee. (The frail health of the chairman, Senator Hayden of Arizona, left Russell, the second-ranking Democrat on the committee, at the center of power.) Longtime service on the Democratic Steering Committee gave Russell an important voice in deciding the committee assignments of other Senate Democrats. Johnson's relationship with Russell stretched back to LBJ's early days in the Senate; recognizing legislative talent when he saw it, Russell had adopted the young Senator Johnson as his protégé, in effect commanding Senate Democrats in the early 1950s to make LBJ their leader. Russell's Senate "style" fit the institution perfectly; he was adept at compromise and displayed courtly manners and evident intelligence. No senator was more respected and none possessed greater power and influence, even though he did not hold a formal leadership position.

Russell was also the acknowledged leader of the southern Democratic delegation in the Senate. From the time he first came to the Senate in 1933, through the mid-1960s, there were at least

---

12. See Murphy, *Fortas*, 316–17; Shogan, *Question of Judgment*, 154–56.
13. Quoted in Murphy, *Fortas*, 325.

eleven votes to invoke cloture in connection with attempts to pass civil rights legislation.[14] Russell successfully led the battle against all of them and also fended off attempts to liberalize the cloture rule itself. When asked how the southern bloc of only eighteen senators could be so successful, Senator John Stennis of Mississippi replied that "we did not have eighteen Senators but that we have seventeen plus Senator Russell—and that plus Russell is the thing which makes the difference." Stennis paid Russell another dubious compliment. After Russell led the futile fight to block the Civil Rights Act of 1964, Stennis wrote him; "[E]xcept for you and your fine leadership, a strong civil rights bill would have been passed . . . as early as 1948 . . . or certainly after the unprecedented Supreme Court decision [*Brown* v. *Board of Education*] of 1954."[15] In the traditional understanding of the way the Senate operated, Russell could deliver votes. In short, he was the quintessential Senate whale.

Johnson thought that Russell's assent would clinch the Fortas nomination. To secure the Russell stamp of approval, Johnson nominated Texan Homer Thornberry, a judge on the Fifth Circuit Court of Appeals, to assume Fortas's associate justice seat. Thornberry was a competent jurist, not the equal of Fortas, but among the reasons for the selection of Thornberry was that he was an old duck-hunting buddy of Richard Russell. "When you sit in a duck blind all day with a man, you really get to know him," and Russell knew Thornberry "to be a good man, an able

---

14. Unlimited debate is perhaps the feature that most distinguishes the Senate from the House, and hence the filibuster is a jealously guarded Senate prerogative. It was not until 1917 that the Senate even adopted a cloture rule to end debate. Rule 22 of the Senate provided that debate be cut off if two-thirds of the senators present and voting agreed to a cloture motion. In 1975 the current cloture rule was enacted, requiring the vote of three-fifths of the Senate—sixty senators—to close debate.

15. Quoted in Gilbert C. Fite, *Richard Russell, Senator from Georgia* (Chapel Hill: Univ. of North Carolina Press, 1991), 407, 416. While a testimony to Russell's immense influence in the Senate, these statements also testify to Russell's unwavering defense of apartheid in America.

man and a fair man."[16] Johnson had no difficulty with the notion of putting Thornberry on the Court, and, if a Thornberry nomination would nail down Russell's vote on Fortas, then it would be done. Therefore it was scarcely a coincidence that Russell was having dinner with Johnson when the president called Thornberry to inform him of his nomination as associate justice. Russell promised Johnson that he would support the Fortas nomination and enthusiastically support Homer Thornberry. Johnson had secured the consent of the two critical whales in the Senate; his understanding of how the Senate worked led him to conclude that Abe Fortas would be the next chief justice.

The Crucible of the Senate Judiciary Committee

The hearings before the Senate Judiciary Committee on the nomination of Abe Fortas to be chief justice of the United States began on July 11, 1968. In the days immediately preceding the hearings, insiders questioned whether the committee would request Fortas to appear personally and whether he would accept the invitation. Edward White and Harlan Fiske Stone, the two previous sitting justices nominated to become chief justice, had not personally testified before the committee. The questioning of a sitting justice raises a host of potential separation-of-powers difficulties, with both the nominee and the committee obligated to avoid discussion of past decisions and pending cases.[17] Nevertheless, the

16. Quoted in Murphy, *Fortas*, 292. Clark Clifford argued against nominating Thornberry, urging Johnson to consider a moderate Republican for the associate justice spot. See Kalman, *Abe Fortas*, 328. With the aid of hindsight, Clifford was, of course, correct. A Republican in place of Thornberry might have done more to avoid Republican opposition than anything Dirksen could provide. In addition, by 1968 Russell's influence in the Senate and his ability to deliver the southern bloc had declined. See, for example, Fite, *Richard Russell*, chap. 20.

17. Technically Fortas was not the first sitting justice to testify before the Judiciary Committee. Recess appointments to the Court, made by the president while the Senate is not in session, permit the justice to be sworn in and engage in the Court's work although not formally confirmed by the Senate. When the Senate returns, the president renominates the individual to secure the advice and consent of the Senate.

chairman of the Judiciary Committee, James Eastland, Democrat of Mississippi, was determined to have Fortas appear personally, and, although the White and Stone precedents offered a gracious and honorable way out, Fortas was outwardly confident of his ability to control the proceedings and win over the Senate and the public.[18]

As a rule, it is easier for an organized minority of senators to delay passage of a measure indefinitely in the U.S. Senate than for a loosely organized majority to secure prompt and decisive action. Delay is a particularly effective strategy in contesting a presidential nomination. Drawing the proceedings out over time permits the opposition to organize, new information to be discovered, the public to be aroused. In the case of the Fortas nomination, prolonging the hearings posed an additional threat to the nominee; the closer a final Senate vote to the November election, the more potent the argument to save the nomination of the new chief justice for the incoming president. With the Senate scheduled to recess in August, extended hearings would allow Fortas's opponents to delay a committee vote until September. The first day of the hearings therefore set the initial tone, producing a listless debate over whether there indeed was a vacancy on the Court. The Warren retirement letter had not set a specific date for his departure; he had retired effective at the pleasure of the president, and Johnson in turn accepted "at such time as a successor

---

The "new" justice is then sworn in a second time. In the modern era, Earl Warren, William Brennan, and Potter Stewart received recess appointments and were subject to Senate proceedings while on the bench. Although Warren declined to appear before the committee, the Stewart hearings saw the nominee make a spirited defense of his commitment to the Court's efforts to desegregate southern school districts. No doubt because of the unseemliness of questioning sitting members of the Court, the Senate adopted a resolution in 1960 requesting the president to avoid recess appointments to the Court.

18. Behind the scenes, however, Fortas had misgivings. He even suggested that a Senate confirmation of a sitting justice as chief justice was unnecessary and urged friends to push that position on friendly members of the Judiciary Committee. See Kalman, *Abe Fortas*, 335.

is qualified." In the view of several of Fortas's opponents on the committee, this conditional resignation meant, in effect, there was no current vacancy on the Court. The debate proved inconsequential, but it consumed a full day of the committee's time. The testimony of Fortas was further delayed when Senator Sam Ervin, Democrat of North Carolina, requested additional time to study all of Fortas's written opinions. It was not until July 16 that the star witness took his place before the committee.

The White House had hoped Fortas could complete his testimony in one day; it would take four. Although wide-ranging, the inquiry was anchored by two general areas of concern. The first was the justice's connections with Lyndon Johnson. When nominated to the Court in 1965, he had been quizzed about his role as adviser to the president, but, as a private citizen, Fortas had been free to serve the president in any mutually agreeable capacity. Now, however, he was a Supreme Court justice and governed by the doctrine of separation of powers. Grilled by the members of the committee regarding his role in the Johnson administration, Fortas, at best, was less than forthright and, at worst, simply lied. He skillfully avoided admitting outright impropriety, but the tone of his testimony cast a pall over the hearings and troubled even his most ardent supporters and friends.

More troublesome still was the effort of several members of the committee to make the Fortas nomination a national referendum on the ideological direction of the Warren Court. Since the 1954 decision in *Brown* v. *Board of Education*, conservative and southern hostility to the Warren Court had grown, stimulated by the Court's continuing commitment to racial integration and its efforts to extend the application of the procedural safeguards found in the Bill of Rights to state criminal proceedings. The Court's criminal process decisions provided several of Fortas's opponents on the committee with their best material. With the explosion in crime and judicial restrictions on police behavior soon to be themes of the Republican drive to the presidency, emphasizing the often gruesome details of these decisions in queries to the nominee appeared to be a no-lose proposition. Fortas might refuse to respond, on the basis of the impropriety of discussing actual cases, and risk appearing evasive, or he could attempt the tasks almost impossible in a public forum of providing technical, legal explanations for what would soon be notorious decisions. In either case, the nominee would make an unfavorable impression, and the strategy quickly developed to place the burden of fifteen years of Supreme Court decision making directly on the shoulders of one man.

His principal antagonist was Senator Strom Thurmond.[19] For hours Thurmond berated Fortas for many of the Warren Court's criminal process decisions, and Fortas, choosing to refrain from discussing these decisions, remained silent. Thurmond then turned the inquiry to *Mallory v. United States*, a 1957 decision in which the Court reversed the conviction of a confessed rapist because the police had failed in a timely manner to bring the defendant before a magistrate as required by federal law.[20] "There was really no question that he committed the crime," Thurmond thundered,

> but when it went to the Supreme Court, they reversed the case and the man went free. Why did he go free? A criminal, a convict, a guilty man, who committed a serious rape on a lady in

19. As governor of South Carolina, Thurmond had bolted the Democratic party in 1948, running for president on the States' Rights ticket. He returned to the Democratic party, only to support Barry Goldwater in 1964 and change party affiliation, becoming one of the leaders of the Republican resurgence in the South. Representing South Carolina in the Senate since 1954, Thurmond was an avid defender of the "southern way of life" and established the modern Senate record for individual filibuster, speaking on the floor of the Senate for twenty-four hours and eighteen minutes in a personal campaign to prevent passage of the 1957 voting rights bill.

20. 354 U.S. 449. Mallory, a nineteen-year-old black man, had been arrested in Washington, D.C., and charged with rape. Police interrogated him for seven hours prior to arraignment and secured a confession. Mallory eventually appealed to the Supreme Court, and the Court, in a unanimous decision, reversed the conviction because the police had intentionally delayed bringing him before a magistrate for arraignment—in direct violation of federal rules of criminal procedure—to obtain a confession. After his release, Mallory was arrested and convicted of assault in Philadelphia.

this city. Simply because the Court said they held him a little too long before arraignment. Do you believe in that kind of justice? Don't you think the main purpose of the courthouses, of the judges, of the jury is to go to the heart of the case and render justice, to convict them when they are guilty, and turn them loose when they are free, and not let technicalities control the outcome? And isn't that what happened in this case?

When Fortas demurred, refusing to respond to inquiries about particular decisions, Thurmond exploded,

Does not that decision, Mallory, I want that word to ring in your ears—Mallory—the man happened to have been from my state incidentally—shackle law enforcement? Mallory, a man who raped a woman, admitted his guilt and the Supreme Court turned him loose on a technicality. And who I was told later went to Philadelphia and committed another crime, and somewhere else another crime, because the court turned him loose on technicalities. Is not that type of decision calculated to bring the courts and the law and the administration in disrepute? Is not that type of decision calculated to encourage some people to commit rapes and serious crimes? Can you as a Justice of the Supreme Court condone such a decision? I ask you to answer that question.[21]

Stunned by the intensity of this outburst, Fortas could do little except decline to discuss the merits of the decision. Regaining his composure, Thurmond continued, in case after case, to demand explanations for a host of Supreme Court decisions that appeared, at least in his view, to turn on mere technicalities and, taken together, to result in a crisis of law and order. It was a theme repeated almost daily in the ensuing presidential campaign. Although Thurmond's outburst may have shocked some observers, his making Fortas the scapegoat for the sins of the War-

21. The Fortas-Thurmond exchange took place during the July 19, 1968, session of the Fortas-Thornberry hearings.

ren Court (*Mallory* had been decided a full seven years before Fortas assumed his seat on the Court) was an effective strategy. Moreover, it took up precious time. When an exhausted Fortas concluded his testimony, the committee had yet to hear from several other witnesses, and the agony of Abe Fortas continued.

One of these witnesses was James Clancy, an attorney representing Citizens for a Decent Literature. Outraged by an alleged increase in pornography throughout the land, Clancy's group had purportedly analyzed Supreme Court obscenity decisions, concluding that in some forty-nine cases Fortas had provided the critical vote permitting a majority of the Court to hold the material in question to be not obscene. To illustrate the depth of this continuing depravity, Clancy had produced a slide show highlighting some of the material involved in these cases, as well as one of the films the Court had held to be constitutionally protected. He invited the members of the committee and other senators to view the evidence, and the committee leadership gratefully accepted, adjourning the hearings and ordering the full committee to delay its report for another week to allow senators to consider Clancy's material. For the next several days, a projector was set up in a room in the Capitol, and senators were invited to review X-rated movies. Not only did this delay the proceedings—by now it was clear the Senate would not vote until after the August recess—but an appearance in the viewing room provided senators with a convenient rationale for opposing the nomination. A conscientious senator, after viewing *Flaming Creatures* (a full-length feature added to the Senate collection after the Clancy testimony), was hardly expected to announce that the experience fortified his support for the embattled Fortas.

In mid-September the Judiciary Committee voted, 11 to 6, to report favorably on the nomination. Liberals formed a majority on the committee, and the favorable vote was not unexpected, but neither was the filibuster that began when the nomination reached the Senate floor. When a cloture vote failed by a substantial margin, the Fortas nomination was dead. Fortas requested

Johnson to withdraw his name from consideration, and a little over a week later the president announced he would make no further nominations to the Court. Earl Warren would remain chief justice, his replacement to be named by the new president.[22]

ABE FORTAS AND THE NEW POLITICS OF JUDICIAL CONFIRMATIONS

The Old World Is Rapidly Changing

The Fortas nomination was undone by events and political considerations that made Fortas the wrong candidate for the wrong position at the wrong time. The fact that Lyndon Johnson was a lame-duck president undercut his celebrated control of the legislative process. Charges of cronyism and Justice Fortas's close connections with the administration raised conflict-of-interest and separation-of-powers problems that transcended simple partisan politics. Conservative outrage at the Warren Court was a major factor. With the wisdom provided by a quarter century of hindsight, however, one must conclude that the Fortas nomination fell victim to circumstances far beyond the power of either Lyndon Johnson or Abe Fortas to control. Although both men had often exhibited an extraordinary ability to shape their own

22. The tragedy of Abe Fortas continued. Following the failed nomination to the chief justiceship, Fortas returned to the Court as associate justice. In May 1969 *Life* magazine released a story detailing Fortas's connection with Louis Wolfson, a man found guilty of conspiracy to violate the federal securities laws. The story is a complicated one, detailed in the Murphy and the Kalman biographies of Fortas. To make a long story quite short, Fortas had represented Wolfson during his years in private practice. Wolfson had established a philanthropic foundation, and when Fortas came to the Supreme Court, Wolfson offered him the position of consultant to the foundation at a stipend of $20,000 a year for life. Fortas accepted the first payment but then reconsidered the arrangement, resigned from the position, and returned the money several months later. The gist of the *Life* story was entirely accurate: A Supreme Court justice had taken money from a foundation headed by a man subsequently found to have violated the federal securities law. Shortly after publication of the story, Justice Fortas resigned from the Court.

destiny, by 1968 these masters of the old political order had been blindsided by sweeping charges that altered the basic structure of American politics and institutions.

It is indeed remarkable that Lyndon Johnson could have been so wrong about the Senate he knew so well. He had cultivated the principal whales, and yet neither Richard Russell nor Everett Dirksen ultimately delivered. Both men had convenient explanations for their defections, but behind the rhetoric was the reality that neither could control and deliver votes as they had in the past.[23] For his part, Johnson, educated in the structured ways of the old Senate, simply could not imagine that a band of renegade young Republican senators would consider defying Everett Dirksen or that Richard Russell was no longer the behind-the-scenes master of the Senate. Evolution in the Senate had taken a strange twist—the whales had fallen victim to the minnows—and one of the primary casualties of the new arrangement was Abe Fortas. In less than a decade following the defeat of Fortas, it would be clear to all that the Senate whale was an extinct species.

The Senate as Johnson knew it was an institution whose membership was constrained by sharply defined and well-understood norms of behavior that rewarded conformity and specialization, demanded that newcomers serve a substantial apprenticeship, and discouraged the maverick. By the last years of his presidency, this model of Senate behavior was out of step with the more open, visible, media-oriented politics of modern America. Indeed, one might easily conclude that the failed For-

---

23. The ostensible reason for Russell reneging on his word to support Fortas was the administration's delay in clearing a federal district court judgeship for one of Russell's friends and supporters. Although the nomination was eventually cleared by the administration, the delay, in the view of Russell, made it appear that he had struck a deal in which he voted for Fortas in return for the district court judgeship. The appearance of such crass political patronage, Russell concluded, released him from any obligation to support Fortas. Dirksen announced right before the cloture vote that the committee hearings on Fortas raised new issues, which demanded greater scrutiny, and hence he was now neutral with regard to the nomination. See Murphy, *Fortas*, chap. 14 and 521–22.

tas nomination was one of the first important indicators of the transformation of the Senate into a more open institution that provides individual members with the resources and motivation to champion diverse interests without regard to state boundaries, seniority, or issue specialization. Today the Senate as an institution is far less hierarchical and stable than it was when Lyndon Johnson was majority leader, and one consequence of this is to make the politics of judicial confirmations highly volatile and quite unpredictable.

The animosity of the Warren Court triggered among conservative senators was, perhaps, the heaviest burden. Linking Fortas to controversial Supreme Court decisions was an astute political strategy, and southern senators like Strom Thurmond played their parts perfectly. Quite apart from strategy and political grandstanding, however, the battle over the Fortas nomination did reveal many senators' deep antagonism to the direction of modern constitutional law. In their opinion the Supreme Court under Earl Warren had provoked explosive change that threatened the stability of their political and social world. They were indeed angry, and, from the perspective of the defenders of the status quo, their anger was quite justified. The Warren Court did bring about a judicial revolution, although the Court's obscenity decisions were a small and insignificant part of that revolution.

Throughout the 1960s the Warren Court reconceived the nature of judicial power by opening the doors of the federal courthouse to a host of new litigants and providing successful litigants with an expanded array of judicial remedies. As will be explained in chapter 2, the Court redefined modern judicial liberalism, rejecting the New Deal model of judicial modesty and restraint for a defiant activism designed to benefit America's disadvantaged. This break with the jurisprudence of the New Deal was the Court's most revolutionary act, because augmenting the ability of the federal judiciary to serve the needs of group litigants ultimately benefited not simply the poor and disenfranchised but many middle- and upper-middle-class interests that found the judiciary a useful arena in which to realize policy goals. Thus a quite unintended consequence of the Warren Court revolution was made to make the nomination and confirmation of federal judges a high-stakes political event with broad policy implications. Not the least of Johnson's miscalculations during the Fortas affair was his failure to appreciate that an appointment to the Supreme Court had become too important to too many potent political forces for insider deals between the president and a few Senate whales to go unchallenged.

Amplifying the impact of these developments was the fact that in 1968 the latent fault lines in the New Deal coalition split wide open. A by-product of the hegemony of the Democratic party in the years following the New Deal was the diminished significance of judicial appointments; during this period there was little incentive for forces in the Democratic party to break ranks and challenge the governing consensus on the appointment of judges. Even the years of the Eisenhower presidency did little to change this understanding of the confirmation process; the appointment of federal judges remained a low-key affair, with senators typically unwilling or unable to invest substantial political capital in any attempt to challenge judicial nominations. When the governing coalition fell upon hard times, however, even the politics of judicial appointments began to reflect the deep divisions within the party. By 1968, for example, the typical southern Senate Democrat saw little political gain in supporting Fortas and little political cost in challenging his own party's presidential prerogative.

The Republican party was also in a period of transition, and, in his campaign to forge a new Republican majority, Richard Nixon attached the Supreme Court in a manner calculated to attract disaffected white Democrats to his party. The image of a federal judiciary protecting the forces of disorder and discontent at the expense of law-abiding citizens became a powerful campaign theme in the resurgence of the national Republican party. Throughout the 1970s and 1980s the Court remained a valuable

bogeyman for many Republican candidates, providing a convenient explanation for the party's inability to enact the social agenda
championed by its most conservative elements. Although in 1968
veteran Senate whales like Everett Dirksen might consider nominations to the Court appropriate for behind-the-scenes deals, a
new generation of Senate Republicans understood that highly visible, public battles to bring the Court back to the "silent majority" could produce real electoral dividends that would outweigh
the consequences of any breach of timeworn patterns of Senate
decorum and behavior.

Back to the Future

The events surrounding the failed Fortas nomination thus provide a benchmark for the study of the new politics of judicial
selection and confirmation. With very few exceptions, previous
judicial confirmations in the twentieth century were characterized by low-key, insider politics in which a handful of participants made the critical decisions with minimal public scrutiny or
participation. Following the Fortas nomination came the modern
era of conflict in which open, public confrontations over the selection of our judges made confirmation to the Court a highly unpredictable enterprise. Fortas links these two eras, providing a
window on both the past and the present. And the tale of Abe
Fortas, despite its seductive combination of triumph and tragedy,
human virtue and foible, does compel the observer seeking a
greater understanding of contemporary American politics to
eschew, at least for a moment, the fascination with the particular
and to direct attention to several recent changes in American politics and law that have combined to alter the general political
landscape.

Chapter 2

THE JUDICIARY: THE CHANGING NATURE OF JUDICIAL POWER

Since the days of John Marshall, the political effectiveness of the federal judiciary has rested on the ability of astute judges to use the great power of judicial review to link the judiciary to powerful social and political forces. Throughout a good deal of American history, the courts have been aligned with the forces of capital and, for the first 150 years of the nation's development, constitutional litigation offered a most effective means of protecting property against the regulatory power of the state. During these periods, efforts at reform invariably included efforts to weaken the Court or to constrict the scope of judicial review. To the generation of reformers associated with the New Deal, for example, breaking the link between the judiciary and capital became a touchstone of successful liberal reform.

Beginning with the decision in Brown v. Board of Education *in 1954, the Supreme Court under Chief Justice Earl Warren transformed the nature of judicial power in the United States. The Warren Court directly challenged the traditional progressive conviction that a diminished judiciary was a necessary precondition for reform. Indeed, the judicial "activism" so often associated with the Warren Court of the 1960s was in fact a dramatic judicial campaign to further progressive goals, empowering the politically disadvantaged and redirecting the central concern of constitutional law from property to equality. The justices of the Warren era redefined modern judicial liberalism and in so doing altered the nature of the politics of the nomination and confirmation process for the decades that followed.*

There is, as this chapter will illustrate, a direct connection between the Warren Court and the politics of the modern confirmation process. As the Court of the 1960s eased the requirements for entertaining federal lawsuits and expanded the array of available remedies for successful litigants, a multitude of groups—including many affluent and upper-middle-class interests—found the judiciary an important ally in the battle to secure their political goals. In short order, politically potent groups considered the staffing of the Supreme Court and the lower federal judiciary to be a matter of great concern, worthy of the expenditure of substantial resources. Moreover, in the decades following the resignation of Earl Warren, his Court materialized as an icon of modern American politics. The political right evoked the Warren Court as a symbol of the evil of rule by judges and vowed to rectify this democratic aberration through the appointment of judges who would not "legislate from the bench." The political left lionized the Warren Court and in subsequent decades mobilized to protect its rulings from the vicissitudes of electoral politics and the appointment of less than sympathetic judges.

Perhaps it is Earl Warren's ultimate legacy; thirty years after his retirement from the bench, the image of his Court still resonates in American politics and shapes the debate for both the left and right in the modern confirmation process,

The Crisis of the Old Order

Judicial Activism in Defense of Property

Political power in the United States is inevitably a function of constituency. In a nation with a strong commitment to popular rule, mass support is often the crucial component in the struggle for political supremacy. Institutions typically grow more politically dominant as they come to represent the interests of larger portions of the electorate. Political actors that lack a direct link to a sizable constituency play a secondary role. During much of the twentieth century, for example, the executive branch has dominated political life, principally because the presidency has proven best suited to using modern technology to reach out to a nation-wide constituency. Recent congressional challenges to the power of the modern presidency, on the other hand, highlight the height-ened capacity of individual senators to attract national attention through the skillful use of the media and to extend their popular support beyond state borders.

The framers also understood well the significance of con-stituency; the judiciary was thought to be "the least dangerous branch" precisely because of the limited capability of the courts to cultivate and mobilize mass support. Article III of the Consti-tution, for example, grants federal judges lifetime tenure, a unique bequest of political independence. But autonomy is not neces-sarily synonymous with political power. Elected officials in the United States may periodically face the harrowing prospect of defeat at the polls, but victory provides a measure of democratic legitimacy unavailable to appointed judges. The framers were confident that the judicial branch lacked both the political valid-ity conferred by popular sovereignty and the institutional resources to develop strong and lasting bonds to important con-stituent groups. In the grand design of the Constitution, they believed, the judiciary would play a secondary role in the devel-opment of the American state.

Had the Supreme Court been content with its initial, peripheral position, the selection of justices would be of little consequence even today. Establishing the Court as a primary, national political institution, however, called for a judiciary able to forge alliances with important political and economic forces.[1] John Marshall's famous opinion in *Marbury* v. *Madison* was a critical first step, because in announcing the power of judicial review—the power of the federal judiciary to declare the acts of

1. See Mark Silverstein and Benjamin Ginsberg, "The Supreme Court and the New Politics of Judicial Power," *Political Science Quarterly* 102 (1987): 371, for a discus-sion of the links between federal judiciary power and constituency support.

other branches null and void as contrary to the Constitution—
Marshall set in motion a constitutional evolution that would
make the Court the final arbiter of the meaning of the Constitution and the federal judiciary an attractive institutional ally
for powerful groups.[2] Max Lerner astutely noted that the genius
of Marshall was in forging "the strategic link between capitalism and constitutionalism."[3] During Marshall's thirty-four years
as chief justice, the Court emerged as the prime protector of private property against democratically elected state legislatures
thought to be too sympathetic to the leveling impulses of the
propertyless masses. By joining the judiciary's role of interpreting the Constitution with the political power of the prosperous,
the Marshall Court was able to transcend the institutional constraints on judicial power.

Marshall's legacy (he died in 1835) to future generations of
American judges was to establish the potential for active judicial
intervention in the affairs of state. Less skillful jurists or those less
favored by historical circumstance would still find the assertion
of judicial power a risky endeavor. Marshall's successor, Roger
Taney, shared his vision of an activist judiciary, but the social and
economic life of America had become vastly more complicated
by midcentury and the exercise of judicial power a more intricate
undertaking. The Court was forced to temper its defense of property in the face of growing popular support for state regulatory
activity that impaired private economic rights in the cause of
expanding economic opportunity for the community at large. Reconciling the tension between the conservative insistence on stable, predictable laws governing economic relations on the one
hand, and the progressive quest for more flexible constitutional
interpretation to release creative economic energy on the other,
proved a formidable challenge to the judges of the post-Marshall

2. *Marbury* v. *Madison*, 1 Cranch 137 (1803).
3. Max Lerner, "John Marshall and the Campaign of History," in Leonard Levy,
ed., *American Constitutional Law: Historical Essays* (New York: Harper & Row, 1966), 57.

era.[4] The rising tide of states' rights sentiments and the explosive issue of slavery left the Taney Court unable to fashion enduring bonds with powerful social and economic forces. The Court's attempt to settle these issues in the infamous *Dred Scott* was a political and legal disaster.[5] Abandoned by its supporters and stripped of the prestige it had so carefully cultivated, the Court entered a period of decline and quiescence.

The Civil War stands as the critical divide in American political and economic history. The grand debates over the very nature of the Union that dominated the Marshall and Taney eras of Court history were ultimately settled not in the courtroom but on the battlefield. The nation that began as an agrarian society, where most citizens scratched out a living from the land, witnessed in the war's aftermath a great migration to the cities and the coming of the Industrial Revolution. A period of unprecedented economic development followed, producing extremes of wealth and poverty unsurpassed in America's history. At the turn of the century, it was reported that Marshall Field, the Chicago department store magnate, was clearing approximately $600 an hour from the operation of this store while paying the average clerk $12 for a sixty-hour workweek. The Census Bureau estimated that 9 percent of the nation's families owned 71 percent of the nation's wealth. As the transformation of America's economic life proceeded at a dizzying pace, the triumph of capital was aided by a sympathetic Supreme Court that found in the Constitution stringent limits on the

4. The best example of this tension appears in the famous case of *Charles River Bridge* v. *Warren Bridge*, 36 U.S. 420 (1837), and the debate in that case between Chief Justice Taney and Justice Story over the relationship between the state and private property rights in a capitalist society remains a classic. See Stanley I. Kutler, *Privilege and Creative Destruction: The Charles River Bridge Case* (New York: Norton, 1978).

5. *Dred Scott* v. *Sandford*, 60 U.S. 393 (1857). Taney's opinion, perhaps the most disastrous one the Supreme Court has ever issued, held that blacks were not citizens under the meaning of the Constitution and that the Missouri Compromise Act, prohibiting slavery in the territories of the United States, was unconstitutional. The decision provoked outrage in the North and subjected the Court to a blizzard of abuse.

power of government to regulate private enterprise. An expensive interpretation of the due process clause of the Fourteenth Amendment and a narrow construction of the powers of the national government made the Supreme Court the darling of the new industrial capitalists of the Gilded Age. Armed with the support of this powerful political ally, the Court could again return to center stage.

The Age of Reform

In the last quarter of the nineteenth century, the Supreme Court championed the cause of entrepreneurial liberty through a series of decisions that limited the reach of governmental power and directly linked the Court with the new forces of industrial and finance capitalism.[6] The ascendancy of this new industrial order ignited a determined opposition, and, beginning with the agrarian uprisings of the 1890s, the demand for a more effective use of state and federal governments to control the reach and abuses of private power provided an attractive alternative to the dogma of free markets and laissez-faire capitalism. Progressives of this era, however, could hardly be described as Jeffersonian romantics, animated by a faith in the wisdom of the populace and the dream of the return to an idyllic, agrarian America. Accepting industrialization and economic inequality as facts of modern life, they sought in big government administered by trained, disinterested experts the means to control and regulate capitalist development to further the public good. "The democrat," wrote Walter Lippmann in 1922, "has always assumed if political power can be derived in the right way, it would be beneficent." This naïveté was "the democratic fallacy." In the initial decades of the twentieth century, Progressives like Lippmann lived by the credo that

6. For a highly readable account of the Court's interpretation of constitutional protections property, see James W. Ely, *The Guardian of Every Other Right: A Constitutional History of Property Rights* (New York: Oxford Univ. Press, 1992), particularly chap. 5, detailing the Court's decisions during the Gilded Age.

"what determines the quality of civilization is the use made of power."[7]

The major obstacle to the effective use of governmental power to further the public good was the Supreme Court. From the very outset of the twentieth century, judicial activism on behalf of industrial capitalism and government regulation in the name of economic and social welfare were on a collision course. As the Progressive reformer increasingly looked to the state to control the expanding private sector, the industrial capitalist looked to a sympathetic Supreme Court to use the power of judicial review and constitutional interpretation to shield private power from state control. While the National Association of Manufacturers was passing resolutions praising the Supreme Court for its defense of economic liberty, the champions of reform were pressing a campaign to limit the scope of judicial review, on the basis of a growing conviction that an activist judiciary was the enemy of progressive reform.

Renovating a constitutional jurisprudence keyed to the protection of private property in light of the demands of modern industrial life became the intellectual passion of many of America's best and brightest during the initial decades of the twentieth century. The early career of Felix Frankfurter provides a prime example. Years before his appointment to the Supreme Court, Professor Frankfurter of the Harvard Law School was a respected advocate of progressive politics. Joining a defense of a powerful state run by impartial, expert administrators with expressions of grave misgivings concerning the exercise of judicial power, Frankfurter often employed the pages of the popular press to champion judicial restraint as an important step toward progressive reform. Repeatedly he sought to disabuse the populace of "the mischievous assumption that our judges embody pure rea-

---

7. Walter Lippmann, *Public Opinion* (New York: Free Press, 1965; original copyright 1922), 196. The classic work that inspired many of the Progressive reformers of the era was Herbert Croly's *The Promise of American Life* (New York: Macmillan, 1909).

son, that they are set apart from the concerns of the community, regardless of time, place and circumstances, to become the interpreters of self-determining words with fixed content, yielding their meaning to a process of inexorable reasoning."[8] The exercise of constitutional adjudication and interpretation was, at bottom, a political event, and in matters of politics the judiciary had consciously to defer to the reasonable judgments of the other branches of government. Diminishing the role of the federal judiciary, he believed, was necessary to allow democratic government to respond to the needs of a modern industrial society. Active judicial intervention in the affairs of state was incompatible with progressive politics. Even when judicial activism produced the occasional liberal result, Frankfurter counseled caution. "For ourselves," he wrote after one such decision, "we regard the cost of this power of the Supreme Court on the whole as greater than its gains."[9]

The judiciary's determined defense of industry led some reformers a step further, to support congressional proposals, ranging from requiring a specified number of justices to agree before a federal law might be declared unconstitutional to requiring the direct election of federal judges for ten-year terms, all designed to restrict the ability of the federal judiciary to declare legislative acts unconstitutional. The measures prompted vigorous debate in Congress, scholarly journals, and the popular press. Although none of the measures were ever enacted, the idea of formally restricting the power of judicial review was not without popular support. Even Frankfurter succumbed to the reformer's

8. "The Nomination of Mr. Justice Brandeis," *New Republic*, February 5, 1916. Although unsigned, this editorial piece was written by Frankfurter. See Philip Kurland, ed., *Felix Frankfurter on the Supreme Court* (Cambridge, MA: Harvard Univ. Press, 1970), 43, where the piece is reprinted.

9. "Can the Supreme Court Guarantee Toleration?" *New Republic*, June 17, 1925, reprinted in Kurland, *Felix Frankfurter*, 176. This piece was written in response to the decision in *Pierce* v. *Society of Sisters*, 268 U.S. 510 (1925), in which the Court used an expansive interpretation of due process to strike down an Oregon law that would have abolished private schools.

frustration with hyperactive judicial review. So great was his disaffection with the Supreme Court's use of the Fourteenth Amendment to strike down innovative state legislation that in 1922 he announced in the pages of the *New Republic* his support of the drastic step of repealing that amendment's due process clause.[10]

THE NEW DEAL AND A NEW JUDICIAL LIBERALISM

Holmes and Brandeis

Frankfurter eventually moderated his views, concluding that "panaceas like the recall of judicial decisions or the requirement that more than a majority of the Court should declare legislation unconstitutional" were not the answers.[11] Eschewing direct limitations on judicial power, Frankfurter, with a host of liberals in the years prior to the New Deal, championed a jurisprudence of self-restraint that demanded that judges proceed in a statesmanlike manner, moderating the impact of judicial review through a real deference to the decisions of the elected branches of government. In the years that followed, the doctrine of judicial self-restraint became the centerpiece of a new understanding of judicial liberalism and the hallmark of the jurisprudence of the New Deal.

The role model for this generation of liberals was Justice Oliver Wendell Holmes. The judges of the old order measured social legislation against fixed, immutable principles such as that

10. "An informed study of the work of the Supreme Court of the United States will probably lead to the conclusion that no nine men are wise enough and good enough to be entrusted with the power the unlimited provisions of the due process clauses confer. We have had fifty years of experiment with the Fourteenth Amendment and the centralizing authority lodged with the Supreme Court over the domestic affairs of forty-eight widely different States is an authority which it simply cannot discharge with safety to either itself or the States. the due process clause ought to go." "The Red Terror of Judicial Reform," *New Republic*, October 1, 1924, unsigned editorial; see Kurland, *Felix Frankfurter*, 166–67.

11. Ibid., 226.

of liberty of contract, without apparent regard for new economic and social conditions. Progressives, on the other hand, believed that modern civilization was in a state of constant flux and required governments capable of adapting policies to the shifting needs of a dynamic society. From their perspective a judiciary that found in the Constitution a set of unchanging first principles that severely circumscribed legislative attempts to grapple with the social ills of a changing society was anathema. The appeal of Holmes to liberals like John Dewey lay in his refusal to settle "matters of social policy by dialectic reasoning from fixed concepts."[12] For Holmes the core principle of majority rule defined the judicial role; unless the actions of the sovereign majority were entirely reasonable, the task of the modern judge was to defer to the legislative choice, whatever the apparent wisdom of the challenged legislation.[13]

Holmes's jurisprudence of restraint freed the governing process from judicial control and placed ultimate responsibility for governing in the hands of the elected branches. Although a friend and mentor to many of the most influential liberals of the times and beloved by millions of Americans, Holmes had little faith in legislative efforts to aid the poor and weak; in his world view the strong and powerful would inevitably win out and social welfare legislation designed to alter this outcome was doomed to failure. Despite his own fatalistic outlook, Holmes became the archetype of the ideal judge to a generation of reformers because his understanding of the judicial role diminished the scope of

12. John Dewey, "Justice Holmes and the Liberal Mind," *New Republic*, January 11, 1928, 210.

13. An often recounted story about Holmes illustrates the point. Encountering John W. Davis, the solicitor general, after he had argued an antitrust case before the Court, Holmes asked if there were many additional antitrust cases the solicitor general intended to bring to the Court. When Davis answered quite a few, Holmes responded, "Well bring 'em on and we'll decide 'em. Of course I know and every sensible man knows that the Sherman law is damned nonsense but if my country wants to go to hell, I'm here to help it." Quoted in Mark Silverstein, *Constitutional Faiths: Felix Frankfurter, Hugo Black, and the Process of Judicial Decision Making* (Ithaca: Cornell Univ. Press, 1984), 44.

judicial control while expanding that of the legislative and executive branches, and this fit nearly with the goals of those championing change and reform.

Liberals might differ over the means to achieve their goals, but in the years preceding the New Deal almost all agreed on the necessity of decreasing the sphere of judicial decision making as an important step in permitting the elected branches the flexibility to deal effectively with issues of the day. Justice Louis Brandeis, for example, unquestionably lacked Holmes's skepticism but joined in his colleague's efforts to moderate judicial authority over economic and social legislation. Acutely aware of the Supreme Court's tenuous claim to democratic legitimacy, Brandeis constantly reminded his brethren on the bench that "the most important thing we do is not doing" and strove to develop judicially enforced rules to carry out the ideal of restraint. His efforts in a case arising out of congressional attempts to control child labor illustrate this point.

During his career as a private attorney, Brandeis had been an outspoken leader in the progressive movement and a tireless campaigner to end the social and economic inequities of American life, including the evils of child labor. On the Court he often joined with Holmes to protest the conservative majority's zeal in protecting private property against legislative efforts to combat the social ills of a modern industrial society. In 1918, for example, he joined Holmes's famous dissent in *Hammer* v. *Dagenhart*, protesting the majority's holding that Congress lacked power under the commerce clause to exclude goods produced by child labor from interstate commerce.[14] Following the setback of *Hammer*, Congress attempted to limit child labor by imposing a substantial tax on any goods produced by children under the age of sixteen.[15] In *Atherton Mills* v. *Johnston*, the father of a young boy

---

14. 247 U.S. 251 (1918).
15. This act was eventually struck down in *Bailey* v. *Drexel Furniture Co.*, 259 U.S. 20 (1922).

employed at Atherton Mills brought an action against the company alleging that because of the Child Labor Tax Act the company was about to discharge his son.[16] He sought a declaration
that the act was unconstitutional and injunctive relief preventing
the company from firing the boy. Atherton Mills acknowledged the
proposed termination, but defended it on the basis that it was
simply conforming to the federal act. A federal district court held
the tax invalid and granted the requested relief.

Even though he was a constant critic of the evils of child
labor and no doubt believed that the federal government had the
constitutional authority to outlaw the practice, Brandeis wrote a
memo to his fellow justices urging that the case be dismissed for
lack of jurisdiction, without their deciding the merits of the constitutional claim. An employer under the existing law, he noted,
was free to discharge an employee at will, and as a result the
father and the son had no cause of action against the company.
Their dispute was with the government of the United States,
which was not a party to the case. This defect could not be cured
simply by amending the complaint to include the government as
defendant, because a congressional act foreclosed any actions
against the United States to restrain the collection of a tax. In this
context, the constitutionality of the act could be tested only by
the employer's first paying the tax and then raising the constitutional claim in an action against the government for a refund.
Concluding that *Atherton* failed to present a "case" within the
meaning of Article III of the Constitution, Brandeis urged the
Court not to rush to judgment on the merits but simply to dismiss the action. He closed his memo as follows:

> For nearly a century and a quarter Federal courts, as an inci-
> dent to deciding cases rightfully before them, have necessarily
> exercised at times the solemn duty of declaring acts of Congress
> void. But the long continued, uninterrupted exercise of this

16. 259 U.S. 13 (1922).

power has not sufficed to silence the doubt originally expressed whether the framers of the Constitution intended to confer it. On the contrary, the popular protest against its exercise has never been as vehement, nor has it ever secured the support of so many political thinkers and writers, as in the last decade. At a time like the present, when the fundamental principles upon which our institutions rest are being seriously questioned, those who have faith in their wisdom and desire to preserve them unimpaired, can best uphold the Constitution by careful observance of the limitations which it imposes. As this court declared in the *Sinking Fund Cases*, "One branch of the Government cannot encroach upon the domain of another without danger. The safety of our institutions depends in no small degree on a strict observance of this salutary rule."[17]

The "careful observance of the limitations" on judicial decision making quickly became an article of faith for liberals of the day. They believed that the rigid observance of the rules of justiciability—the technical term used to describe the constitutional as well as the self-imposed, prudential limits on judicial power— would best preserve the separation of powers and ensure that the federal courts did not gratuitously exercise the power of judicial review. By confining the sphere of judicial influence through essentially discretionary rules, the judiciary could avoid more draconian limitations while allowing a powerful president and executive branch the constitutional "space" to provide the flexible leadership necessary in a modern industrial state. Judicial modesty, in short, must replace judicial arrogance. Sixteen years after he first explored these ideas in *Atherton*, Brandeis wrote his famous concurring opinion in *Ashwander* v. *TVA*, in effect codifying the various rules developed by the advocates of judicial

17. Alexander Bickel, *The Unpublished Opinions of Mr. Justice Brandeis* (Chicago: Univ. of Chicago Press, 1967), 13–14. After holding the case for two terms without issuing an opinion, the Court finally declared the case moot. By this time the boy had reached the age of sixteen, and his continued employment would no longer trigger the application of the tax.

restraint to avoid constitutional decisions in cases unquestionably within the Court's jurisdiction:

> The Court will not pass upon the constitutionality of legislation in a friendly, non-adversary, proceeding. . . . The Court will not "anticipate a question of constitutional law in advance of the necessity of deciding it." . . . The Court will not "formulate a rule of constitutional law broader than is required by the precise facts to which it is to be applied." . . . The Court will not pass upon a constitutional question . . . if there is also present some other ground upon which the case may be disposed of. . . . The Court will not pass upon the validity of a statute upon complaint of one who fails to show that he is injured by its operation. . . . The Court will not pass upon the constitutionality of a statute at the instance of one who has availed himself of its benefits. . . . "When the validity of an act of the Congress is drawn in question, and even if a serious doubt of constitutionality is raised, it is a cardinal principle this Court will first ascertain whether a construction of the statute is fairly possible by which the question may be avoided."[18]

With Justice Holmes and Brandeis providing leadership from the high court and academics like Frankfurter training a new generation of lawyers, judicial restraint coupled with strict application of the rules of justiciability emerged as the defining characteristic of judicial liberalism and progressive politics on the eve of the New Deal.

Judicial Modesty Triumphant

The election of Franklin Roosevelt in 1932 and the explosion of legislative activity during the first hundred days of his administration fanned the flames of the controversy surrounding the proper role of the judiciary. A conservative majority on the Court

18. 297 U.S. 288 at 346 (1936).

continued in the tradition of activism in defense of property, but economic emergency and increased public demands for government action placed this understanding of the judicial role in serious jeopardy. As the economic and political crisis deepened, judicial activism increasingly came to be seen as the old order's most effective tool for checking reform and regulation, despite overwhelming popular support for government action. In 1936 the Court actively employed judicial review to veto federal and state legislation designed to combat the depression, while in the November election Roosevelt won a stunning reelection victory. With the battle lines between the judiciary and the popularly elected branches starkly drawn, FDR in 1937 announced his plan to "pack" the Court with additional justices.[19] The motives behind the plan were apparent to all. Although the proposed legislation was never enacted by Congress, judicial retirement and death soon presented Roosevelt with the opportunity to transform the Supreme Court.

The Roosevelt appointees—a total of eight nominated and easily confirmed between 1937 and 1943—were all heirs to the tradition of restraint championed by Holmes and Brandeis. To a man, these justices came to the Court with a mandate to diminish the scope of judicial intervention in the policymaking arena and with an abiding faith that deference to the economic and social decisions of the elected branches would in the long run best serve the needs of the nation. With the judiciary in glorious retreat, liberalism emerged triumphant, and judicial deference to Congress and the executive became an integral part of the New Deal's legacy to future generations. Thus the passion for judicial restraint that reached its zenith during the New Deal was born

19. The proposal would have permitted the president to appoint one new justice for each sitting justice who, upon reaching the age of seventy, declined to retire. The maximum number of judges on the Court would have been set at fifteen. In short, Roosevelt's plan would have permitted a president to name from one to six new justices, depending on how many sitting justices had reached the age of seventy and refused to step down.

not of a fear of state power but of an appreciation of it, and the confining of judicial activism was a mark of liberal reform and not of conservative counterreaction.

A general acceptance of the jurisprudence of restraint and the limited institutional role of the judiciary united the judges and lawyers of the New Deal. Even those championing a more active role in the protection of civil liberties paid homage to the model of restraint, seeking only to carve out a narrow exception to protect against majoritarian abuses of the democratic process.[20] Many prominent New Dealers later taught at the nation's most prestigious law schools, and the lessons they passed on to their students stressed the importance of a strong president and judicial deference to the elected branches. The saga of FDR's confrontation with the Supreme Court and the constitutional battles that marked the New Deal soon transcended more history and became, in effect, a set of parables used to instruct future generations about the proper balance among the branches. The modern state, it was said, functioned best when a triumphant president could lead a submissive Congress in quest of enlightened policies. The received wisdom was equally unequivocal in demanding of the judiciary acceptance of the self-imposed limitations on the exercise of judicial review; to liberals whose political truths were formed during the era of the New Deal, judicial activism was simply incompatible with progressive politics. Their mission in the following decades was to ensure that this lesson was not lost on the generations that followed.[21]

20. The classic statement remains that of Justice Stone in *United States* v. *Carolene Products Co.*, 304 U.S. 144, 152, no. 4. See text accompanying note 50, below.

21. The impact of generational change on the New Deal's understanding of judicial liberalism is explored in several essays by Martin Shapiro. See his "Fathers and Sons: The Court, the Commentators, and the Search for Values," in Vincent Blasi, ed., *The Burger Court: The Counter-Revolution That Wasn't* (New Haven: Yale Univ. Press, 1983); "The Supreme Court: From Warren to Burger," in Anthony King, ed., *The New American Political System* (Washington, DC: AEI Press, 1978); "The Supreme Court and Economic Rights," in M. Judd Harmon, eds., *Essays on the Constitution of the United States* (Port Washington, NY: Kennikat Press, 1978).

For a brief period the Roosevelt Court functioned smoothly and without rancor, the shared belief in judicial deference to the elected branches being the unifying theme. By 1943 good will was, for the most part, long past, and the Court was divided by personal disputes and ideological splits. Frankfurter was often at the heart of these divisions. His habit of lecturing his fellow justices much as he did his law students, coupled with a willingness to personalize any dispute, strained relations among the brethren. The justices of the Roosevelt Court remained firm in their acceptance of deference to the elected branches on matters of economic and social policy, but the unexpected rush of cases involving individual rights and liberties during World War II and thereafter shattered the ideological consensus of the justices. Frankfurter continued in his dedication to self-restraint, while Justice Hugo Black became the titular leader of a group advocating a more positive judicial role in the protection of individual rights.[22] Although this conflict divided the justices, it did not thrust the Court into open confrontation with the other branches. By the 1960s, however, judicial modesty and the active defense of civil liberties would prove to be essentially incompatible.

THE WARREN COURT

The Court and Its Critics

The triumph of the New Deal and the ideal of judicial restraint rendered the politics of judicial confirmations rather mundane. A vacancy on the Supreme Court might still produce partisan, insider wrangling, but as America approached midcentury the distinguished and the mediocre found their way to the Court with

---

22. By the early 1940s Frankfurter was referring to Black and his supporters on the Court—William Douglas, Wiley Rutledge, and Frank Murphy—as "the Axis." See Silverstein, *Constitutional Faiths*, for a description of the different paths taken by Black and Frankfurter.

confirmation proceedings that were—at least by today's standards—little more than formalities. The federal judiciary's acceptance of its limited institutional role meant that the federal courts
would no longer intervene in policy matters close to the heart of
the New Deal, and the slowly emerging activism in the area of
personal rights was in basic accord with the philosophy of the
New Deal and did not seriously challenge executive power and
prerogative. With the liberalism of the New Deal ascendant, the
political profile of the federal courts receded and the judiciary
returned to a secondary position in determining the direction and
fate of national policy.

From this perspective the appointment of Earl Warren as
chief justice in 1953 marked a turning point in the history of the
Supreme Court, surpassed in significance only by John Marshall's
appointment 152 years earlier.[23] Renouncing the modest judicial
role propounded by the theorists of the New Deal, the Court
under Warren's leadership embraced the tradition of judicial
assertiveness that began with the great Marshall. Marshall had
established the possibility of extraordinary judicial power when
judicial activism could be linked to the interests of powerful
social, economic, and political forces. The crisis of the old order
had been set in motion by a judicial arrogance founded on the
mistaken belief that the resolute exercise of judicial review could
withstand the dominant political impulses of the times. The justices of the Warren Court were not nearly so presumptuous. They
set out to employ the federal judicial power to serve the interests

23. At the time of his appointment by President Dwight Eisenhower, Warren
was in his third term as governor of California. He had previously served fourteen
years as the district attorney for Alameda County and one term as the state attorney
for Alameda County and one term as the state attorney general. In the 1948 presidential election he had been Tom Dewey's running mate and had been seriously considered as a Republican presidential candidate in 1952. Surprisingly many (including the
president who appointed him), Warren became the leader of the new liberal activism
of the Supreme Court. This may have sorely disappointed the Republican Eisenhower,
but history's assessment of Earl Warren is far kinder; Warren is considered to be one
of the Court's great justices. For a sympathetic biography see G. Edward White, *Earl
Warren: A Public Life* (New York: Oxford Univ. Press, 1982).

of important components of the New Deal governing coalition, particularly America's ethnic and religious minorities. By linking the federal judiciary with Kennedy's New Frontier and Johnson's Great Society, the justices of the Warren Court were confident that judicial activism in the service of the disadvantaged would be embraced as the new definition of judicial liberalism.[24]

The Court's return to an unabashed activism was not without controversy. Criticism from traditional conservative interests was expected and not particularly troublesome. Censure from the liberal community struck much closer to home. Throughout the era of the Warren Court, a steady stream of criticism emanated from the pens of many prominent scholars whose understandings of the proper role of the judiciary had been honed during the battles of the Roosevelt presidency.[25] These critics condemned judicial activism in the modern democratic state even if the efforts of the Warren Court furthered many policies and substantive goals championed by the critics. The problem was not *what* the Court was doing but that it was a *court* that was doing it. Even a redemptive decision like *Brown* v. *Board of Education* was not immune from criticism; in the words of Professor Kurland, the desegregation decisions illustrated the hubris of the Warren justices in forgetting that "the Court, by itself, is incapable of effecting fundamental changes in society."[26] Martin Shapiro, who has written extensively of the impact of the New Deal on modern judicial review, captures the irony of the situation perfectly: "To an outsider, if often seemed wondrous indeed that so much

24. For a recent work that seeks to place the Warren Court in a political perspective, see Lucas A. Powe, Jr., *The Warren Court and American Politics* (Cambridge, MA: Harvard Univ. Press, 2000).

25. A classic example of such scholarship is Philip Kurland, *Politics, the Constitution, and the Warren Court* (Chicago: Univ. of Chicago Press, 1970). See also Alexander Bickel, *The Supreme Court and the Idea of Progress* (New Haven: Yale Univ. Press, 1978). An article by Robert Bork, much discussed during his Senate confirmation hearings, broadly fits this description. See his "Neutral Principles and Some First Amendment Problems," *Indiana Law Journal* 47 (1971): 1.

26. 347 U.S. 483 (1954); Kurland, *Politics, the Constitution, and the Warren Court*, 113.

energy was expended in seeking to persuade a particular organ of government not to act to achieve a goal that the would-be persuader was so anxious that other parts of government achieve."[27]

These critiques from the academic community suggest the magnitude of the revolution wrought by the Warren Court. A decade after Earl Warren's retirement from the Court, Judge J. Harvie Wilkinson began his history of the Supreme Court's campaign to end segregation in the nation's public schools with the sweeping conclusion that the Warren Court's decision in *Brown* v. *Board of Education* "may be the most important political, social, and legal event in America's twentieth-century history."[28] *Brown* was unquestionably a most decisive battle in the movement to end apartheid in America, and Judge Wilkinson can hardly be charged with overstatement in seeing it as a transforming moment in American history. But the Warren Court's commitment to equality and social change obviously did not stop with the decision in *Brown*. Throughout the tumultuous 1960s, the Supreme Court linked constitutional decision making to the demands of a changing American society. In applying the critical provisions of the Fourth, Fifth, Sixth, and Eighth Amendments to the states, the Court revolutionized the practice of criminal law in the states.[29] Throughout the era, the protections of the First

27. Shapiro, "Fathers and Sons," 219. See other citations in n. 21, above.

28. J. Harvie Wilkinson, *From Brown to Bakke: The Supreme Court and School Integration: 1954–1978* (Oxford: Oxford Univ. Press, 1979), 6. In 1984, Ronald Reagan named Wilkinson to the U.S. Court of Appeals for the Fourth Circuit, and Wilkinson is often mentioned as a possible nominee to the Supreme Court during Republican administrations.

29. The debate over whether any or all of the provisions of the Bill of Rights limited state governments began with the passage of the Fourteenth Amendment and continued with varying degrees of intensity through much of the twentieth century. See Henry Abraham, *Freedom and the Court*, 5th ed. (New York: Oxford Univ. Press, 1988), chap. 3, for a brief history. The Warren Court's principal contribution was in the area of criminal procedure, applying to state criminal proceedings the Fourth Amendment search-and-seizure provisions, in *Mapp v. Ohio*, 367 U.S. 43 (1961); the Fifth Amendment's protections against self-incrimination, in *Malloy v. Hogan*, 378 U.S. 1 (1964), and double jeopardy, in *Benton v. Maryland*, 395 U.S. 784 (1969); the Sixth Amendment's guarantees of a jury trial, in *Duncan v. Louisiana*, 391 U.S. 145 (1968); confrontation, in

Amendment were expanded to protect unpopular activities ranging from mass demonstrations to the viewing of sexually explicit
movies. The Court energized a hitherto dormant Equal Protection Clause, and in a decision of momentous significance, the
Court for the first time recognized a constitutionally sanctioned
right of privacy.[30] The Court's participation in the political and
social life of the nation, in short, was broad and deep.

The judicial theorists of the New Deal had formulated the
rules of justiciability and jurisdiction to narrow the sphere of judicial influence and free the elected branches from judicial control.
Their guiding principle throughout the first half of the twentieth
century was that judicial power was ultimately destructive of progressive politics. The heart of the Warren Court's revolt against the
old order was its rejection of this ideal of judicial modesty. The
results of any number of Warren era decisions might inflame conservative critics, but for an older generation of liberals, the Court
was now guilty of the worst kind of judicial hubris. In renouncing
the New Dealer's belief that judicial power should not be employed
as an agent of social change, the justices of the Warren era confidently thrust the Supreme Court and the federal judiciary into the
maelstrom of American politics. Whatever its merits, the consequences of that undertaking would be felt for generations to come.

Baker *v.* Carr: *The Warren Court at Work*

Although Earl Warren came to the chief justiceship in 1953, the
Warren Court did not reach full speed until the mid-1960s. Even

---

Pointer v. *Texas*, 380 U.S. 400 (1965), counsel, *Gideon* v. *Wainwright*, 372 U.S. 335 (1963);
and speedy trial, in *Klopfer* v. *North Carolina*, 386 U.S. 213 (1967); and the Eighth Amendment ban on cruel and unusual punishments, in *Robinson* v. *California*, 370 U.S. 660
(1962). The excerpts from the Fortas hearings in chapter 1 are striking examples of the
controversy these decisions engendered.

30. A description of the Warren Court's efforts in each of these areas can be found
in Powe, *The Warren Court*, as well as Morton J. Horwitz, *The Warren Court and the Pursuit of Justice* (New York: Hill and Wang, 1998). The privacy decision is the famous *Griswold* v. *Connecticut*, 381 U.S. 479 (1965).

the famous 1954 *Brown* decision did not begin to suggest the sweeping changes in the nature of judicial power that would take place in the next decade. It was not until the 1962 decision in *Baker* v. *Carr*, a case raising the difficult legal and potentially divisive question of whether malapportioned state legislatures violate the Constitution, that the real measure of the impending judicial revolution became readily evident.[31]

With the end of the Civil War began the great migration to America's cities. This general demographic trend, however, was not reflected in the makeup of most legislative and congressional districts in the nation. By the turn of the century, urban and suburban voters were seriously underrepresented in the state legislatures as well as in the House of Representatives. Since most state legislators were predictably unwilling to alter the electoral systems that placed them in office, those seeking to stem the disenfranchisement of urban voters sought judicial relief. State courts, however, often proved hesitant in ordering meaningful changes in the makeup of legislatures, and litigants who pursued similar claims in federal courts were met with a holding that the constitutionality of malapportioned legislatures was a political question and therefore nonjusticiable.

The political-question doctrine remains a fundamental example of a prudential rule intended to ensure that the federal courts avoid unnecessary conflict with other units of government. Stated much too simply for its complexity to be captured, the doctrine requires a federal court to refuse to rule on an issue properly before the court upon a determination that such an issue is unsuitable for judicial resolution. A claim that a particular issue constitutes a political question requires a court to determine whether it has the institutional competence to render judgment. A favorite of New Deal advocates of judicial modesty, the doctrine enables judges to avoid unnecessary clashes with the other branches and to soften the impact of the power of judicial review

31. 369 U.S. 186 (1962).

on the democratic process, by holding that particular issues are not amenable to judicial determination and better resolved by the other branches of government.[32]

For many years the apportionment of seats in state legislatures and congressional districting was considered just such a political question. During the 1940s, for example, Illinois congressional districts varied in population from 112,116 to 914,053. When neither the state legislature nor the state courts showed any willingness to redress the imbalance, a federal lawsuit was filed contending that the disparity in the size of Illinois congressional districts ran afoul of the U.S. Constitution. In *Colegrove* v. *Green*, Justice Frankfurter, writing for a four-judge plurality, denied relief, asserting that the Constitution conferred upon Congress the authority to guarantee fair representation in the House.[33] Although the federal courts had the jurisdiction (that is, the power and authority to decide the matter), judicial respect for the authority of another branch of government and the frank acknowledgment of the judiciary's limited competence in these matters compelled the conclusion that this was an issue best left unresolved by the federal courts. "Due regard for the effective working of our Government," Frankfurter noted, "revealed the issue to be of a particularly political nature and therefore not for judicial determination." He concluded with his soon-to-be-famous warning: "Courts ought not to enter this political thicket."

Frankfurter's conclusion in *Colegrove* that apportionment was a political question and thus nonjusticiable is hardly surprising; it is entirely consistent with the dominant New Deal phi-

32. The term "political question" often confuses neophytes in the at times arcane world of constitutional law. Because virtually every constitutional decision rendered by a federal court has political implications, relying on everyday parlance might lead one to believe that every constitutional issue presents a potential "political question." In the field of constitutional law, however, "political question" has a specialized meaning, although any attempt to nail down a precise definition is bound to fail. For an interesting essay on the political-question doctrine, see Louis Henkin, "Is There a Political Question Doctrine?" *Yale Law Journal* 85 (1976): 597.

33. 328 U.S. 549, 552 (1946).

losophy that a passive judiciary would best serve the needs of progressive politics. Finding that the case presented a political question permitted the Court to dispose of a difficult, politically charged issue without facing the Hobson's choice of holding the shamefully malapportioned Illinois scheme constitutionally valid or invalidating it and assuming the herculean task of measuring the democratic legitimacy of every elected body at the national, state, and local level. Hardly a champion of legislatures weighted to favor rural interests, Frankfurter nonetheless believed *Colegrove* to be an example of farsighted decision making, certainly consistent with the teachings of Holmes and Brandeis. Not only would judicial intervention deny the elected branches the primary responsibility for progressive change, but the perilous task of deciding what constituted fair representation might ultimately subject the federal judiciary to serious political reprisals.

Sixteen years later Frankfurter's continual admonitions regarding the teachings of Holmes and Brandeis and the lessons of the New Deal found a less receptive audience among his brethren on the Court. In March of 1962 the Court, over his vehement protests, essentially swept away the constraints of the political-question doctrine, holding in *Baker* v. *Carr* that the issue of malapportioned legislatures presented a justiciable claim under the equal-protection clause. Since 1901 not one reapportionment law had been passed in Tennessee, and, with urban voters seriously underrepresented in the state legislature, the plaintiffs in *Baker* sought a federal court decree holding the Tennessee apportionment scheme unconstitutional. A lower federal court dismissed the claim on the basis of *Colegrove*. In reversing and finding the issue of apportionment to be appropriate for judicial consideration, Justice Brennan's lengthy majority opinion marked the demise of the political-question doctrine as a significant limit on judicial power. In an internal memo to the chief justice and to Justices Black and Douglas, Brennan explained the necessity of his extended discussion of the political-question doctrine in the *Baker* opinion. "[A]fter much thought," he wrote, "I believe that

the full discussion of 'political question,' and its bearing on apportionment suits, is required if we are effectively and finally to dis-
pel the fog of another day produced by Felix's opinion in
Colegrove v. Green."[34] The "fog of another day"—that is, the
abiding faith that the judiciary could best serve progressive politics by playing an essentially secondary role—was at odds with
a new model of government that partnered an activist judiciary
with a dynamic executive branch in the quest to redefine American politics.

Immediately following the announcement of the result in
Baker, two events occurred that proved to be turning points in the
history of the Warren Court. Frankfurter had warned that entering the political thicket of reapportionment would expose the
Court to a political backlash that the judiciary was ill equipped
to resist. Such fears, however, proved groundless when the White
House embraced the outcome in *Baker*. Equality of representation,
President Kennedy noted in a news conference, was basic to a
democracy, and the attorney general, Robert Kennedy, also publicly defended the decision.[35] When the debate over reapportionment sharpened, presidential support for the judiciary
permitted the courts to weather the storm, and the reapportionment of the nation's legislatures took place with very little damage to the federal courts. Apart from the dire warnings of Justice
Frankfurter, the lesson of the reapportionment cases appeared to
be that judicial activism, when linked to presidential politics and
constituencies, could serve the cause of progressive politics.

The second event was of still greater import. Within days of
the decision in *Baker* v. *Carr*, Frankfurter suffered a debilitating

34. Bernard Schwartz, *Super Chief: Earl Warren and His Supreme Court—A Judicial
Biography* (New York: New York Univ. Press, 1983), 419–20.
35. Following the decision in *Baker* v. *Carr*, Dean Acheson, a Frankfurter friend,
asked Kennedy what he thought about the decision. Acheson reported the president
as saying "that legislatures would never reform themselves and that he did not see
how we were going to make any progress unless the Court intervened." Quoted ibid.,
425. Robert C. Cortner discusses the response to the reapportionment cases in his *The
Apportionment Cases* (Knoxville: Univ. of Tennessee Press, 1970), 176–77.

stroke and, in August of 1962, formally announced his retirement from the Court. In his twenty-three years of service, he had been the Court's most vocal and articulate (and, at times, most irritating and pedantic) champion of a jurisprudence of restraint. Justices Hugo Black and William Douglas, the remaining Roosevelt appointees, continued to serve, but their vision of the Court as a powerful nationalizing force in American politics was diametrically opposite to that of Frankfurter. Others would continue the battle for judicial restraint, but Frankfurter's departure snapped the Court's last remaining link with the New Deal ideal of judicial deference.[36] The Warren Court revolution was about to gather steam.

The Real Warren Court Revolution

In August of 1962 President Kennedy nominated his secretary of labor, Arthur Goldberg, to fill the Frankfurter seat. Easily confirmed by the Senate, Goldberg remained a justice of the Supreme Court for only three years. In 1965, at the behest of Lyndon Johnson, he resigned to become U.S. ambassador to the United Nations, and Johnson named Abe Fortas as his successor. The addition of Goldberg and then of Fortas solidified a working majority on the Court in favor of expanding federal judicial power to its constitutional limits. The chief justice's announced retirement in 1968 and the failure of the Fortas nomination marked the beginning of the end of this coalition, but, in the six years between Frankfurter's retirement and the Fortas hearings, the Court re-defined liberal assumptions concerning judicial power and in a profound, albeit indirect, way altered the politics of judicial confirmations.

36. Saying that Frankfurter's retirement from the Court hastened the activism of the Warren Court is not meant to suggest that the voiced of restraint was not absent from the Court. Justice John Harlan, for example, quickly emerged as Frankfurter's intellectual heir and as a superb advocate of restraint. Harland, however, lacked Frankfurter's all-consuming passion, as well as his irritating manner, and the Court functioned quite smoothly with Harlan as the spokesman of the loyal opposition.

Baker signaled what was to follow; within months of Frank-furter's departure, an energized Supreme Court resumed the cam-paign to dismantle the lattice of rules erected by the progressive jurists of the 1930s and 1940s to restrain judicial power. In short order the warnings of Brandeis in *Atherton* and *Ashwander* became quaint reminders of a bygone era. For example, the abstention doctrine provides that a federal court should decline to exercise jurisdiction and decide a constitutional issue when there are ques-tions of state law that are unsettled and may be dispositive of the case. Although the federal courts have the power to rule on both constitutional and state law questions, the proper course for the cautious federal jurist is to abstain while the parties litigate the state claims in state court. Resolution of the state law issues in the state courts may prove dispositive and make the federal court proceedings unnecessary. The doctrine in the 1940s and 1950s loomed as a significant weapon for avoiding constitutional issues linked to cases clearly within the jurisdiction of the federal courts.[37] With the retirement of Frankfurter the doctrine became, in the words of one law review commentator, a "judicial orphan" in the Court's haste to secure federal court adjudication of impor-tant constitutional rights.[38]

The Court's interpretation of the limits imposed by the standing-to-sue doctrine provides another important example. The standing doctrine directs a court's attention to whether the particular party seeking relief has a sufficient stake in the out-

---

37. For example, in *Harrison* v. *NAACP*, 360 U.S. 167 (1959), the Court invoked the abstention doctrine to avoid reaching the constitutional merits of a claim that Vir-ginia statutes regulating lobbying and litigation efforts by organized groups were being employed to harass the NAACP. A majority concluded that the Virginia courts might possibly construe the statutes in such a manner as to avoid the necessity of a consti-tutional ruling. The NAACP was required to file a new action in Virginia state court and, following a set of adverse rulings there, return to the Supreme Court, which ulti-mately ruled in its favor, *NAACP* v. *Button*, 371 U.S. 415 (1963). The four-year delay was simply considered a price paid for federalism and the need to restrain the exer-cise of judicial review.

38. See Note, "Federal-Question Abstention: Justice Frankfurter's Doctrine in an Activist Era," *Harvard Law Review* 80 (1967): 604.

come of the litigation to justify judicial resolution of the controversy. At a minimum, federal courts require a plaintiff to show "injury in fact" and that the injury is the result of the conduct challenged in the lawsuit. Deciding precisely what makes up the requisite injury and how close the nexus between the injury and the complained-of conduct must be has been the subject of countless suits and scholarly commentaries. To the jurist schooled in the judicial liberalism of the New Deal, limiting access to the federal courts through strict application of the standing doctrine is an important technique for avoiding difficult and perhaps unnecessary constitutional decisions.

In 1943, for example, the Court denied a Connecticut physician standing to challenge a state statute prohibiting the use, or assistance in the use, of contraceptive devices, because the physician asserted that the statute infringed the constitutional rights of his patients who were not party to the case.[39] The complaint failed to allege any injury to the doctor, and therefore the majority concluded he lacked the requisite interest in the outcome to satisfy the requirements of the standing doctrine. When, in 1961, a husband and wife and their doctor sought a declaration that the same statute was invalid, Justice Frankfurter, writing for the Court, again avoided a decision on the merits, by emphasizing that because the Connecticut statute had never been enforced against similar plaintiffs, the case was a hypothetical one and not appropriate for adjudication by the federal courts.[40] A decision on the constitutional merits of the Connecticut anti-birth-control law finally came in 1965 in *Griswold* v. *Connecticut*, when the Warren Court, undeterred by concerns of judicial vulnerability, swept aside any justiciability problems and held the statute invalid, recognizing for the first time a constitutional right of privacy.[41] By the mid-1960s the activist core of the Warren Court had relaxed

39. *Tileston* v. *Ullman*, 318 U.S. 44 (1943).
40. *Poe* v. *Ullman*, 367 U.S. 497 (1961). Frankfurter's opinion quoted extensively from the Brandeis opinion in *Ashwander*. Four justices dissented.
41. 381 U.S. 579 (1965).

the requirements of the standing doctrine to give a wide assortment of litigants the opportunity for a federal court determination of their constitutional claims.

The Court's rulings on abstention and standing as well as the other rules of justiciability, according to Professor Laurence Tribe, provide a "description of an institutional psychology: an account of how . . . the Justices of the Supreme Court view their own role."[42] In the case of the Warren Court, the role was that of an active partner with the executive branch in the transformation of American politics. The erosion of the judicially created limitations on judicial power expanded the reach of the federal judiciary, enhancing the opportunity of the courts to promote a new social and political agenda. In 1966, for instance, the Court amended Rule 23 of the Federal Rules of Civil Procedure to facilitate class action suits and thereby increased access to the federal courts for group litigants. To virtually no one's surprise, civil rights cases made up the vast majority of new class actions as the Court championed the causes of the racial and ethnic minorities of America, fusing the bond between the judiciary and the 1960s variant of the New Deal coalition.

All of this was a bit too much for those whose intellectual ties to the jurisprudence of the New Deal remained intact. "The [Warren] Court has substantially loosened the definition of a lawsuit," lamented Alexander Bickel, Frankfurter's most brilliant protégé; "it has opened the door wider to more litigants and has indeed come near to making the lawsuit something of a formality, still an expensive one, but within the reach of just about all who can afford it, at just about any time of their choice."[43] In Bickel's view the *unmistakable* lesson of the New Deal era was that expansion of the judicial role was incompatible with lasting reform and would ultimately threaten the institutional inde-

42. Laurence Tribe, *American Constitutional Law*, 2d ed. (Mineola, NY: Foundation Press, 1988), 68.
43. Bickel, *Supreme Court*, 108.

pendence of the judiciary. To the justices of the Warren Court, however, throwing off the shackles of a constricted view of the Court's power simply brought a greater diversity of litigants before the Court and rendered a wider range of issues subject to judicial determination.

Easing the rules governing justiciability was not the only transgression of the Warren Court, in the view of those who supported the model of judicial modesty; among its other sins they counted its opinion-writing technique and its eagerness to expand the nature and scope of judicial remedies. Brandeis in *Ashwander* urged the justices to focus their attention narrowly and render judgment only on questions necessary to the outcome of the case. Avoiding broad constitutional decrees, it was thought, would lessen the potential conflict between the federal judiciary and the democratic system, reserving most issues for resolution by majority rule. As the Warren revolution progressed, this admonition was all but forgotten, for the Court often moved beyond simply deciding a case and delivered broad and sometimes controversial policy pronouncements. The important decision in the 1966 case of *Miranda* v. *Arizona* provides a convenient example.[44]

Ernesto Miranda had been arrested and taken to a police interrogation room and, without being advised of his right to have an attorney present, questioned for several hours. At his trial on charges of rape and kidnapping, Miranda's statements to the police were admitted into evidence, over the objection of his attorney. The basic issue presented in *Miranda* and its companion cases was whether self-incriminating statements made without full warning of the suspect's constitutional rights could be used at trial to secure a conviction. In a 5-to-4 decision, the Court held the statements inadmissible. Assigned the task of crafting the majority opinion, a proponent of judicial modesty might have carefully fashioned a narrow opinion closely tailored to the facts of the case, relying on future cases to develop incrementally a

44. 384 U.S. 436 (1966).

comprehensive set of constitutional rules governing the questioning of criminal suspects. Chief Justice Warren's opinion, however, seized the opportunity to establish a detailed code of police behavior designed to govern all future police-suspect confrontations. Thirty-two pages of the opinion were dedicated to the discussion and formulation of the famous *Miranda* warnings—the explicit statement of the suspect's rights that henceforth would be required to be given to the suspect prior to police interrogation—while less than nine pages dealt with the constitutional authority for the result. Furthermore, by holding that some newly announced constitutional standards applied only prospectively, the Warren Court bypassed a very real inhibition on the Court's willingness to alter rules of criminal procedure.[45]

The explosion of public law litigation and litigants in the 1960s created the need for innovative remedies to effectuate the expanded judicial role. The transition from a judiciary primarily engaged in resolving private disputes to one confronting many of the most pressing and intractable of society's problems required a change in the nature and scope of judicial decrees.[46] The Warren Court encouraged judges throughout the federal system to fashion innovative remedies that often required public officials to implement complex and varied policies designed by the court to square the defendant's practices with constitutional requirements. As a result, federal courts assumed the day-to-day

45. Consider the problem presented by *Miranda*. The Court's alteration of the constitutional standards of police-suspect confrontations would naturally trigger a subsequent case contending that a prisoner who did not receive the proper warnings—even though tried and convicted before the decision in *Miranda*—should be entitled to a habeas corpus hearing and perhaps release from prison. The prospect of thousands of hearings and retrials for convicted prisoners imposes an enormous constraint on a Court contemplating a change in the constitutional rules of criminal procedure. Holding that *Miranda* applied only prospectively—see *Johnson* v. *New Jersey*, 384 U.S. 719 (1966)—freed the Court from this constraint.

46. See, for example, Phillip Cooper, *Hard Judicial Choices; Federal District Court Judges and Local Officials* (New York: Oxford Univ. Press, 1988); Donald Horowitz, *The Courts and Social Policy* (Washington, DC: Brookings Institution, 1970); Abram Chayes, "The Role of the Judge in the Public Interest Litigation," *Harvard Law Review* 89 (1976): 1281.

operation of public schools, prisons, public housing, and state mental institutions. By the 1970s the federal judiciary had carved out the power to detail the manner in which other governmental units would conduct their business and was thus able to provide successful litigants with remedies similar to those previously available only through the executive or legislative branches.[47]

The most striking decisions of the Warren era—the desegregation cases, the efforts to enlarge the protections afforded by the First Amendment, and the continued nationalization of the Bill of Rights—remain that Court's most important legacies. These were the decisions that captured the headlines, galvanizing the Court's supporters, infuriating its critics, and challenging a scholarly tradition skeptical of the judiciary's capacity to bring about redemptive social change. The substructure for this constitutional revolution was far less visible but no less significant and certainly as revolutionary. The arcane and complex world of justiciability standards and federal court jurisdiction did not lend itself to newspaper headlines or facile editorial commentary, but the Warren Court's work in these areas posed a weighty challenge to the old order. By the mid-1960s, the advocates of judicial activism had no doubt that a dynamic federal judiciary could further progressive objectives, particularly by linking the fate of the disadvantaged and electorally powerless with that of the Court. A judiciary sensitive to the needs of racial, ethnic, and religious minorities, employing the equal-protection clause and the First Amendment to simplify mass politics and communication, would also be assured the political support of the Kennedy and Johnson administrations. When asked, Earl Warren invariably pointed to *Baker* v. *Carr* as the Court's most important decision during his tenure as chief justice. *Baker* was not only the opening gambit in the Court's campaign to constitutionalize the "one man, one vote" principle but also a direct assault on the citadel of judicial restraint

47. For a conservative's critique of this development, see Gary McDowell, *Equity and the Constitution* (Chicago: Univ. of Chicago Press, 1982).

and an unequivocal proclamation that the standards of justiciability would no longer stand as a bar to the Court's defense of enlightened self-government.

THE BURGER COURT

A New Constituency for the Federal Courts

The failed Fortas nomination of 1968 symbolized the end of the Warren Court revolution, but the impact of the Warren years on the nature of judicial power survived the passing of the men who gave the revolution life. The jurists of the New Deal had hoped to harmonize judicial review with the needs of a modern, progressive society by obliging judges to observe a stringent assortment of restrictions on the exercise of judicial power. Shrinking the scope of judicial influence, they believed, would create greater constitutional space for the other branches to govern effectively. The Warren Court revolution of the mid-1960s constituted a frontal attack on this essentially passive understanding of the judicial role. The judicial theorists of the New Deal valued strict adherence to the rules of standing because rigorously confining who could properly invoke the jurisdiction of the federal courts would diminish the judiciary's impact on the political system. The justices of the Warren Court, however, liberalized the standing rules with precisely the opposite outcome in mind. Likewise, the political-question doctrine narrowed the range of issues federal courts could properly decide; disregarding it as a limitation broadened the capacity of the federal courts to pass judgment on novel claims. Historically the exercise of judicial review had involved the exercise of a negative power, basically returning the parties to the situation that existed before the enforcement of the challenged government action. By the late 1960s, decisions like *Miranda* and the development of new judicial remedies had made the federal courts active participants in reform, permitting judges to direct other political actors on precisely how to achieve the policy outcomes sought by the court.

In opening the doors of the federal courthouse to a multitude of new litigants and constitutional claims and providing potent remedies to those who prevailed, the justices of the Warren Court established the federal judiciary as a commanding force in the policymaking process. Whatever the merits of this development—and much may be said both pro and con—an unanticipated consequence was to make the selection of the men and women who would sit on the federal bench a matter of vast importance and concern to an array of groups and interests far wider than ever before in American history. The Fortas defeat was simply one of the first manifestations of the new state of affairs. The appointment of Warren Burger the following year as chief justice did not alter this new reality. Although Burger did not share his predecessor's soaring vision of the Court as the protector of the weak and disenfranchised, the Burger Court did not significantly tighten access to the federal court or surrender the tools of judicial power fashioned during the Warren era.[48]

Scholars have long recognized that groups unable to compete in the legislative or executive arena often turn to the courts for access to government power.[49] The first tentative acknowl-

48. Although the Burger Court is generally considered more moderate in its actions than is its predecessor, it did not seriously alter the Warren Court's liberalized justiciability standards. See Bernard Schwartz, *The Ascent of Pragmatism: The Burger Court in Action* (Reading, MA: Addison-Wesley, 1990), chap. 2; William Atkin and Burton Taggart, "Substantive Access Doctrines and Conflict Management in the U.S. Supreme Court: Reflections on Activism and Restraint," in Stephen Halpern and Charles Lamb, eds., *Supreme Court Activism and Restraint* (Lexington, MA: Lexington Books, 1982). Although specific decisions, such as Justice Powell's discussion of standing in *Warth* v. *Sedlin*, 422 U.S. 490 (1975), might contrast with effort of the Warren Court, access to the federal courts was not significantly confined by the Burger Court, and the expansive decisions of the Warren era were not overruled. As a result, the current Court find itself in a uniquely powerful position, blessed with recent precedent that can be used to grant or deny litigants access to the federal courts without flagrant disregard for judicial standards.

49. See Richard Cortner, "Strategies and Tactics of Litigation in Constitutional Cases," *Journal of Public Law* 17 (1968): 287.

edgment of a duty to act on behalf of such groups came from the Supreme Court in 1938.[50] By the 1960s, the judicial obligation to the politically powerless had led to much of the activism of the Warren Court, including the drive to reexamine the justiciability standards. This "out-group" understanding of interest group litigation, however, fails to capture the Warren era's extraordinary impact on judicial power. Throwing the doors of the courthouse wide open and providing an extensive range of remedies to those who entered ultimately benefited not only the disadvantaged but many affluent, middle- and upper-middle-class interests. With the coming of the Burger Court, in the early 1970s, an assortment of these interests—for example, environmentalists, feminists, consumer groups, political reformers—found in the judiciary an attractive alternative to the other branches in the battle to secure their goals. Thirty years previously the majority of those groups seeking access to the federal courts may well have been the politically impotent; in the modern era, however, increased access to the courts has combined with the new tools of judicial power to make the judiciary an attractive ally for a host of powerful constituent groups.[51]

50. *United States* v. *Carolene Products Co.*, 304 U.S. 144 (1938), was an unremarkable decision upholding a federal statute excluding "filled milk" from interstate commerce. It was based on the New Deal wisdom that the Court would not interfere with congressional decisions unless the legislature had acted without a rational basis. In the famous footnote 4 to that decision, however, Justice Stone suggested that judicial activism might be justified when (1) the legislation was within a specific prohibition of the Constitution (for example, the Bill of Rights), (2) the legislation restricted the ability of groups and individuals to influence the political process, and (3) the legislation was aimed at disadvantaging "discrete and insular minorities" unable to protect their interests in the political process.

51. This is not to suggest that comparatively affluent, progressive groups shunned court action prior to the late 1960s. During the early twentieth century the National Consumers League frequently appeared in court, often represented by Louis Brandeis and Felix Frankfurter in their pre-Court days, in litigation to improve working conditions. Typically, however, the NCL was engaged in *defensive* litigation to protect enacted legislation against constitutional attack. See Clement Vose, "National Consumers League and the Brandeis Brief," *Midwest Journal of Political Science* 1 (1957): 267.

The Legacy of the Warren Court: Roe *v.* Wade

The failure of the Senate to confirm Justice Fortas as chief justice in 1968 also set in motion a series of events that altered the makeup of the Supreme Court. To succeed the retiring Earl Warren, the newly elected Richard Nixon selected Warren Burger, a judge on the Court of Appeals for the District of Columbia Circuit, who had attracted Nixon's attention through his unrelenting criticism of the Warren Court's criminal procedure decisions. Before Nixon announced the Burger nomination, however, another vacancy opened up on the Court as Justice Fortas announced his resignation.[52] Burger was easily confirmed as chief justice, but the old civil rights establishment dramatically reasserted itself on the question of who would replace the newly departed Fortas. The Senate's repudiation of first Clement Haynsworth and then G. Harrold Carswell to succeed Fortas is chronicled later in this volume; ultimately Harry Blackmun, a childhood friend of the new chief justice and an appellate judge on the federal bench in the Midwest, was the compromise choice of an exhausted Senate and a furious president. Within a year of his coming to the Court, the quiet and unassuming Justice Blackmun would have his baptism of fire.

Roe v. *Wade* provides perhaps the starkest example of the Warren Court's impact on its allegedly more cautious successor.[53] There is little need to chronicle here the controversy engendered by *Roe* since the decision was announced, early in 1973. In the minds of those with degrees from the Frankfurter school of constitutional jurisprudence, the tumult was the result of yet another judicially self-inflicted wound, because in their view *Roe* was a case that cried out for judicial avoidance. In the years preceding *Roe*, a significant reform movement advocating the liberalization of the nation's abortion laws appeared in several states. Between 1967 and 1973, nineteen states had reformed their abortion

52. See chap. 1, note 22, for the events surrounding the Fortas resignation.
53. 410 U.S. 113 (1973).

statutes, with New York, Hawaii, and Alaska repealing criminal restrictions through the twentieth week of a pregnancy.[54] The emergence of several important women's groups intensified the political debate; for example, the National Organization for Women was established in 1966 and a year later voted to include reproductive freedom in NOW's women's bill of rights. Although reform may not have been immediate or sweeping, by the early 1970s debate over abortion was part of mainstream American politics, and even the most sympathetic of judges might, in good faith, avoid reaching a difficult and novel constitutional issue in deference to the workings of the democratic system.

Abortion was, moreover, not an issue that lent itself to easy judicial resolution. Many of the nation's abortion statutes made performing an abortion a crime. The party directly affected was the doctor, but old justiciability decisions could be cited to bolster the conclusion that the doctor lacked standing to assert the constitutional rights of her patients. The claim of a pregnant woman that the Constitution guaranteed her the abortion choice might be met by a dismissal for mootness; none other than Brandeis himself had urged progressive jurists to pay particular attention to whether controversial cases posed a live, ongoing controversy and the human gestation period is far shorter than that of a constitutional case.[55] In short, the claim that the Constitution protected a woman's right to an abortion was precisely the type of case that a generation of judges had been schooled to avoid.

54. See Laurence Tribe, *Abortion: The Clash of Absolutes* (New York: Norton, 1990), chap. 3, for a brief review of the history of restrictions on abortion in the United States.

55. The flip side of mootness is ripeness, another limitation imposed by standards of justiciability. Mootness asks whether the controversy that existed between the parties has been concluded, that is, whether there continues to exist a "live" controversy. Ripeness, on the other hand, demands that federal courts determine whether the controversy has become sufficiently focused and concrete to warrant judicial intervention. Very simply, a finding of mootness is a finding that judicial intervention is coming too late in the game, while the ripeness requirement asks whether it is coming too early. For an example of the cautious jurist attempting to use ripeness to avoid a constitutional issue, see Justice Frankfurter dissenting in *Adler* v. *Board of Education*, 342 U.S. 485 (1952).

Just before the commencement of the 1971 term of the Court, Justices Black and Harlan retired because of failing health. With little likelihood that replacements could be nominated and confirmed in quick order, the Court was faced with proceeding through a good part of the term with only seven sitting justices. Chief Justice Burger appointed justices Stewart and Blackmun to review the docket and determine which of the cases presented controversies that could adequately be handled by seven justices. In what in hindsight can only be seen as the classic judicial understatement, *Roe v. Wade* was one of the cases designated by Stewart and Blackmun.[56]

In both *Roe* and its companion case, *Doe v. Bolton*, pregnant women sought a declaration that state abortion laws were unconstitutional. The three-year delay between the filing of the cases and Supreme Court review meant that the cases could easily be found to be moot and subject to dismissal, because the petitioners no longer had a personal stake in their outcomes. Following in the tradition of the Warren Court, however, not one justice on the Burger Court gave more than a passing thought to avoiding this complex (not to mention politically divisive) constitutional issue through the expedient route of a dismissal for mootness.[57] The chief justice assigned the opinion to Justice Blackmun, a decision no doubt in part motivated by the belief that although the Court had passed on any procedural disposition of the case, Burger was confident that Blackmun would write a "narrowly focused opinion that would discharge the Court's duty without doing or saying anything more than necessary."[58] Justice Blackmun's original draft opinion for the Court sought just this outcome by holding that the Texas statute was too vague in describing

56. See Linda Greenhouse, *Becoming Justice Blackmun: Harry Blackmun's Supreme Court Journey* (New York: Times Books, 2005), 80. A subsequent memo written by Justice Blackmun suggests that at least prior to argument and conference Justice Stewart thought the cases could be disposed of on procedural grounds.

57. At the first conference following the initial argument in *Roe*, all the justices agreed without much discussion that none of the possible justiciability arguments foreclosed a decision on the merits. Schwartz, *Ascent of Pragmatism*, 47.

58. Greenhouse, *Becoming Justice Blackmun*, 82.

when an abortion could and could not legally be performed.[59] Such a holding would have accomplished much the same as a dismissal for mootness: disposing of the case without a binding determination of the basic issue of whether the constitution protected from state interference a woman's decision regarding abortion.

The circulation of the Blackmun draft opinion prompted Justices Douglas and Brennan immediately to respond with "Dear Harry" letters reminding Blackmun that a majority in the conference had voted to reach the core constitutional issue.[60] The reaction of Douglas and Brennan (who, along with Justice Thurgood Marshall, made up the Court's unreconstructed liberals) was perhaps to be expected; more enlightening was the fact that Blackmun's vagueness argument, like the mootness point, failed to attract any significant support among his other colleagues. Liberals and conservatives appeared equally disposed to confront the merits of the abortion claim. As a result, Justice Blackmun's majority opinion, issued a year later, simply dispenses with the justiciability problems in a few sentences. The remainder of the opinion, following the *Miranda* technique, not only unequivocally establishes the constitutional protection for a woman's right to choose, but describes at some length an elaborate, judicially created framework to govern state efforts to regulate abortion in the future.[61]

59. Schwartz, *Ascent of Pragmatism*, 301. A criminal statute is considered constitutionally "void for vagueness" when it fails to provide adequate notice of what behavior is considered criminal. The Texas statute permitted abortions "to save the life of the mother." Blackburn concluded that this criterion did not inform the physician whether an abortion could be performed only when the patient would certainly die without it or whether an abortion was permissible when there was simply a possibility that the patient would die without it.

60. Ibid., 303.

61. When his colleagues failed to enthusiastically embrace his "void for vagueness" argument to dispose of the case, Justice Blackmun agreed to have the cases held over to allow the newly appointed justices—Rehnquist and Powell—to participate. While the liberals such as Douglas and Brennan had grave misgivings about holding the case over, reargument ultimately did not affect the outcome, as Powell joined Justice Blackmun's majority opinion and Justice Rehnquist dissented. What is interesting is that the newly appointed Powell encouraged Blackmun to ground the case on a broad right to abortion rather than the narrow vagueness argument. See Greenhouse, *Becoming Justice Blackmun*, 93; John Jeffries, Jr., *Justice Lewis F. Powell, Jr.* (New York: Scribner's, 1994), chap. 11.

Reaching the merits of a similar case in a similar posture would have been unthinkable twenty-five years earlier. A decade of increased access to the courts coupled with the emergence of a politically potent women's movement made the abortion issue palatable to the justices of the Burger Court. The Warren Court, in its quest to serve the disadvantaged, had opened the doors of the federal courthouse, and during the Burger years a multitude of interests, including upper-middle-class citizens and professional groups, marched right in. Following *Roe*, groups such as NOW, the American Civil Liberties Union, the Women's Equity Action League, the Women's Legal Defense Fund, and Planned Parenthood devoted substantial time and effort to litigation in the federal courts in the effort to realize substantive goals broadly identified with the women's movement. Even groups not typically associated with court action—for example, the American Association of University Women and the League of Women Voters—were soon filing briefs and sponsoring litigation to further their particular policy agenda.[62] Their adroitness in using the federal courts provoked opposition groups like the Americans United for Life and the United States Catholic Conference to develop countervailing litigation strategies. Quite rapidly, federal courthouses became the principal battlefields in the war to define the depth and breadth of gender equality in the United States. To those who had kept the faith with the New Deal idea of restraint—regardless of their position on gender equality—this was precisely the outcome they had fought so hard to avoid.

Feminists and their rivals were, of course, not the only groups to focus attention on the federal courts. Indeed, during the years of the Burger Court the overall group presence in the federal judicial system increased substantially.[63] Although tradi-

---

62. See Tracy George and Lee Epstein, "Women's Rights Litigation in the 1980s: More of the Same?" *Judicature* 74 (1991): 314.

63. See Lee Epstein, "Courts and Interest Groups," in John B. Gates and Charles A. Johnson, *The American Courts: A Critical Assessment* (Washington, DC: CQ Press, 1991), for a discussion of the scholarly literature and data pointing to the increase in

tional business interests continued to be the most frequent participants, there was a marked increase in the participation rates of citizens' groups reflecting essentially middle- and upper-middle-class concerns. The expectations of the Warren Court notwithstanding, increased access, whether to the judiciary or to Congress, eventually benefits the affluent and the educated. Thus beyond women's right advocates, groups promoting consumer and environmental causes, for example, quickly established impressive litigation records during this period. Several commentators reviewing this period have noted that *organized* environmental interests, as opposed to individuals seeking redress for alleged environmental transgressions, found the federal courts particularly receptive to their claims.[64] The considerable body of environmental and consumer protection case law now on the books was nonexistent a mere thirty years ago, and the plethora of law school offerings in these subjects today is testimony to the willingness of the modern courts to consider novel claims on behalf of organized, affluent litigants.[65]

Another indicator of expanded group influence during the 1970s and 1980s is the explosive growth in the number of amicus curiae (friend of the court) briefs filed with the Supreme Court. The amicus brief was originally intended to offer a means by which a

interest group activity during the last twenty years. Professor Epstein's essay also discusses the value of the amicus curiae brief to groups seeking to influence the Supreme Court. One measure of the increased use of the courts in the 1970s and 1980s might well be the escalating critical rhetoric of those clinging to the New Deal understanding of the role of the courts. In this vein see Richard Morgan, *Disabling America: The Rights Industry in Our Time* (New York: Basic, 1983).

64. On the success of organized groups like the Sierra Club, as opposed to individual or ad hoc interests in environmental litigation, see Lettie M. Wenner, *The Environmental Decade in Court* (Bloomington: Univ. of Indiana Press, 1982), chap. 3.

65. "The environmental plaintiff of the 1970s found a sympathetic reception in the [federal] courts." J. William Futrell, "The Ungreening of the Court," *Environmental Forum* (January–February 1992): 13. Mr. Futrell places special emphasis on the willingness of the federal judiciary in the 1970s to interpret federal environmental statutes broadly, at times seemingly moving well beyond the apparent intent of Congress in enacting the measure.

person or organization not party to a case could bring to the attention of the Court facts or legal matters that would not be adequately
presented by the parties. Relatively easy and inexpensive to file,
the amicus brief has in recent years proven to be an extremely popular medium for groups with an interest in the outcome of a particular case to register their preferences with the Court. For
example, in the famous 1978 *Bakke* case, in which the Court confronted the controversial question of the constitutionality of affirmative action programs, 120 organizations joined in the filing of
fifty-eight amicus briefs.[66] In the 1982 term of the Court, 1,400
organizations submitted or joined in the sponsoring of amicus
briefs. By the 1987 term, amicus briefs were filed in 80 percent of
the cases decided by the Court on the merits.[67] This trend has continued uninterrupted. A not untypical 1991 case, *United Mine Workers* v. *Johnson Controls*, turned on the question of whether the Civil
Rights Act of 1964 barred employers from excluding fertile women
from jobs out of concern for the fetus the woman might conceive.[68]
Participating through the amicus process were such disparate
groups as the American Nurses Association, the National Resources
Defense Council, and the United States Catholic Conference.

   When groups broadly located on the left of the political spectrum (see the discussion of "New Progressives" in chapter 3)
found the judiciary a sympathetic ally in the battle to secure policy goals, interests with a conservative agenda took steps to
develop their own litigation program. The growth of conservative public-interest law firms and legal foundations, another phe-
nomenon of the last two decades, is further testimony to the
federal judiciary's increased significance to an entirely new set of
interests.[69] When, during the early 1970s, several liberal groups

---

66. *Regents of the University of California* v. *Bakke*, 438 U.S. 265 (1978).
   67. Lawrence Baum, *The Supreme Court*, 4th ed. (Washington, DC: CQ Press,
1992), 86–87.
   68. 111 S. Ct. 1196 (1991).
   69. See, for example, Lee Epstein, *Conservatives in Court* (Knoxville: Univ. of Tennessee Press, 1985).

sponsored litigation challenging then Governor Ronald Reagan's attempts to impose substantial cuts on the California welfare system, conservatives founded the Pacific Legal Foundation to provide a conservative counterpart to liberal public-interest law firms. The success of the Pacific Legal Foundation spawned other conservative litigation groups. The Mountain States Legal Foundation, for example, sponsored several important legal actions on behalf of conservative interests and supplied a pool of unabashedly conservative lawyers to Republican administrations.[70] The Capital Legal Foundation supported and litigated General Westmoreland's libel action against *60 Minutes* and the Columbia Broadcasting System. Without undue exaggeration it can be said that the federal courts now form a crucial theater of operations for a wide array of upper-middle-class interests seeking to use a receptive and activist judiciary to promote policy goals. What began as the Warren Court's effort to empower the underdogs now often serves the interests of the affluent and politically powerful.

Judge Bork and the Modern Confirmation Process

Simple observations often provide the most satisfactory explanations for complex phenomena. The crescendo of voices demanding to be heard in the modern confirmation process is in no small measure a by-product of the expanded role of the federal judiciary in late-twentieth-century America. The Warren Court altered not only the nature of judicial power but the nature of the confirmation process as well. Powerful groups from all points along the ideological spectrum now consider a sympathetic judiciary essential to the development and achievement of important policy goals. Nominations to the Supreme Court and, to a lesser degree, to the lower federal courts thus command the attention

70. For example, Mountain States provided the Reagan administration James Watt (secretary of the interior) and Rex Lee (solicitor general).

of a wide range of interests, provoke sophisticated campaigns to mobilize grassroots support, and trigger the expenditure of substantial sums of private money in the effort to sway public opinion. Given the expansion of judicial power and influence over the last three decades, it should hardly be surprising that the process of selecting and confirming federal judges increasingly resembles a national electoral campaign.

The clash over the nomination of Robert Bork to the Supreme Court offers the most distinctive example of the new politics of judicial power. For our limited purposes it is important not to lose sight of the fact that Judge Bork not only had unchallenged professional qualifications for the high court but also was one of his generation's most vocal (and prominent) critics of the activism of the Warren Court. This fact alone assured a substantial level of opposition to his nomination. Early on, opponents of the nomination set about to compile a collection of Bork's scholarly writings and his opinions while a judge on the U.S. Court of Appeals. Exposure to what came to be known as the "Book of Bork," it was thought, would energize numerous groups with no predisposition to oppose Bork but with a growing interest in the staffing of the federal judiciary.[71] For example, in a 1985 interview Bork asserted that an expansive understanding of the standing-to-sue doctrine "would so enhance the power of the courts as to make them the dominant branch of government." He concluded the interview as follows: "Every time a court expands the definition of standing, the definition of interests it is willing to protect through adjudication, the area of judicial dominance grows and the area of democratic rule contracts.[72]

The real task of the groups initially opposing Bork was to use his derision of the broad expansion of judicial power of the

---

71. Michael Pertschuk and Wendy Schaetzel, *The People Rising* (New York: Thunder's Mouth Press, 1989), chap. 3 of which describes the evolution and the content of the "Book of Bork."

72. Quoted in Patrick McGuigan and Dawn Weyrich, *Ninth Justice* (Washington, DC: Free Congress, 1990), 297.

last several decades as the catalyst for propelling into the fray groups not normally associated with confirmation battles. During the course of the Bork proceedings, for example, the general counsel of the Audubon Society was moved to write to the members of the Senate Judiciary Committee and illustrate how Bork's interpretation of the rules of standing and justiciability might seriously constrict the ability of citizen groups to challenge in federal court "the weakening of national surface mining regulations" or to require the government "to issue regulations protecting visibility in our national parks to protect some unique and threatened resources like Mono Lake, the Alaska Coastal Plain or whooping cranes in Central Nebraska."[73] Similar concerns united many organizations opposing Judge Bork. The alliance that formed in 1987 to defeat the nomination was extraordinary, if only because of the diversity of interests that united in a common endeavor.[74] Building an effective coalition with interests ranging from the United Mine Workers to the National Gay and Lesbian Task Force is obviously no easy matter. In the Bork campaign the adhesive that bound these groups together was Bork's cramped conception of the role of the federal judiciary in modern America. In the 1960s the Warren Court's expansion of access to the federal courts was revolutionary; by the mid-1980s it was considered simply business as usual, and a vast array of interests was prepared to defend what was already part of the status quo. Bork was easily portrayed by his opponents as a radical conservative precisely because he was considered by many a threat to a dynamic and active federal judiciary.

The political moral of the Bork nomination battle is that there is a substantial reservoir of support for (or opposition to, for that matter) most nominees to the Court and that victory belongs to the side that most effectively mobilizes its active and potential

73. Quoted in Pertschuk and Schaetzel *People Rising*, 184.
74. The number of groups campaigning to defeat Bork numbered in the neighborhood of three hundred. See ibid., appendix B, for a "representative sampling" of these groups.

supporters. Notwithstanding cries of foul by many passionate Bork supporters, his failed nomination was hardly the handiwork of a cabal of liberal activists, perverting the normal politics of judicial selection.[75] The roots of Bork's defeat reached back thirty years, to the activism of the Warren era, and the particular circumstances of the Bork nomination (a lame-duck and weakened Republican president, a particularly controversial nominee, a Senate controlled by Democrats) simply added fuel to an already raging fire. The nomination of Robert Bork was defeated because the opposition understood the reality of modern judicial confirmations better than did his supporters. Little wonder that an ardent Bork supporter and conservative activist vowed in the wake of the Bork defeat "to prepare for every confirmation battle to be the legislative equivalent of a senatorial campaign with high dollar media expenditures, vigorous negative advertising, and polemical theatrics."[76]

The shattering defeat of Judge Bork energized the right wing of the Republican party. In the months following the failed nomination, organizations connected with the New Right searched out potential candidates for judicial positions and began to develop strategies for securing their nomination and eventual confirmation.[77] Clarence Thomas was the product of just such a talent search. During his days as the head of the Equal Employment Opportunity Commission, Thomas met with several New Right organizations to assure them of the soundness of his views on the social and legal issues of the day. These same organizations actively promoted his appointment to the court of appeals in 1989 and two years later assisted in securing his nomination to succeed the retiring Justice Marshall on the Supreme Court. The Thomas nomination supplied conservative activists not sim-

75. See Suzanne Garment, "The War against Robert Bork," *Commentary* (January 1988): 17–26, for an example of the "liberal conspiracy/perversion of normal process" approach.
76. McGuigan and Weyrich, *Ninth Justice*, 221–22.
77. For a discussion of the New Right, see below, chap. 3.

ply with the long-awaited occasion to avenge the Bork defeat, but also with the opportunity to carry out new strategies for judicial confirmation. Applying the lessons learned during the Bork defeat, conservative groups began a major fund-raising and lobbying campaign to secure Senate confirmation and energize grassroots support.[78] Pat Robertson's Christian Coalition, for example, spent over one million dollars on behalf of the Thomas nomination, producing a television ad said to have generated over 100,000 letters and telephone calls in his favor. On the other hand, the opposition was stymied; liberals went out of their way to "like" Clarence Thomas. As the Bush administration correctly calculated, his Horatio Alger success story and his race undercut opposition to the nomination.

The allegations of sexual harassment on the eve of the Senate confirmation vote transformed the confirmation of a Supreme Court justice into a revelatory moment in American history. Even before Anita Hill's testimony fascinated a worldwide audience, however, the Thomas nomination was of signal importance. In 1987 the New Progressives had engineered a major political campaign to defeat the nomination of Robert Bork, a man whose professional qualifications would at first blush have seemed to guarantee him a seat on the Court. Four years later the New Right activists masterminded a similar crusade to place on the Court an individual with embarrassingly meager professional qualifications and substantial links to fringe rightwing political groups.

---

78. Timothy Phelps and Helen Winternitz, *Capitol Games: Clarence Thomas, Anita Hill, and the Story of a Supreme Court Nomination* (New York: Hyperion, 1992), details at some length the efforts of conservative groups on behalf of Thomas. Among these groups were Gary Bauer's Family Research Council, Phyllis Schafly's Eagle Forum, Beverly LaHaye's Concerned Women for America, the Reverend Louis Sheldon's Coalition for Traditional Values, and Pat Robertson's Christian Coalition. Although all these groups were united in their opposition to abortion, many reflected the extreme positions of the fringe radical Right. For example, LaHaye's group does not accept any separation of church and state, arguing that government officials who do not use the Bible as their guide to public life do not belong in office.

A Conservative Judicial Revolution?

With the confirmation of Clarence Thomas in 1991, the Republican reconstruction of the U.S. Supreme Court appeared complete. Thomas filled the seat of the legendary Thurgood Marshall. Marshall, appointed twenty-four years earlier by Lyndon Johnson, was the last justice with a direct connection to the Warren Court. Republican control of the White House, broken only by the four years of the Carter administration—and Carter did not have the opportunity to name a justice to the Court—had transformed the Court. During the decades between the appointment of Marshall and the confirmation of Clarence Thomas, Republican nominees to the Court came to the confirmation process portrayed as men and women who stood firm against the excesses of the Warren era. The would-be justice was invariably described by supporters as an advocate of "judicial restraint," a "strict constructionist" who would defer to the popularly elected branches and who would be loath to inject the judiciary into matters of public or social policy. The election of Democrat Bill Clinton in 1992 and his appointments of Ruth Bader Ginsburg and Stephen Breyer did not significantly alter this basic ritual; both Democratic nominees professed a similar diminished faith in the power of the judiciary to effect progressive social change.[79] In an age of Republican ascendancy, the Warren era's archetype of a judiciary enmeshed in the affairs of state seemed thoroughly repudiated.

The reality of American politics has always differed from its rhetoric, and this seems particularly the case with judicial confirmations. Republican resurgence produced a new Court, but it did not deliver a Court of modesty and deference. Speechifying aside, liberals and conservatives alike had learned to live quite comfortably with an activist judiciary; the Frankfurter model of

---

79. For example, Justice Ginsburg, well prior to her appointment, had challenged *Roe* v. *Wade* for the sweeping nature of the opinion, suggesting that a narrower opinion would have not preempted state legislative efforts at reform and would have not triggered the bitter controversy that followed. See, e.g., Ginsburg, "Some Thoughts on Autonomy and Equality in Relation to *Roe* v. *Wade*," *North Carolina Law Review* 63 (1985): 375–86.

judicial restraint simply did not serve the needs of partisan interests in the highly contentious, media-dominated world of modern American politics. The Warren justices had thrust the Court into the heart of American politics, and by the 1990s interests across the political spectrum had deduced that an activist judiciary could be an important ally in the fight to further policy objectives. The nation's gradual turn to the right in the last quarter of the twentieth century thus resulted not in a return to jurisprudence of deference but in the seeming anomaly of an *activist conservative* Court. As Thomas Keck, a political scientist who has best chronicled this development observed, the demands of the modern conservative movement in American politics have moved Republican justices to create "a Court that is playing an ever-broader role in the American political system."[80]

The examples are legion. Deference to a popularly elected coequal branch was not a guiding principle, to put it mildly, for the men and women of the Rehnquist Court; indeed the Court in the last decade or so has invalidated congressional statutes at a record-breaking rate.[81] Nor has a respect for *stare decisis* been a significant constraint on judicial activity; the Rehnquist justices had little hesitancy in reexamining settled law, particularly when the reexamination furthered the goals of the new Republican majority. Arguments, for example, grounded on judicial restraint and respect for established precedent fell on deaf judicial ears as the Court discovered in the Takings Clause a significant limit on governmental action, reset the balance in federal-state relations, reinterpreted the religion clauses of the First Amendment, and eviscerated the exclusionary rule as a means of enforcing Fourth Amendment constraints.[82] And, in a stunning display of judicial

80. Thomas Keck, *The Most Activist Supreme Court in History: The Road to Modern Judicial Conservatism* (Chicago: Univ. of Chicago Press, 2004), 13.

81. See Keck, *Most Activist Supreme Court*, 40.

82. On the Takings Clause consider, e.g., *Lucas* v. *South Carolina Coastal Council*, 505 U.S. 1003 (1992); on federal-state relations, *United States* v. *Morrison*, 529 U.S. 598 (2000); on religion, *Employment Division* v. *Smith*, 494 U.S. 872 (1990) and *Mitchell* v. *Helms*, 530 U.S. 793 (2000), and on the Fourth Amendment see *Arizona* v. *Evans*, 514 U.S. 1, (1995).

hubris, a majority on the Rehnquist Court cast the deciding vote in the 2000 presidential election. *Bush* v. *Gore* will most assuredly stand as one of one of the most divisive of Supreme Court decisions; that it was also the work of justices who came to the Court pledging to repudiate the activism of an earlier age makes it all the more remarkable.[83]

The electoral and legal fight to determine who would succeed Bill Clinton as the president of the United States ended on December 12, 2000, when the United States Supreme Court held that a recount of the Florida popular vote ordered by the Florida Supreme Court violated the Equal Protection Clause of the Fourteenth Amendment and hence should be halted. Stated quite simply, seven justices concluded that the procedures for the recount lacked sufficiently specific standards to ensure that questionable ballots were treated in a similar and consistent manner throughout the recount. Having found the procedures for the recount to be constitutionally suspect, the Court then refused to allow the Florida courts the opportunity to refashion the procedures for the recount and instead ordered the recount halted. On this hotly debated issue of the appropriate remedy, Justices Souter and Breyer broke with the majority and joined Justices Ginsburg and Stevens in dissent. Thus seven justices found issue with the nature of the recount, but only five agreed to the draconian step of halting the recount and in effect awarding Florida's electoral votes and the presidency to George W. Bush.

Not the least of the controversy engendered by *Bush* v. *Gore* could be found in the voting alignment of the justices; on the critical issue of the halting the recount, the most conservative justices on the Court (Rehnquist, Scalia, Thomas, Kennedy and O'Connor) formed a consistent and stable bloc of votes on behalf of Bush, suggesting to some that the outcome of the case was dictated by politics and not constitutional law. The discord, however, runs even deeper. As Professor David Strauss has noted,

83. 531 U.S. 98 (2000).

while the vision of the Equal Protection Clause relied on by the majority was not entirely implausible—it was an understanding of equal protection that the Warren Court might embrace—it was "wildly out of character" for a majority of the Rehnquist Court.[84] Putting aside, however, the question of whether the majority relied on a novel interpretation of the Equal Protection Clause, this was a controversy that appeared to cry out for judicial avoidance. The case presented several justiciability issues that might have provided a more cautious Court with a convenient way of avoiding the definitive political thicket.[85] Nevertheless, from the Court's grant of certiorari (many observers were certain the Court would deny certiorari and allow the Florida courts and the Constitutional provisions regarding contested electors to sort things out) to the fashioning of a remedy that precluded resolution by state institutions or ultimately the Congress, the Rehnquist Court aggressively—and perhaps even enthusiastically—interceded in the quintessential political process of electing a president. It was a breathtaking display of judicial activism.[86]

The Warren Court and the Transformation of Judicial Power

Much like Woodstock or the Black Panthers, the Warren Court recedes into historical memory as the symbol of an age. But the justices of the Warren era have also transcended mere symbol-

84. David A. Strauss, "*Bush* v. *Gore*; What Were They Thinking," in Cass R. Sunstein and Richard A. Epstein, eds., *The Vote: Bush, Gore, and the Supreme Court* (Chicago: Univ of Chicago Press, 2001), 187.

85. For example, standing to sue (was George W. Bush the correct plaintiff to represent the uncounted voters in Florida counties?) and the political question (was the Supreme Court the institution best suited to determine the outcome of a presidential election?). See Pamela Karlan, "Nothing Personal: The Evolution of the Newest Equal Protection from *Shaw* v. *Reno* to *Bush* v. *Gore*," *North Carolina Law Review* 79 (2001): 1345; and Garrett, "Institutional Lessons from the 2000 Election," *Florida State University Law Review* 29 (2001): 975.

86. For the contrary view, that indeed Court intervention saved the nation from political chaos, see Richard A. Posner, *Breaking the Deadlock: The 2000 Election, the Constitution, and the Courts* (Princeton: Princeton Univ. Press, 2001).

ism; the Court under Earl Warren revolutionized the nature of judicial power and constitutional law, and it continues to shape legal and political discourse to this day. In opening the doors of the courthouse to a vast assortment of interests and expanding the array of judicial remedies available to secure constitutional rights, the Warren Court radically altered the nature of judicial power. Transforming the very nature of the judiciary also worked to change the process of nominating and confirming our judges. But the impact of the unintended changes wrought by the Warren Court on the confirmation process must be considered in the context of developments in the larger political setting. The fragmentation of the New Deal coalition during the 1960s and 1970s and the tensions inherent in the Republican majority of the 1980s enhanced the potential rewards for groups adept at cultivating new forums for the enactment and implementation of policy goals. In a political environment often marked by gridlock and delay, the stakes surrounding judicial appointments rise rather quickly. It is to these developments at the "macro level" of national politics that we now turn.

Chapter 3

THE DEMOCRATS: THE COMING OF THE NEW PROGRESSIVES

From the days of the New Deal through the fateful election of 1968, the Democratic party set the tone and direction of American political life. With the Roosevelt coalition in place, attention focused on the building of a powerful administrative state, and appointments to the federal courts, even at the level of the Supreme Court, excited only minimal investigation and public interest. The dissolution of this coalition, however, altered not only American politics on the grand scale but the process of judicial selection and confirmation as well. The passing of Democratic hegemony forced elements of the party to seek alternative forums and means for the achievement of their policy agenda. Beginning in the late 1960s an activist judiciary emerged as an important institutional ally of powerful groups associated with the Democratic party, thereby substantially raising the political stakes in the selection and confirmation of Supreme Court justices.

THE DEMISE OF THE NEW DEAL COALITION

The Legacy of the New Deal

In the years following the New Deal, the legacy of Franklin Roosevelt shaped national political life, and the Democratic party emerged as the dominant political force in the United States.[1]

1. William E. Leuchtenburg, *In the Shadow of FDR: From Harry Truman to Ronald Reagan* (Ithaca: Cornell Univ. Press, 1983).

Democrats far outnumbered Republicans; in 1954, 46 percent of the electorate identified with the Democratic party, compared with 34 percent who considered themselves Republicans.[2] The New Deal produced a new public philosophy that transformed the relationship between the citizen and the national government. For the first time in the history of the Republic, the federal government assumed primary responsibility for the redistribution of wealth and the regulation of economic life.[3] The resulting growth in the size and responsibilities of the centralized government during this period furthered Democratic hegemony by linking the interests of a diverse mass constituency to the party through the development of a host of federal programs administered by an expanding executive branch. The electorate accepted Washington, D.C., as the guardian of the economic and social well-being of the country and the Democratic party as the prime proponent of national action to solve the nation's domestic problems.

To compete successfully, Republicans were forced to acknowledge the reality of American's limited welfare state. Even during the eight years as the Eisenhower presidency, the Democratic majority in Congress often set the agenda for domestic policies.[4] "Should any political party attempt to abolish Social Security, unemployment insurance and eliminate labor laws and farm programs," wrote Dwight Eisenhower in 1954, "you would

2. In 1956, 20 percent of those polled were independents. By 1989 the percentages had changed to Democrat 38 percent, Republican 34 percent, and independent 28 percent. See James Ceasar, "Political Parties—Declining, Stabilizing or Resurging?" in Anthony King, ed., *The New American Political System*, 2d version (Washington, DC: AEI Press, 1990), 87–137.

3. See Theodore Lowi, *The End of Liberalism: The Second Republic of the United States*, 2d ed. (New York: Norton, 1979), 273–74, for a discussion of the impact of the New Deal on the coming of the "Second Republic."

4. V. O. Key, *Politics, Parties, and Pressure Groups*, 4th ed. (New York: Crowell, 1958), 205. James Sundquist concluded that during the Eisenhower years the modern notion of president-congressional relations was reversed; the initiative for most policy measures belonged to the Democratically controlled Congress. See James Sundquist, *Politics and Policy: The Eisenhower, Kennedy, and Johnson Years* (Washington, DC: Brookings Institution, 1968).

not hear again of that political party in our political history."[5] Indeed, the crushing defeat of Republican Barry Goldwater in the 1964 presidential election was a reminder of the fate of those who challenged the wisdom of Eisenhower's assessment. Held together by the harrowing memories of the Great Depression, a shared faith in the redemptive powers of a powerful national government led by an activist president, and a steady stream of programs and benefits flowing from Washington, the coalition of minorities forged by Roosevelt—unionized labor, Catholic ethnics, Jews, public-sector employees, white southerners, and northern blacks—proved to be a remarkably stable and powerful governing regime in post-World War II America.

Although the New Deal would have a profound impact on the constitutional jurisprudence of the twentieth century, the politics of judicial confirmations during this period, notwithstanding Roosevelt's famous Court-packing plan of 1937, were actually rather uneventful. Roosevelt may have lost the Court-packing battle—the plan was never enacted—but he did ultimately win the war. In the spring of 1973 the Court reversed positions, upholding a state minimum-wage law and validating several key New Deal measures, including the National Labor Relations Act and the Social Security Act of 1935.[6] The Court's famous "switch in time that saved nine" coupled with the long-anticipated retirement of recalcitrant justices defused the conflict and shifted the focus of New Dealers—and their opponents—from the staffing of the Supreme Court to the building of a powerful administrative state.

---

5. Quoted in Michael Barone, *Our Country: The Shaping of America from Roosevelt to Reagan* (New York: Free Press, 1990), 279.

6. *West Coast Hotel* v. *Parrish*, 300 U.S. 379 (1937) (sustaining a Washington State minimum-wage law); *NLRB* v. *Jones and Laughlin Steel Corp.*, 301 U.S. 1 (1937) (upholding the National Labor Relations Act); *Stewart Machine Company* v. *Davis*, 301 U.S. 548 (1937) (upholding the unemployment excise tax provisions of the Social Security Act); *Helvering* v. *Davis*, 301 U.S. 619 (1937) (upholding the old-age tax and benefits provision of the Social Security Act). For a highly readable account of the Supreme Court and the emerging welfare state of the New Deal, see Robert McCloskey, *The American Supreme Court* (Chicago: Univ. of Chicago Press, 1960), especially chap. 6.

Between 1937 and 1943, for example, Roosevelt named eight justices to the Supreme Court and elevated Harlan Fiske Stone to the chief justiceship. In retrospect, what is particularly remarkable about Roosevelt's new Court is the ease—especially in light of the brouhaha over the Court-packing plan—with which several controversial figures were placed on the Court. Felix Frankfurter, for instance, was American's most famous law professor, a founder of the American Civil Liberties Union, defender of Sacco and Vanzetti, and a close, as well as controversial, adviser to Roosevelt.[7] His "paper trail" was far longer and his politics more controversial than Robert Bork's were fifty years later. Hugo Black was a contentious New Deal senator from Alabama and a former member of the Ku Klux Klan. William Douglas, as chairman of the Securities and Exchange Commission, had made few friends in the financial community and was characterized as a "radical" by the *New York Times*. Wiley Rutledge, while dean of the Iowa University School of Law, had so infuriated Iowa legislators with his support of the Roosevelt Court-packing plan that they had threatened to withhold university salary increases.

Each nomination gained the advice and consent of the Senate handily. Roosevelt anticipated opposition only with the Frankfurter appointment, but, aside from some allegations that Frankfurter was a Communist, the appointment passed the Senate easily. During this era of its dominance, the Democratic party concentrated on linking its diverse components through patronage, compromise, and vote trading. Ideological conflict was sub-

7. Sacco and Vanzetti were Italian immigrants charged with the murder of a paymaster and a guard in Braintree, Massachusetts, in 1920. Coming at the height of the Red scare following World War I, the trial saw the prosecution play to the jury's bias against immigrants and fear of political radicalism (the defendants were both admitted anarchists and draft evaders). Both men were convicted and sentenced to death despite substantial evidence of their innocence, and the case became a cause célèbre among American intellectuals and progressives. Frankfurter wrote a scathing analysis of the case in the *Atlantic Monthly*, documenting the legal errors and prejudice that produced the guilty verdicts. The article galvanized supporters of the two men to continue to fight to keep Sacco and Vanzetti alive. The article also enraged conservatives and produced in many a lifelong hatred for Frankfurter. Despite the efforts of Frankfurter and others, the men were eventually executed.

merged beneath a pragmatic concern with the distribution of goods and services. The coalition could ill afford protracted battles over judicial appointments, and, thanks to the expansion of the administrative branch of the Supreme Court's retreat from economic policymaking, such battles were largely unnecessary.

Roosevelt's death in 1945 brought Harry Truman to the White House, and, although his four appointments to the Court were mediocre by any measure, they too elicited little opposition. Even the Republican capture of the presidency in 1952 scarcely ruffled the apparent calm that marked judicial confirmations of the era. The moderate Eisenhower administration coexisted quite well with the Democratic Congress, and Eisenhower made no effort to use his personal popularity to spearhead a Republican challenge to Democratic hegemony. Even when he was confronted by a Democratic Congress, his appointments to the Court secured confirmation by wide margins. The courts of this era constituted a primary concern only when they thwarted the policy goals of the New Deal coalition, and after 1937 the federal judiciary studiously avoided intervention in the policy areas closest to the heart of the governing regime.

The Pervasive Problem of Race

Hence one explanation for the lack of conflict over nominations to the Court in the years following the New Deal lies in the relative strength of the Democratic governing coalition. The slow dissolution of this coalition, however, is a basic plot line in the saga of American politics over the last four decades. Again 1968 is a pivotal year. In the presidential election Richard Nixon and independent candidate George Wallace combined for 57 percent of the vote and dealt a devastating defeat to the Democratic party and its candidate, Hubert Humphrey. The capacity of the Wallace candidacy to attract almost ten million votes, a substantial number from traditional white Democratic voters, was a harbinger of the fate that awaited future Democratic candidates for national office. During the early 1960s a substantial black vote had become requisite to Democratic success in presidential elections, and the party responded by trying to weld black voters to the party through the promotion of civil rights legislation. The strategy proved strikingly successful, and blacks formed a solidly Democratic bloc of voters. Today, although blacks make up only about 11 percent of the electorate, they provide approximately 20 percent of the Democratic vote in national elections.[8]

The backlash triggered by this strategy among white voters, however, has been a defining characteristic of modern American politics.[9] In 1952 some 70 percent of all white southerners considered themselves Democrats; during the next thirty years that percentage was cut in half. In 1980 and 1984 southern whites gave Ronald Reagan solid majorities and in 1988 preferred Bush to Dukakis by a margin of almost two to one. White southerners, an important component of the New Deal coalition, provided the bedrock of support for George Wallace in 1968. The Wallace campaign, in effect, provided a way station for white southern voters making the ideological journey from "the party of their fathers" to the new Republican majority, in response to what political scientist Robert Weissberg has termed "the blackening of the Democratic party."[10]

8. From 1948 through 1960, blacks constituted, at the most, one in twelve Democratic votes. In 1988 almost one in five Dukakis voters was black. See Paul Abramson et al., *Change and Continuity in the 1988 Elections* (Washington, DC: CQ Press, 1990), 135. In 2004, the Democratic candidate, John Kerry, received 88 percent of the African American vote and only about 42 percent of the white vote. Phrased most simply, African Americans have throughout recent decades overwhelmingly supported Democratic national candidates as whites have increasingly drifted away from the Democratic party.

9. See Thomas Edsall and Mary Edsall, *Chain Reaction: The Impact of Race, Rights, and Taxes on American Politics* (New York: Norton, 1991). For a similar view of the impact of race on the New Deal coalition, see Benjamin Ginsberg and Martin Shefter, *Politics by Other Means: The Declining Importance of Elections in America* (New York: Basic, 1990). Whether the election of Bill Clinton in 1992 marks the arrival of a "new" Democratic party and coalition, or merely a monetary return of white "Reagan-Democrats" to the fold, remains to be seen.

10. Robert Weissberg, "The Democratic Party and the Conflict over Racial Policy," in Benjamin Ginsberg and Alan Stone, eds., *Do Elections Matter?* (Armonk, NY: Sharpe, 1986).

The migration of the civil rights movement during the 1960s from the rural South to the urban North intensified the exodus of whites from the Democratic party. The ethnic voter who populated America's northern and midwestern industrial cities was another important ingredient in Roosevelt's Democratic party. From the years of the New Deal through 1960, approximately one-third of the Democratic votes came from white union members and their families. Between 1964 and 1988 this base of support steadily eroded; in the 1988 election only one in five Democratic votes came from white union members. The significance of this development can be further illustrated from the perspective of class, irrespective of union membership. In 1948 almost 50 percent of the Democratic vote came from working-class whites; in 1988 only 28 percent of the vote did.[11] Democratic voting among white Catholics has shown a similar long-term decline. Increasingly, urban ethnics came to identify the Democratic party with the redistribution of benefits to black interests. By the late 1980s academic studies had confirmed what many observers of American politics had long suspected: Among voters, attitudes regarding race had become a critical variable in determining party identification.[12]

Racial antagonism, of course, is not the only explanation for the decline in the Democratic vote during the last three decades. Broad social and economic changes combined with shifts in the political environment to take a heavy toll on the New Deal coalition. Union membership in the United States has declined markedly, and the income distinctions between working and mid-

11. Abramson et al., *Change and Continuity*, 139, 141.

12. Edward G. Carmines and James A. Stimson, *Issue Evolution: Race and the Transformation of American Politics* (Princeton: Princeton Univ. Press, 1989); Robert R. Huckfeldt and Carol Kohfeld, *Race and the Decline of Class in American Politics* (Urbana: Univ. of Illinois Press, 1989). So important is this development to Republican success at the national level that the task for Republican presidential candidates is how to make the appropriate appeal without opening themselves to charges of overt racism. I will argue in the following chapter that, beginning with Richard Nixon in 1968, appeals and promises regarding the staffing of the federal courts in general and the Supreme Court specifically have provided Republican candidates with a convenient vehicle for delivering the racial message without breaching political good taste.

dle class have blurred. Because most voters now identify with a
broad, well-to-do middle class, the traditional Democratic appeal
to working-class interests apparently falls on deaf ears.[13] Memories of Roosevelt and the New Deal link fewer voters to the Democratic party; by the late 1960s younger voters, lacking a personal
connection to the Democrats, began to replace the generation of
voters emotionally wedded to the party of Franklin Roosevelt. To
the older generation the New Deal was a defining political event;
the label "New Dealer" or "Anti–New Dealer" signified one's
position across a broad range of political, social, and economic
issues.[14] To the new generation of voters, the New Deal is merely
a term encountered in history books. Generational change coupled with broad alterations in the political landscape, including
the demise of patronage and the advent of television, had by 1968
clearly taken their toll on the national Democratic party.

The New Progressives

Roosevelt's political genius found expression in forging a majority coalition out of competing minority interests. By the late 1960s,
however, the coalition was in disarray. In the aftermath of the
1968 election debacle, a battle for the heart (and mind) of the party
developed between the traditional New Deal Democrats with
roots in the union halls and Democratic clubs and a new generation "who had earned their political spurs in the civil rights

13. For example, 66 percent of Americans considered themselves part of the
working class in 1966; by 2000 only 46 percent made a similar assessment. What is particularly interesting about this development is that while Americans increasingly identified with a broad middle class, during the same time period income disparities and
inequalities increased. From the 1960s through the 1990s, for example, the percentage
of low-income Americans grew significantly. See Nicole Mellow, "Voting Behavior: The
2004 Elections and the Roots of Republican Success," in Michael Nelson, ed., *The Elections of 2004* (Washington, DC: CQ Press, 2005), 76.

14. "The point about the ideas of the New Deal was not that they constituted a
source of political division in America, but that for more than thirty years they constituted *the* source of political division" (emphasis in original). Anthony King, "The American Polity in the Late 1970s: Building Coalitions in the Sand," in Anthony King, eds.,
The New American Political System (Washington, DC: AEI Press, 1978), 372.

movement and later in the antiwar movement" and who sought to refocus the party's priorities to fit the needs of an expanding suburban middle class.[15] The violence of the Chicago national convention and the results of the 1968 election hastened a movement to "democratize" the party's candidate selection procedures by broadening the groups and opinions represented in the process. A not unanticipated result of this effort was to diminish the power of old-line party regulars. The new guidelines for delegate selection adopted before the 1972 convention changed the demographics at the convention—the proportion of blacks, youth, and women dramatically increased—and showcased the emergence of a new and powerful force in the party. The appearance of what I term the New Progressives not only transformed the nature of the Democratic party but also had a profound, albeit unexpected, impact on the politics of judicial selection.[16]

In her important study of the delegates to the 1972 political conventions, Professor Jeane Kirkpatrick wrote of the emergence of a new "presidential elite," political activists with higher income, higher education, higher social status, and less religious commitment than both party voters and old-line party activists.[17] At the 1972 Democratic National Convention, over 80 percent of the delegates had never attended a previous convention; approximately one-third had less than five years' experience in politics. By income, occupation, and status, the new delegates formed a

15. Thomas Byrne Edsall, *The New Politics of Inequality* (New York: Norton, 1984), 49.

16. Although social scientists have acknowledged the existence of this new "elite," there has been little agreement on precisely what to call it. Neoconservatives have written of a new class. See B. Bruce-Briggs, eds., *The New Class?* (New Brunswick, NJ: Transaction, 1979). And political scientists Benjamin Ginsberg and Martin Shefter used the phrase "New Politics Movement." See their "A Critical Realignment? The New Politics, the Reconstituted Right, and the 1984 Election," in Michael Nelson, ed., *The Elections of 1984* (Washington, DC: CQ Press, 1985). Neither "class" nor "movement" seems quite right, and I will use "New Progressives" because, as upper-middle-class, educated, cosmopolitan professionals dedicated to good government and reform, this group broadly resembles the Progressives of the early twentieth century. The similarities are not exact but close enough to justify the title.

17. Jeane Kirkpatrick, *The New Presidential Elite* (New York: Russell Sage Foundation, 1976).

representative sample not of the American electorate but of America's skilled professionals.[18] The ascendancy of the New Progressives, Professor Kirkpatrick predicted, would alter our understanding of Democratic party politics:

> Politics conducted by . . . [this group] will probably feature more emphasis on the symbolic aspects of politics and less on the output of goods and services. . . . Politics denominated by [such] professionals is likely to have a higher ideological content and the political process is more likely to be conceived as an arena for setting public agendas and resolving more problems than as an arena for winning and compromising material interests.[19]

Throughout the 1960s and 1970s the issue that had galvanized the New Deal coalition—the scope and nature of the American welfare state—receded in significance, and a cluster of new problems keyed to race, crime, and the Vietnam War created deep divisions in what remained of the old coalition. On many of these social and cultural issues, the New Progressives held positions more liberal than those of old-line Democratic delegates and considerably more liberal than those of Democratic electorate.[20] Furthermore, the New Progressives gave party unity and cohesion a low priority. In the view of these activists, one did not support a candidate simply out of party loyalty or the pragmatic need to win elections; on the contrary,

18. At the 1972 Democratic convention, the characteristics defining the New Progressives were most prevalent among the supporters of George McGovern. For example, 40 percent of the female and 49 percent of the male McGovern delegates held professional jobs or were highly qualified technical experts. Among the delegates of McGovern's chief rival for the nomination, Hubert Humphrey, the percentages were 31 percent and 42 percent. Some 43 percent of the male McGovern delegates had graduate degrees, while only 22 percent of the male Humphrey delegates had achieved similar academic status. Ibid., 385–86.

19. Ibid., 71–72.

20. For example, on the issue of the balance between protecting the rights of the accused and fighting crime, 95 percent of the McGovern delegates generally favored the rights of the accused, compared with 78 percent of all the delegates to the 1972 Democratic convention. Only 36 percent of rank-and-file Democrats, however, favored the rights of the accused. By way of comparison, 21 percent of the delegates at the

political activity was inextricably linked to policy preferences and ideological goals. The coming of age of the New Progressives markedly increased divisive disputes within the party; compromise, in the end, is more difficult when principle rather than patronage must be accommodated.

The nomination of George McGovern as the party's standard-bearer in the 1972 campaign marked a dramatic change in the Democratic party, and, despite his decisive defeat the hands of Richard Nixon, McGovern remains an important figure in modern American history. His nomination testified to the capacity of the New Progressives to challenge the party bosses; no longer a small, isolated fringe group contesting American involvement in Southeast Asia, McGovern and his supporters quickly became a dominant force in the party. The reform of the nominating procedures adopted by the Democrats in the early 1970s gave life to the McGovern candidacy and continues to this day to skew the process in favor of the New Progressives, despite the persistent efforts of the old guard to redress the balance.[21] Furthermore, the McGovern campaign accentuated the redirection of the party's primacy focus from the urban blue-collar worker, who formed the backbone of support for Roosevelt and Truman, to the professional living in America's expanding suburbs.[22]

Republican convention chose the rights of the accused. Similar findings on issues like attitudes toward the military and political demonstrations led Professor Kirkpatrick to conclude that the policy preferences of the typical rank-and-file Democrat actually were closer to those of the delegates at the Republican convention than to those of the delegates at the Democratic convention. While delegates to national conventions are traditionally more politicized than the average Republican or Democrat, the distinctions found by Kirkpatrick between Democratic delegates and identifiers were noteworthy, and the distinctions between the rank and file and McGovern delegates were extraordinary. Ibid., chap. 10.

21. The ebb and flow of reform in both parties is discussed in William Crotty, *Party Reform* (New York: London, 1983).

22. In the 1974 elections voter disgust with Watergate produced a crop of new legislators, reflecting the background and outlook of the New Progressives. There were ninety-two freshman representatives in what became known as "the class of '74," seventy-five were Democrats, and two-thirds of the newly elected Democrats were from districts previously represented by Republicans. For the majority of the class of '74, the

The McGovern campaign of 1972 may have heralded a new force in the Democratic party, but the cruel reality of the Nixon landslide in the general election showcased the insurgents' failure to appeal to a broad, national electorate. The liberalism of the New Progressive was built upon a tolerance for changing social values and lifestyles and was preoccupied with curtailing American intervention abroad while ignoring, for the most part, the bread-and-butter economic concerns that united the New Deal with working-class America. The crisis of Democratic party identification, made so manifest in the 1972 campaign, continued to haunt the party for the next two decades: although the tone and direction of the party remained with the New Progressives, electoral success every four years depended on a large voter turnout among more socially conservative, lower-income voters. In effect, from 1968 through the election of Bill Clinton in 1992, the Democratic party was a political party at war with itself.[23]

THE NEW PROGRESSIVES AND THE JUDICIARY

Electoral Defeats, Litigation Victories

Whether Bill Clinton's 1992 victory actually represented the birth of a "new" Democratic party awaits the judgment of history. What is certain is that the period from the 1968 campaign through the

---

civil rights movement and opposition to the Vietnam War were the defining events of their political lives, and the 1972 McGovern campaign constituted their introduction to organized Democratic politics. A fair number were political or social activists prior to their election. Upon their arrival in Congress in 1974, the new Democrats worked to limit the power of the party leadership and reform the committee system. Whereas the traditional Democratic leadership often reflected either the Old South or big-city politics, the class of '74 had a more polished suburban image, often mixing moderate economics with social liberalism. One skill shared by almost all the newcomers was an appreciation of the power of the media in modern American politics.

23. For a brilliant analysis of the confusion of ideology in both the Democratic and Republican parties, see E. J. Dionne, Jr., *Why Americans Hate Politics* (New York: Simon & Schuster, 1991).

Reagan-Bush era witnessed the unraveling of the old Democratic coalition. The disorder in the party produced among other things a new attention to the staffing of the federal judiciary. Repeated Democratic losses in presidential campaigns combined with the party's domination of Congress produced a presidential-legislative gridlock that made control of the third branch more important. Even the victory of the Democrat Jimmy Carter in the 1976 presidential election and the return of party government did not significantly alter the stalemate of national politics. The disdain of the New Progressives for the politics of patronage and vote trading led to congressional reforms that curtailed the ability of the leadership to cut the deals that formed the lifeblood of the old coalition, and the courts became a viable alternative forum for advancing segments of a progressive policy agenda. As the behind-the-scenes power of the leadership diminished, the likelihood of polarizing public battles over nominations to the federal courts naturally increased. But neither divided government nor a change in politics as usual adequately accounts for the highly divisive and bellicose politics of modern judicial confirmations.

In spite of their drubbings in national elections, the New Progressives have proven remarkably adept at securing many of their policy goals. To an extraordinary degree, the judiciary has been the institution responsible for these successes, in effect permitting the New Progressives to substitute court victories for electoral failures. For example, during the Nixon years the progressive wing of the Democratic party employed the judiciary to frustrate the expansion of executive power, establishing significant legal precedents limiting the authority of the executive to impound funds, to engage in domestic surveillance, and to halt the desegregation of the South. The Supreme Court's opinion in the Watergate tapes case was the coup de grâce to the Nixon presidency.[24]

24. See, generally, Mark Silverstein and Benjamin Ginsberg, "The Supreme Court and the New Politics of Judicial Power," *Political Science Quarterly* 102 (1987): 371.

Following the resignation of Nixon, the New Progressives continued to use the federal courts to advance policy preferences ranging from safer working conditions to containment of the nuclear power industry. By the early 1970s, the judiciary had become the institutional ally of an important segment of the Democratic party; as a result, appointments to the federal bench quickly evolved from being matters of political patronage to being decisions fraught with significant political consequences.

The crusade against pervasive and long-standing gender discrimination serves as an illuminating example of the New Progressives' heightened reliance on the federal courts to counter defeats in the electoral arena. Gender equality was (and continues to be) a central, defining policy goal of these activists, and the defeat of the Equal Rights Amendment (ERA) in 1982 dealt a bitter below to forces aligned with the New Progressives. The failure of the ERA in the democratic process, however, was offset at least partly by the Supreme Court, the national institution that evidenced the greatest commitment to gender equality during the 1970s and 1980s. In a 1973 case, four justices reached the conclusion that gender, like race, was a "suspect classification" triggering the strictest level of judicial scrutiny. Had an additional justice voted to support this position, the New Progressives would have been spared the agony of the ERA defeat; in subjecting claims of gender discrimination to strict judicial scrutiny, the Court, in effect, would have judicially enacted the ERA ten years before its eventual defeat in the political arena.[25]

Notwithstanding the Court's ultimate refusal to treat gender discrimination as the legal equivalent of discrimination on the basis of race, a solid majority of the Court has continued to agree that claims of gender inequality should be judged by a heightened standard of review and, during the 1970s and 1980s, invalidated

25. *Frontiero* v. *Richardson*, 411 U.S. 67 (1973). The fifth judicial vote to make gender a suspect classification has not been forthcoming, and gender discrimination is reviewed under a judicial standard more lenient than that for racial discrimination. But consider the following note and the accompanying text.

a broad assortment of statutes that drew distinctions on the basis of gender.[26] The federal judiciary has also proven quite willing to interpret federal statutes to further the goal of gender equality, particularly when the alleged discrimination strikes directly at matters of the most immediate professional concern to the New Progressives. In 1984, for example, the Court extended the federal law barring discrimination in the workplace to forbid sexual discrimination in a law firm's decision on whether to promote a female associate to the position of partner.[27]

Thanks to the active intervention of the federal courts, the New Progressives, despite the defeat of the ERA, were remarkably successful in the war against sex discrimination. Indeed, by the 1970s the federal courts were often the arena most receptive to the policy goals of the New Progressives across a wide range of issues, and even the election of Democrat Jimmy Carter did little to counter this development. Carter was unable to reunite the old coalition, and therefore, throughout his administration, the factions in the Democratic party pursued their own agendas by whatever means and in whichever forums best served their interests. The fact that Democrats controlled both Congress and the executive had little impact; by the mid-1970s the Democratic party was so divided that the strategy and behavior of its disparate

26. For the last twenty years the Court has required the government to show that a challenged gender classification bears a close and substantial relationship to important governmental objectives. See *Craig* v. *Boren*, 429 U.S. 190 (1976). One measure of the potency of this standard of review was the Reagan administration's determined efforts to compel the Court to accept a more deferential standard. See *Mississippi University for Warren* v. *Hogan*, 458 U.S. 718 (1982), a 5-to-4 decision upholding heightened scrutiny for claims of gender discrimination. Throughout the 1990s, the Court continued to subject claims of gender discrimination to heightened scrutiny. Indeed the modern Court has suggested that gender discrimination might be subject to a degree of scrutiny akin to the strict scrutiny applied to racial discrimination. See *United States* v. *Virginia*, 518 U.S. 515 (1996) ("The reviewing court must determine whether the proffered justification [for the differing treatment of women and men] is 'exceedingly persuasive'" 518 U.S. at 533).

27. *Hishon* v. *King & Spaulding*, 467 U.S. 69 (1984). Consider also *Meritor Savings Bank* v. *Vinson*, 477 U.S. 57 (1986), concluding that sexual harassment in the workplace is actionable under Title VII of the Civil Rights Act of 1964.

parts were only marginally altered by Democratic control of the White House.[28]

As a consequence, the New Progressives' attention to the staffing of the federal courts increased rather than decreased during the Carter years. For decades the civil rights establishment had carefully scrutinized judicial nominees, with varying impact on the process. With the coming of the Carter administration, both the degree of scrutiny and the number and political influence of the groups engaged in the endeavor increased materially. Groups with a professional, upper-middle-class focus such as the Women's Legal Defense Fund, the Center for Law and Social Policy, Common Cause, and the National Organization for Women began regularly to set aside funds and staff for the express purpose of keeping watch on nominees to the federal bench. Through sympathetic advocates on the Senate Judiciary Committee (chaired then by Senator Edward Kennedy), these groups were in a position to ensure that nominees were often quizzed on matters of particular concern to the New Progressives, including support for affirmative action and the Equal Rights Amendment.[29]

---

28. E. J. Dionne, Jr., describes the Carter presidency in this way: "His administration became a battleground in which all the tendencies of the Democratic Party, and all of the wings of liberalism, struggled for influence. Carter's appointees to regulatory commissions tended to be younger liberals much influenced by Ralph Nader–style public advocacy. Thus, on issues such as occupational health and safety, the environment, and consumer protection, the Carter administration had a decidedly progressive tinge. Carter himself was not always comfortable with this, commenting once that he was the most conservative member of his own administration. . . . On the social issues, the contradictions were between Carter's conservative personal behavior and his deep and genuine religious feeling, which had made him so attractive to Southern conservatives in his election campaign, and his relatively liberal views on issues relating to civil rights, women's rights, and civil liberties. . . . Social liberals mistrusted Carter's religiosity and his 'Southernness,' sensing that he did not fully share their cosmopolitan worldview. Social conservatives, in the meantime, saw Carter as betraying them." Dionne, *Why Americans Hate Politics*, 134.

29. In 1977 President Carter announced the creation of the Circuit Court Nominating Commission. The commission was divided into panels, one for each judicial circuit, and was charged with recruiting and screening candidates for vacancies on the courts of appeals and submitting a recommendation to the president. The idea behind the commission was to remove the more blatant aspects of political patronage from the

With Jimmy Carter in the White House, the New Progressives' efforts to promote the consideration of judicial "activists" as well as "nontraditional" nominees (that is, people of color and women) to the federal bench were enormously successful. Although denied an opportunity to nominate a Supreme Court justice, Carter appointed more women and minority judges than had all previous presidents combined.[30]

THE NEW PROGRESSIVES IN THE REPUBLICAN ERA

The Reagan Years

The 1980 victory of Ronald Reagan and the Democratic loss of the Senate for the first time in twenty-eight years drove the final nails into the coffin of the New Deal coalition. Reagan drew substantial support from white southerners, blue-collar workers, and Catholics, while many Democratic progressives rejected Carter for the independent candidacy of the Republican liberal John Anderson.[31] Once in office, Reagan inspired tax and spending

---

judicial selection process. In practice, however, the panels of the commission provided New Progressives with an additional forum to screen candidates for judicial appointments. See Larry C. Berkson et al., "A Study of the U.S. Circuit Judge Nominating Commission: Findings, Conclusions, and Recommendations," *Judicature* 63 (1980): 105; Elliot E. Slotnick, "The Changing Role of the Senate Judiciary Committee in Judicial Selection," *Judicature* 62 (1979): 502. One of the first actions of the Reagan administration was to discontinue the nominating commission.

    30. The Carter administration's extraordinary efforts on behalf of affirmative action in the federal judiciary are detailed in Sheldon Goldman, *Picking Federal Judges: Lower Court Selections from Roosevelt through Reagan* (New Haven: Yale Univ. Press, 1997), chap. 7.

    31. Although Reagan essentially split the blue-collar vote with Carter in 1980, this was a substantial improvement over Gerald Ford's showing with these voters in 1976. In 1984 Reagan garnered 53 percent of the blue-collar vote. In short, from 1976 to 1984 the Republican share of blue-collar voters increased by approximately 12 percent. In the case of white southerners, the increase from 1976 to 1984 was nearly twenty percent. A substantial portion of Anderson's support came from upper-income, college-educated voters. See Gerald M. Pomper, *The Election of 1984: Reports and Interpretations* (New York: Chatham House, 1985), 67–69.

policies that further interred any hopes of resurrecting Democratic hegemony. A substantial reduction in the top federal income tax rates linked many of the newly affluent to the Republican party, while the deep cuts in government revenue diminished the distributive capacity of the national government and the Democrats' ability to disburse the goods and services necessary to the maintenance of the old coalition. Republican dominance of the executive branch heightened the intensity of conflict among factions in the Democratic party, as increasing budget deficits and decreasing revenues forced the beneficiaries of federal programs to fight for a smaller piece of an ever-diminishing pie.[32]

The coming of the Reagan presidency made the staffing of the federal judiciary even more important to the New Progressives and focused much of their political energy. The loss of the Senate in 1980 left liberals off balance, and the initial Reagan appointments to the lower federal courts produced limited conflict. The burden of investigating these initial nominees fell to the civil rights establishment, led by the Leadership Conference on Civil Rights.[33] By 1984, however, groups broadly associated with the New Progressives had identified the federal courts as essential points of conflict and organized the Judicial Selection Project to coordinate efforts in the battle against Reagan's judicial appointments. Counting among its members progressive interests as diverse as the Women's Legal Defense and Education Fund, Consumers Union, the National Wildlife Federation, the Children's Defense Fund, the National Education Association, and People for the American Way, the Judicial Selection Project joined with the LCCR to scrutinize nominees to the federal bench, investigating their records,

32. See, for example, Ginsberg and Shefter, *Politics by Other Means*, 102–8.
33. The LCCR was established by the NAACP in 1950 to coordinate lobbying campaigns on behalf of civil rights measures and quickly emerged as the preeminent coalition of civil rights organizations in the country. Its longtime general counsel was Joseph Rauh, who, until his death in 1992, was one of the giants of the civil rights movement in the United States, and its executive director, Ralph Neas, is generally acknowledged to be one of the most sophisticated students of the legislative process in Washington, D.C.

organizing grassroots opposition, and maintaining important links to key Democrats on the Senate Judiciary Committee.[34] In 1986 the citizens' group Common Cause joined the effort, publishing a report that admonished the Senate Judiciary Committee, in the name of responsible, democratic government, to examine with great care the Reagan nominees to the federal judiciary.

That same year the efforts of the progressive interests to direct liberal attention to the staffing of the federal courts gained momentum when Reagan nominated Daniel Manion of Indiana to the Seventh Circuit Court of Appeals. A strident conservative with the slimmest of professional qualifications, Manion enraged liberals with his links to the John Birch Society and his abiding faith that the Constitution permitted the posting of the Ten Commandments in the nation's classrooms. New Progressives united with traditional civil rights groups to form a potent opposition to the Manion nomination. For example, funds for full-page ads in national newspapers and television spots opposing the nomination were provided by People for the American Way, a well-financed New Progressive organization founded by the television producer Norman Lear in 1981 to counteract the influence of the religious Right. Although Manion was ultimately confirmed by the Senate, thanks to the tie-breaking vote of Vice President George H. W. Bush, the surprisingly effective and well-financed battle against the nomination displayed the political strength and

34. The project was established under the auspices of the Alliance for Justice, a coalition of approximately twenty public-interest groups formed in the early 1980s to facilitate lobbying and organizing efforts on behalf of progressive concerns. Although the NAACP and the LCCR were included in the Judicial Selection Project, a tension quickly developed between the old-line civil rights organizations and several of the New Progressive groups associated with the Alliance for Justice. Many traditional civil rights organizations, often with links to church groups like the Catholic Conference, were anti-abortion, while reproductive choice was a paramount concern of many important New Progressive groups such as NARAL and Planned Parenthood and a goal generally supported by almost all professional, upper-middle-class interests. This tension surfaced during the organization phase of the battle against the nomination of Robert Bork. See Mark Gitenstein, *Matters of Principle* (New York: Simon & Schuster, 1992), 170ff.

skills that New Progressives could bring to the contesting of judicial nominations.[35]

For decades civil rights groups monitored judicial appointments. They tended to exercise their at times considerable influence quietly, relying on carefully cultivated contacts with senators and staff, developed through years of playing the Washington power game. The impact of the New Progressives, however, on the traditional, insider politics of judicial selection was electrifying. Substantial resources and a keenly developed appreciation of media politics all but transformed the old system. During the Manion confirmation fight, for example, Senator Slade Gorton, Republican of Washington, was battling for his political life in a tough campaign for reelection. Gorton struck a deal with the Reagan administration, agreeing to vote for Manion's confirmation in return for the administration's support of Gorton's nominee to the federal bench in the state of Washington. Throughout the history of the Republic, similar deals had been made thousands of times without any attendant publicity or adverse electoral consequence. The reality of the modern politics of judicial confirmations, however, is that what was once mundane is now remarkable. Gorton's Democratic opponent seized on the deal to support Manion, and it quickly became an important factor in the defeat of an incumbent senator.[36] That a senator from the state of Washington might be held accountable for a vote to approve an appointment to a midwestern federal judgeship was a startling development that caught the collective attention of Gorton's Senate colleagues.[37] In the aftermath of the Manion battle, few sen-

35. For a description of the tactics and strategy of the groups opposing Manion, see Philip Shenon, "Praise and Pillory for a Liberal Lobby Group," *New York Times*, August 6, 1986, A1, A16.

36. For a description of the reaction of Washington voters and newspapers to the Manion vote, see Bill Prochnau, "Vote Swap Blows Up in Senate Gorton's Face; Deal on Judgeships Is Political Dynamite in Washington State," *Washington Post*, July 11, 1986, A1.

37. More recently, a Bush nomination of an Alabama prosecutor to the Eleventh Circuit Court of Appeals raised similar problems for Republican Arlen Specter of Penn-

ators would disagree with Ann Lewis, the director of the Americans for Democratic Action, when she observed that a "senator's actions on judges is [*sic*] becoming a salient issue" to many important interests.[38]

By the end of Reagan's first term, the New Deal coalition lay in the distant political past. The various factions in the Democratic party had adapted their goals and methods to the reality of Republican domination of the executive branch. The New Progressives made an activist judiciary an indispensable ally in formulating and securing their policy agenda. The linkage between the federal courts and politically potent middle- and upper-middle-class interests is a very significant development in modern American politics. It explains, for example, a good deal of the turmoil generated by Reagan's nomination of Robert Bork to the Supreme Court in 1986. From the perspective of the New Progressives, Bork was unacceptable on the Supreme Court because he was most accomplished, forceful, and unrelenting critic of judicial activism of his generation. The defeat of his nomination therefore became a matter of overwhelming importance to liberal interests and demanded a strategy designed to highlight the potential impact of his narrow interpretation of the federal judicial role on the policy objectives of numerous New Progressive groups.

---

sylvania. The nomination of Edward Carnes, known for his skill and tenacity in arguing against death sentence appeals while an assistant attorney general in Alabama, triggered opposition by civil rights groups contending that in his zeal to defend executions Carnes was insensitive to racial issues. Democrats promised a filibuster, but a cloture motion succeeded and the Senate confirmed Carnes by a 62-to-36 vote. Senator Specter, a member of the Senate Judiciary Committee and engaged in a tough reelection battle, had voted for the confirmation of Carnes when his nomination was before the Judiciary Committee. His Democratic opponent in the Senate race in Pennsylvania made the nomination of Carnes an important campaign issue, and Specter switched positions and voted against the Carnes nomination when it reached the floor of the Senate. See Neil A. Lewis, "Court Nominee Is Confirmed after Angry Senate Debate," *New York Times*, September 10, 1992, A16.

38. Quoted in Howard Kurtz, "Votes on Judge Nominees Become Politically Risky," *Washington Post*, June 28, 1986, A5.

The task was to frame the terms of the debate in a manner calculated to capture the attention of the myriad groups with a substantial stake in an activist judiciary without engaging in heavy-handed, extremist rhetoric certain to alienate many potential opponents of the nomination. To accomplish this difficult balancing act, activists opposing the Bork nomination relied upon the technology of modern electoral politics to find which of the issues associated with Bork resonated most powerfully among important interests. Polls and focus group studies, for example, showed a growing unease with Judge Bork's forceful critiques of the Supreme Court's guardianship of the unenumerated constitutional right to privacy. This right of privacy, first articulated by the Supreme Court in 1965 in *Griswold* v. *Connecticut*, became the constitutional linchpin for judicial protection of the abortion choice in *Roe* v. *Wade*.[39] Abortion, however, was a potentially divisive issue even among some New Progressives, while support of a protected right of privacy tapped into a widely shared belief among liberals and conservatives that government should not dictate personal lifestyle decisions. Because of polling data, opponents of Bork made *Griswold*, rather than the far more familiar (at least to the public at large), *Roe* a key "talking point" in the battle against Bork.[40] Modern technology gave Bork's opponents not simply data to convince senators of constituent opposition to the nomination but, even more important, the means to generate this opposition by linking the concerns of politically important groups to the Bork record.

In the end the Bork nomination was turned aside because the power and resources of numerous New Progressive groups combined with the efforts of the traditional civil rights community to form a potent political force. That over three hundred

39. *Griswold* v. *Connecticut*, 381 U.S. 479 (1965); *Roe* v. *Wade*, 410 U.S. 113 (1973).

40. For a discussion on the evolution of privacy as a key element in the campaign to defeat Bork, see Michael Pertschuk and Wendy Schaetzel, *The People Rising* (New York: Thunder's Mouth Press, 1989), especially chap. 6; Gitenstein, *Matters of Principle*, chap. 8.

organizations, ranging from the National Black Leadership Roundtable to the Association of Flight Attendants and SANE/ FREEZE, actively opposed Bork was due largely to the struggle of the LCCR and the Judicial Selection Project to turn the concerns of the New Progressives with the staffing of the federal judiciary into concrete political action. The prevalence of professional women's groups, for example, among the many interests opposing Bork testified to the power of the New Progressives and the significance in the 1980s of the judiciary to a new constituency beyond the civil rights community.

The National Federation of Business and Professional Women's Clubs is a case in point. The organization, which has many Republican members concentrated in the South and Midwest, actively opposed the Bork nomination. "Here were all the issues we cared about embodied in one fight," explained Monica McFadden, the lobbyist for the association. "Senators know we're not nut cases. We're very moderate as a group. The average age of our members is late forties, early fifties."[41] That a moderately progressive organization could be energized by a campaign against a conservative Republican nominee to the Supreme Court shows the salience of the Court appointments to a far wider range of interests than ever before in its institutional history.

A Kinder and Gentler Politics of Judicial Confirmations?

The coming of George H. W. Bush's "kinder and gentler" politics did not significantly alter the New Progressives' absorption with the shape of the federal judiciary. The failure of the 1988 Dukakis campaign and the stalemate produced by divided rule simply magnified the significance of control of the third branch. The threat to the continued vitality of *Roe* v. *Wade* and the constitutional protection of abortion rights riveted the New Progressives' attention on the judiciary and Bush appointments to the federal

41. Quoted in Ethan Bronner, *Battle for Justice* (New York: Norton, 1989), 186.

bench. Conservative groups were equally attentive to nominations to the federal bench (see chapter 4) and, in the wake of the
Bork defeat, vowed that future conservative nominees would not
suffer a similar fate. In the White House, strategists sought out
nominees who could satisfy conservatives while presenting qualities that would undercut a hostile New Progressive–civil rights
alliance.

These cross-pressures produced David Souter to replace the
retiring Justice Brennan as the first Bush appointment to the
Court. Souter had served as New Hampshire's attorney general
and later as a state trial and appellate court judge before being
appointed to the U.S. Court of Appeals a scant three months
before his nomination to the high court. Most important, he had
left almost no paper trail; he had published no scholarly articles,
written no widely acclaimed books, and produced, as a state
supreme court justice, no distinctive opinions that attracted the
attention of legal commentators. He presented, in the words of
Senator Paul Simon, "as blank a slate as anyone ever offered by
a President for a seat on the Court."[42] Everyone was equally in
the dark regarding Judge Souter. Liberals, however, were quietly
assured by Senator Warren Rudman, the respected Republican of
New Hampshire and a close friend of the nominee, that Souter
was as good as they could possibly hope to get from the Bush
administration. Conservatives eventually were forced to trust the
promises of the president and the judgment of the Department
of Justice. Armed with a quiet, restrained style and doggedly
refusing to engage members of the Senate Judiciary Committee
in a substantive discussion of his judicial philosophy, Souter
(quickly dubbed the "stealth nominee") was easily confirmed.

Souter's nomination reflected the state of the modern process
of judicial selection and appointment. In 1932 President Hoover
had been compelled to bring Benjamin Cardozo to the Court

42. Paul Simon, *Advice and Consent* (Washington, DC: National Press Books,
1992), 76.

because of his renown as a judicial scholar and state court jurist. Almost sixty years later, there was not the slightest suggestion of an outpouring of professional demand for Judge Souter. No one seriously suggested that he was among the most prominent jurists in the land. Nor could the nominee lay claim to a long-standing friendship or professional relationship with the president; indeed, we can be relatively certain that Bush knew little about the nominee in the days before his appointment was announced. Although Judge Souter had the important support of Senator Rudman and White House Chief of Staff John Sununu (the former governor of New Hampshire), the inescapable conclusion is that the White House selected Judge Souter precisely because he was an unknown.

One year later, when Thurgood Marshall announced his retirement from the Court, the Bush administration gambled on a different strategy to achieve the same goal: satisfying conservatives while choosing a nominee with qualities that would forestall significant opposition on the part of the New Progressive and the civil rights community. In the view of the Bush White House, Clarence Thomas fit the bill perfectly. Conservatives were elated. Unlike Justice Souter, Thomas was an avowed conservative, having written and spoken extensively in support of the Right's social agenda. And, despite President Bush's disingenuous claim that the Thomas appointment "has nothing to do with race," it was precisely race and the nominee's humble origins that the White House counted on to deter New Progressive hostility.

To quell liberal opposition, the White House and Thomas supporters offered poignant tales of Thomas's youth in the segregated, backwater town of Pin Point, Georgia, in an initially successful effort to have this rags-to-riches saga define his public persona. During the hearings before the Senate Judiciary Committee, the Pin Point strategy shielded him from a searching examination regarding his mediocre professional background and his limited and undistinguished record as a judge. Given Thomas's personal history, senators normally allied with the New

Progressives found it difficult to probe and challenge either his extremely conservative judicial philosophy or his commitment to civil rights. New Progressives and senators alike were uneasy challenging the credentials of a nominee to the Supreme Court who could speak so movingly of surviving the indignities of apartheid in America. Although his slim professional record and conservative views assured a fair number of negative votes on the Senate floor, Clarence Thomas was well on his way to confirmation until Anita Hill and allegations of sexual harassment appeared on the scene.

A DEMOCRAT IN THE WHITE HOUSE

Democrats Reborn?

After years of Republican occupation of the White House, the election of Bill Clinton in 1992 appeared to herald a new age in American politics. At home in front of an MTV live audience or addressing a Kennedy School of Government seminar on the most arcane policy matter, the young and articulate Clinton stood in stark contrast to his immediate Republican predecessors, who appeared distinctly out of touch with the aspirations of a new generation and the demands of a new economy. Although Clinton often portrayed himself as a "New Democrat"—without really explaining how "new" differed from "old"[43]—the New Progressives, long shut out of executive influence during the Reagan and Bush years, were certainly comfortable with Clinton in the White House. Blessed with Democratic majorities in both the House and Senate, Clinton proclaimed during his inaugural address that "the era of deadlock and drift is over," and he quickly

43. Clinton in his run to the presidency described himself as a centrist Democratic, more fiscally responsible and socially conservative than the New Progressive wing of the party. While in office, Clinton did focus attention on deficit reduction; the social conservative facet of this "New Democrat," however, was not particularly evident during his years as president.

began the herculean task of governing with an ambitious policy agenda headed by the bold aspiration to transform America's out-of-date health care system.

Almost immediately the new administration began to stumble. On his first day at the White House, Clinton faced a firestorm over his nomination of Zoë Baird, a corporate attorney, to be attorney general. Baird, it was revealed, had failed to pay Social Security taxes for household help and hired illegal aliens. Within days, the Baird nomination was dead and the nomination to attorney general would remain a Clinton embarrassment until he finally settled on Janet Reno. Other appointments also went poorly. "New Democracy" failed to provide an ideological center for the new administration. The Clinton presidency slipped badly when it was unable to deliver on a campaign promise to end discrimination against gays in the military. After much fanfare, the Clinton health initiatives disintegrated under Republican attack and a public perception that they constituted a return to big government. The president, in the mode of a New Democrat, successfully championed the North American Free Trade Agreement (NAFTA) and the Omnibus Crime Bill but at the cost of support among traditional Democrats. Scandal erupted over the firing of the White House travel staff and later over the Clintons' alleged involvement in a decades-old land deal in Arkansas. Sadly, the president seemed most effective and compelling when he touchingly consoled a nation after the bombing of a federal courthouse in Oklahoma City in the late spring of 1995.

The staffing of the federal judiciary also appeared to reflect the lack of a consistent governing philosophy on the part of the new administration. Blessed with a record number of vacancies on the federal bench, Clinton made competency, along with ethnic and gender diversity, the cornerstone of his judicial appointments, steering clear of any concentrated effort to shift the ideological focus of the judiciary to the left. "Our mission," explained White House counsel John Quinn, "is not to counteract the appointments of the Reagan and Bush years. The fact is that this President is a moderate who brings mainstream, Main Street values to the job of selecting judges."[44] From the outset, the Clinton strategy consisted of presenting an ever-shifting target to his political enemies, constantly bargaining with foe and friend alike, claiming credit wherever he could and sacrificing any long-term policy agenda to the demands of a defensive approach designed to secure survival (and reelection) at the expense of broad and coherent policy proposals. Within such a governing philosophy, battles over appointments to the federal judiciary were simply not worth the cost.

This approach to judicial appointments succeeded in pleasing almost no one. Clinton's appointments to the federal courts were distinctive in their competency and diversity and decidedly middle-of-the-road in their ideology.[45] New Progressives were, in the words of Nan Aron of the Alliance for Justice, willing to give credit for diversity and skill but nonetheless found themselves disappointed ". . . that the President failed to address the issue of correcting the imbalance of the courts from the previous Republican Presidents."[46] In the modern politics of judicial confirmations, disappointment is not far removed from active opposition, and very quickly the Clinton White House confronted the unsettling reality that resistance could come from friend as well as foe. Seeking to shore up relations with the House leadership, for example, the administration floated the name of Gary Gaertner, a state court judge and friend of House Majority Leader Dick Gephardt, as a potential pick for a vacancy on the federal district court in Missouri. Throughout the history of the nation, federal district court judgeships had been the stuff of political patronage, used to cement alliances between the administration and the polit-

44. Quoted in Neil Lewis, "In Selecting Federal Judges Clinton Has Not Tried to Reverse Republicans," *New York Times*, August 1, 1996, A20.

45. For a statistical comparison of the Clinton appointments to the federal bench with those of his predecessors, see Robert Stidham, Robert Carp, and Donald Songer, "The Voting Behavior of Clinton's Appointees," *Judicature* 80 (1996): 16.

46. Quoted in Lewis, "Selecting Federal Judges."

ically powerful and well beneath the radar screen of national politics. Opposition to Gaertner, however, came not from local Missouri interests nor from Republicans, but from the New Progressives. Characterizing Gaertner as insensitive to the rights of women and gays, New Progressive opposition ultimately doomed the potential nomination.

That a Democratic president's natural constituency had mobilized to oppose the appointment of a federal district judge with ties to important Democratic legislative leaders was yet another step in the evolution of the politics of judicial confirmations.[47] Republican interests, of course, vowed carefully to scrutinize the Clinton nominations and began to develop the techniques for delaying the confirmation of Clinton appointments to the federal bench that they would perfect during the last years of the Clinton presidency. Following the 1992 election, conservatives established the Judicial Selection Monitoring Project to monitor Clinton appointments and mobilize grassroots opposition.[48] Using sophisticated high-tech media and communication devices, the project's stated goal was to contest the elevation of Democratic nominees to the federal courts. "I don't feel we have much of a choice," said Marianne Lombardi, the project's deputy director. "They're going to load up the courts with liberals and activists. We just can't stand by and let them do it."[49] The best-known supporter of the project was Robert Bork. In a fund-raising letter, he sounded an ominous note, warning potential donors that monitoring Clinton appointments to the federal bench was so vital to the nation's future that it demanded that conser-

---

47. Reporting on the Gaertner matter, Daniel Klaidman noted that some Clinton administration officials were "irked" by opposition coming from those on the left. See Daniel Klaidman, "Liberals Hit Clinton Judge Picks," *The Recorder*, October 27, 1993.

48. See W. John Morse, "Judges on the Left Hold that Line," *National Law Journal*, April 22, 1993, 1246.

49. Quoted in Ruth Shalit, "Conservatives Set for Fight on Judicial Nominees," *New Republic*, May 17, 1993, 20.

vatives organize and prepare even before the first Clinton nominee to the federal bench was named.[50]

Big Hearts and Home Runs

In March of 1993, Justice Byron White announced his retirement from the Court.[51] Attention almost immediately focused on New York Governor Mario Cuomo as a possible Clinton nominee to replace White. During a campaign appearance at an MTV town hall meeting, Clinton had named Cuomo as his ideal Supreme Court pick, and George Stephanopoulos, a Clinton White House adviser, later recounted that Clinton's articulated criteria for his first nominee to the Court ("fine mind, good judgment, wide experience in the law and in the problems of real people, and someone with a big heart") had been fashioned with Cuomo in mind.[52] Cuomo would eventually remove himself from any consideration but not before the Cuomo name was prominently displayed by conservative groups in the crusade to raise funds and muster opposition to Clinton judicial nominees. Besides Cuomo, Laurence Tribe, Marian Wright Edelman, and Eleanor Holmes Norton—names certain to produce consternation among conservatives—were, at one time or another, cited by opponents as possible Clinton choices to replace Justice White.[53] That there was no

50. Neil A. Lewis, "Conservatives Set for Fight on Judicial Nominees," *New York Times*, November 13, 1992, B16.

51. Justice White, appointed by President Kennedy in 1962, first came to the public's attention as a football star at the University of Colorado and played for the Detroit Lions while attending law school at Yale. A Rhodes Scholar, White first met John Kennedy when White was at Oxford and Kennedy was in the United Kingdom while his father served as the Ambassador to the Court of St. James. White worked on the Kennedy presidential campaign and was named a deputy attorney general in the Kennedy Administration before his appointment to the Court. Throughout his judicial career, White was a consistent "tough on crime" vote while generally supporting equality and civil rights claims. See Dennis Hutchinson, *The Man Who Once Was Whizzer White: A Portrait of Justice Byron R. White* (New York: Free Press, 1998).

52. George Stephanopoulos, *All Too Human* (Boston: Little, Brown, 1999), 167.

53. Professor Laurence Tribe of the Harvard Law School is perhaps the most prominent constitutional scholar advocating an activist role for the Supreme Court.

evidence that the Clinton administration was seriously considering any of these individuals mattered little; by 1993, the importance of a vacancy on the Supreme Court warranted the galvanizing of opposition even before the identity of the president's nominee was known.

By late spring, Clinton struggled to complete the selection process to permit Senate confirmation before the August Senate recess. Torn between the desire for a "home run" (his word) choice and the reality of the confirmation process, the president allowed the selection process to drag on with more than the usual leaks and rumors. After much public procrastination, Clinton appeared to settle on Bruce Babbitt, the secretary of the interior and former governor of Arizona, as his "home run" choice. Well known (in 1988 he had launched a dark-horse campaign for the Democratic presidential nomination) and popular, Babbitt had the extensive background in politics and public affairs that Clinton, at least initially, sought in his first nominee to the Court. A champion of many liberal causes, Babbitt would please New Progressive groups, while his nomination was certain to trigger the ire of the New Right. When New Right supporters and powerful Republicans such as Orrin Hatch, the ranking Republican on the Judiciary Committee, expressed concern about Babbitt's liberalism and lack of judicial experience (he would be the first nominee since William Rehnquist not to have served as a judge), and conservation groups mobilized to keep the popular Babbitt as interior secretary, the White House quickly retreated. The Clinton White House concluded it could not afford a battle over the nomination; as he had done so often (and would do in the future), Clinton elected to switch rather than fight.

Marian Wright Edelman, a former staff attorney and director of the NAACP Legal Defense Fund, was at the time the president of the Children's Defense Fund. Eleanor Holmes Norton was an assistant legal director of the ACLU and a professor at the Georgetown University Law Center and the District of Columbia's nonvoting member of the House of Representatives. Each, in short, had impeccable New Progressive credentials.

Attention now focused on Judge Stephen Breyer, the chief judge of the First Circuit Court of Appeals. Breyer, a graduate of Harvard Law School, clerked for Justice Arthur Goldberg before working for the Justice Department and serving as an assistant special prosecutor during the Watergate investigation. From 1979 to 1980, he had worked as the respected chief counsel to the Senate Judiciary Committee. When he was nominated to the First Circuit judgeship by President Carter, bipartisan support from the members of the Committee eased the confirmation process. Judge Breyer quickly established a reputation for professional competency and moderation. Although he had apparently failed to pay Social Security taxes for an elderly woman who did housecleaning for his family, powerful Republicans such as Hatch and Minority Leader Robert Dole, who knew Breyer personally from in his work in the Senate, supported his nomination. Publicly summoned to the White House to meet with the president, Breyer apparently failed to impress Clinton, who concluded that he lacked "the big heart" he was seeking in his first appointment to the Court.[54] Thus, three months into the selection process, the Clinton administration found itself with a vacancy but no nominee, and mocking press coverage continuously emphasized the ineptitude of a Democratic administration as it caromed from name to name in an all too public effort to settle on this most momentous choice.

In the end, Ruth Bader Ginsburg was the pick. The first woman editor of the *Harvard Law Review*, Ginsburg taught at Rutgers University Law School before becoming the first tenured woman professor at Columbia University Law School. While at Columbia she also served as general counsel to the American Civil Liberties Union and was instrumental in forming the ACLU's Women's Rights Project. In the latter capacity, she argued six major gender discrimination cases before the Supreme Court, prompting former dean of the Harvard Law School and former solicitor general Erwin Griswold

54. Elizabeth Drew, *On the Edge: The Clinton Presidency* (New York: Simon & Schuster, 1994), 216.

to compare her work in women's rights to that of Thurgood Marshall in the realm of civil rights. Although the comparison appears a bit overblown, the fact remains that throughout the 1970s Ruth Bader Ginsburg was gender equality's most effective constitutional advocate. Nominated to the U.S. Court of Appeals for the District of Columbia Circuit by Jimmy Carter in 1980, Ginsburg won Senate approval despite the misgivings of conservatives, who feared she was a promoter of liberal causes and a champion of judicial activism.

Thirteen years of judicial service, however, transformed the advocate of judicial action into a proponent of New Deal judicial modesty. While serving on the D.C. Circuit, Ginsburg acquired a reputation as a cautious centrist on an appellate court with deep ideological divisions. Her opinions typically were narrowly drawn, seeking to diminish the impact of the judiciary on the political process while eschewing any attempt to articulate a broad constitutional philosophy. Although a supporter of abortion rights (she was refreshingly candid on that point during the Supreme Court confirmation hearings), she also had the temerity to criticize *Roe* v. *Wade*, arguing in several articles and public lectures that equal protection rather than privacy would have provided abortion with a sounder constitutional basis. Expressing an understanding of the judicial role that Felix Frankfurter would have roundly applauded, Ginsburg asserted that the sweeping nature of the opinion in *Roe* preempted legislative attempts at reform and fueled the bitter controversy that followed. In her view, a narrower ruling, permitting the state legislatures some latitude in fashioning abortion statutes, would ultimately have better served the pro-choice cause while conveying the added benefit of redirecting public attention from the judiciary to the popularly elected branches. Indeed, when word leaked that Ginsburg would be the choice, some women's groups hoped to devise a strategy to encourage Clinton to choose Breyer in the hope that he would select a more liberal woman for the next Supreme Court vacancy.[55]

55. Drew, *On the Edge*, 218.

The moderating impact of her years on the federal bench, her gender, and her religion (she would be the first Jewish justice since Abe Fortas) made her, in the words of Republican Senator Charles Grassley of Iowa, a "Democrat that even Republicans can support."[56] Although some New Progressive groups expressed concern about Ginsburg's criticism of *Roe* and her narrow interpretation of the judicial role, and New Right groups lamented her unquestioned defense of abortion, Judge Ginsburg's unchallenged competency, sharp intelligence, and professional demeanor disarmed all but her most zealous critics. Notwithstanding the fact that President Clinton had earlier expressed a preference for a nominee with broad political experience, well known to the general public, and with a "big heart," whose nomination would be greeted with shouts of "Wow! A home run"—qualities not easily associated with Judge Ginsburg—many political pundits quickly concluded that the Ginsburg nomination furnished one of the brightest moments of Clinton's first year in office.

The winter of the also-ran Judge Breyer's discontent, however, would fade quickly from memory. In early April of 1994, Justice Harry Blackmun announced his retirement effective at the conclusion of the current term of the Court. He had apparently informed the president personally of this decision several months earlier, and the administration promised an expeditious and orderly nomination process. Seemingly within hours of the Blackmun announcement, Senator George Mitchell of Maine emerged as the favored choice. The retiring majority leader of the Senate was hailed as an ideal selection; certain of confirmation, Mitchell could be counted upon to champion progressive causes while bringing to the Court the real-life political experience the president continued to seek in a nominee. Mitchell, however, declined the president's eventual offer, citing an obligation in his remaining months as majority leader to champion health care reform

56. Quoted in *Congressional Quarterly*, June 19, 1992, 1571.

and other Democratic causes in the Senate. With Senator Mitchell no longer in the picture, the White House began, for the second time in a year, the daunting task of selecting a nominee for the High Court.

What followed might best be understood as the political equivalent of a war of attrition as one potential nominee after another was floated as a trial balloon only to quickly deflate. Hispanic groups, for example, pressed the case of Jose Cabranes, then a federal district court judge from Connecticut.[57] Although Mr. Clinton was reportedly intrigued by the idea of appointing the first Hispanic to the Court, the Puerto Rican-born Cabranes was deemed too conservative by important liberal interests as well as by several Hispanic groups that preferred a Mexican-American for the appointment. The civil rights community pushed the candidacy of Solicitor General Drew Days, a former Yale law professor and head of the Civil Rights Division of the Justice Department during the Carter years. Solicitor General Days, however, had signed a brief urging the Supreme Court to reverse a lower appeals court decision upholding a novel and extraordinarily broad interpretation of a federal child obscenity statute. Commenting on a possible Days appointment, Clint Bolick, the head of a New Right think tank, stated: "It would cause a messy fight. His pornography position makes many of our sister organizations absolutely apoplectic."[58] Nervous about the issue of "kiddie porn," administration sources quickly squelched talk of Days as a possible nominee.

In early May, Senator Biden, the chair of the Senate Judiciary Committee, warned the White House that his committee would need at least six to eight weeks to prepare for the hearings on a nominee to the Supreme Court. If the president intended to have

57. Judge Cabranes was eventually appointed to the Court of Appeals for the Second Circuit. His name continues to appear on "possible" lists when commentators write of potential George W. Bush nominees to the Court.

58. Bolick is quoted in John A. Farrell, "Partisan Jockeying Besets Hunt for Justice," *Boston Globe*, May 2, 1994, 3.

the new justice confirmed prior to the congressional summer recess, a choice would have to made quickly. The selection process promptly turned even more frenetic and open to public scrutiny. And once again, President Clinton was forced to confront the unsettling reality that the selection of a nominee to the Court was a more difficult enterprise than he might ever have anticipated.

In the final rush to judgment, the frontrunner by all accounts was again Secretary of the Interior Babbitt. The previous year, environmental interests had lobbied hard to keep Babbitt at Interior, but his recent efforts to mediate battles over western grazing lands earned him the enmity of conservationists and ranchers alike. Babbitt, of course, had the broad political and real-life experience Clinton said he wanted on the Court, and the president was reported to be discussing whether Babbitt might turn out to be another Hugo Black.[59] But the president's ardor for Babbitt quickly cooled when Senator Hatch announced he would again oppose Babbitt because his actions at Interior indicated he would be a liberal judge who would legislate from the bench. Conservative groups promised a serious confirmation battle, and White House strategists were also alarmed over the prospect of selecting and confirming a new interior secretary. Although Senator Biden assured Clinton that Babbitt had the votes for confirmation by a substantial margin, for the second year in a row the secretary was passed over.

Babbitt's demise revived the candidacy of Judge Richard S. Arnold, the chief judge of the Eighth Circuit Court of Appeals based in Little Rock, Arkansas. A personal friend of the Clintons, Judge Arnold was a judicial moderate with wide support in the legal community; he had even been considered by Republican administrations as a possible nominee. Women's groups, however, expressed concern about Arnold's vote in several abortion

---

59. Hugo Black was a United States Senator from Alabama when he was appointed to the Supreme Court by FDR in 1937. Black served as associate justice until 1971, and his place as one of the great justices in Court history is secure. See Roger K. Newman, *Hugo Black: A Biography* (New York: Pantheon, 1994).

cases and asserted that Arnold would be a poor choice to succeed Harry Blackmun—the author of *Roe* v. *Wade* and the Court's most stalwart defender of a woman's right to choose. Also working against the selection of Arnold was the president's wish to avoid charges of cronyism and media scrutiny of the often troubling particulars of Arkansas state politics. Throughout the spring and summer of 1994 Clinton was dogged by allegations regarding his family's involvement in the insolvent Whitewater Land Development Company and that funds from a failed savings and loan were passed through Whitewater to the Clinton campaign fund during his time as governor of Arkansas. Judge Arnold suffered from cancer and, although the disease was in remission, this fact apparently influenced the president to look elsewhere.

Eventually the only candidate left standing was Stephen Breyer. A noncandidate throughout the entire tortuous process—Breyer's name had rarely been mentioned up until the moment of the president's announcement of his selection—he came up a winner because he posed the fewest problems. The political cost of nominating Judge Breyer was minimal. Republicans were elated—this was an appointment they could easily support—and liberals, aside from Ralph Nader and Senator Howard Metzenbaum of Ohio, who complained that Breyer too often favored the haves over the have-nots in his judicial rulings and scholarly writings, maintained a somewhat uneasy silence. His moderation and acknowledged legal skills, together with his friendship with key senators, helped smooth out any bumps he encountered during the confirmation process. He was easily confirmed by the full Senate in a 87–9 vote.

Bill Clinton and the Federal Judiciary

The ease with which both Ginsburg and Breyer gained Senate approval must not obscure the degree to which their appointments were the product of political conflict and weakness. That Ginsburg and Breyer are extremely competent jurists with impressive intellects and distinguished records is beyond question. They did not, however, represent the home run that President Clinton claimed he wished to hit. Prior to their respective appointments, neither Stephen Breyer nor Ruth Bader Ginsburg was a figure of great public stature, well known to the citizenry and endowed with a feel for political life at the grass roots. By 1994, individuals of such stature and promise could be brought to the Court only at substantial cost, and the Clinton presidency, even in its first term, lacked the political capital (or mettle) to make such appointments.

In the 1994 elections, the Democrats suffered a stunning setback. Republicans gained control of the Senate as well as the House—for the first time in forty years—and even captured a majority of state governorships. But in a strange twist, the Clinton presidency was reborn with the return of divided government. Resurgent conservative Republicans, flush with electoral success, declared war not only on what remained of America's limited welfare state but on the Clintons as well. The atmosphere on the Hill became even more acid as extreme partisanship and ideological warfare dominated American legislative politics. Battles over the budget, for example, quickly escalated and produced not merely acrimony, but a standoff between legislature and executive that resulted in the shutdown of the national government over the Christmas holidays.[60] The President found the room to maneuver as a "third way" between the radical Republicans controlling Congress and the old "tax and spend" Democrats. Called

---

60. In 1995, a Republican House and Senate passed a budget reconciliation bill that cut taxes as well as domestic spending and several entitlement programs dear to the hearts of Democrats. Attaching a number of these controversial provisions to appropriations bills that enable the federal government to continue in operation, the Republicans in effect challenged the president to veto the measures. Clinton did veto the reconciliation bill as well as several appropriations bills. The government shut down and, in a masterly bit of politics, Clinton emerged as a symbol of competence and moderation amidst the political squabbling of congressional Republicans and Democrats. Public opinion quickly began to build in support of the president. See Elizabeth Drew, *Showdown: The Struggle between the Gingrich Congress and the Clinton White House* (New York: Simon & Schuster, 1996).

"triangulation" by the Clinton strategist Dick Morris, this essentially defensive strategy steered clear of big policy initiatives and permitted the president to portray himself as the voice of reason and compromise among the warring factions. As the economy improved and the stock market soared, so did Clinton's standing with the public. In the end, despite Whitewater, Paula Jones, Monica Lewinsky, and impeachment, Bill Clinton ultimately left the White House in 2000 more popular than when he arrived in 1992.

But a Democratic president who boldly proclaims that "the era of big government is over" (the words are those of President Clinton in the 1996 State of the Union address) and seeks to govern from the middle (a perhaps popular but nonetheless politically weak position) is unlikely to put political capital at risk over the appointment of judges. Blessed with a Democratic Senate in his initial years in office, Clinton picked moderate judicial candidates who often frustrated New Progressive stalwarts. After the 1994 midterm elections, the Clinton administration hewed even closer to the strategy of steering clear of partisan battles over judgeships, and his nominees to the federal bench were distinguished by their competency, diversity, and, to the often expressed dissatisfaction of those on the left, moderation.[61] Republicans responded to Clinton's failure to provide any meaningful leadership on judicial appointments by using their majority control of the Judiciary Committee to block and delay action on many of the Clinton nominees. By the end of Clinton's first term in office, his caution in selecting judges, coupled with the Republican's tactics of delay and obstruction, meant that the New Progressive goal of recasting the federal judiciary was largely unfulfilled.

Clinton's second term produced more of the same. For the president, governing from the middle became an art form, and the prerogative of the appointment of judges was seemingly sac-

---

61. See, e.g., David Kairys, "Clinton's Judicial Retreat; When Naming Judges He Is Quick to Cave," *Washington Post*, September 7, 1997, C1.

rificed to the strategy of continual compromise and very selective combat. Republicans found persistent opposition to the appointment of lower court judges selected by Clinton a tactic that resonated strongly among the party's conservative base.[62] Indeed the pattern of delay and obstruction became so entrenched that it evoked a response by the chief justice. In January of 1998 in his annual year-end report on the judiciary, William Rehnquist asserted that the major problem facing the federal judiciary was too much work for too few judges. This situation was a product both of the Clinton administration's delay in naming judges to fill lower court vacancies and Senate delays in the confirmation process. Evoking a perhaps fairy-tale image of the modern confirmation process, Rehnquist urged a process in which "the President should nominate candidates with reasonable promptness, and the Senate should act within a reasonable time to confirm or reject them."[63] Needless to say, the chief justice's admonition went unheeded.

Thus Clinton's years in office, so eagerly anticipated by New Progressives, produced not a new judiciary but the further evolution of the new politics of confirmation. Conflict continued to define the politics of nomination and confirmation of Supreme Court justices. While the Clinton appointments to the High Court encountered little public opposition in the confirmation proceed-

---

62. In what could be a case study in the sometimes bizarre reality of American electoral politics, Republicans labored mightily to make the "radical" Clinton nominations to the federal bench an issue in the 1996 campaign, while New Progressives castigated the president for the moderation of his judicial picks. The Republican presidential candidate, Robert Dole, continually chastised Clinton over the appointment of "liberal judges" in his basic stump speech, often seeking to energize the Republican base by evoking the horrifying specter of a return to the Warren Court era if Clinton were reelected. See e.g., Joan Biskupic, "GOP Presidential Candidates Stage Full-Court Press Against Justices," *Washington Post*, March 9, 1996, A10; Bill Rankin, "Campaign '96" *Atlanta Constitution*, October 24, 1996, A. An overview of these developments can be found in Stephan O. Kline, "The Topsy-Turvy World of Judicial Confirmations in the Era of Hatch and Lott," *Dickinson Law Review* 103 (Winter 1999): 247.

63. Quoted in John H. Cushman, "Senate Imperils Judicial System, Rehnquist Says," *New York Times*, January 1, 1998, A1.

ings (a result, no doubt, of their own moderation and the return of unified government), strife continued to mark the process of selecting Supreme Court justices. The battleground, however, shifted from the confirmation to the nomination process. During the Clinton years, the president found it as difficult to select a nominee as his predecessors had found it to confirm one.[64] Furthermore, conflict migrated not only horizontally (from confirmation to nomination) but vertically as well. Appointments to the Supreme Court have always been special moments in American history; the theme of this book is that these moments have become ever more special during the last forty years. But during the Clinton administration, the conflict over judicial nominations drifted vertically down to the level of the Court of Appeals. The same combination of forces that transformed the politics of the confirmation of Supreme Court justices has now found expression in the confirmation of lower court federal judges as well. And, when Clinton sought to avoid conflict and placate opposition by selecting the politically moderate to staff the judiciary, he not only failed to neutralize the expected opposition but also triggered the unexpected ire of his own constituency.[65]

64. See Mark Silverstein and William Haltom, "You Can't Always Get What You Want: Reflections on the Ginsburg and Breyer Nominations," *Journal of Law and Politics* 12 (1996): 459.

65. For a review of Clinton's judicial legacy, particularly with respect to the lower federal courts, see David M. O'Brien, "Judicial Legacies: The Clinton Presidency and the Courts," in Colin Campbell and Bert A. Rockman, *The Clinton Legacy* (New York: Chatham House, 2000).

Chapter 4

THE REPUBLICANS: THE ASCENDANCY OF THE NEW RIGHT

Judicial appointments to the Supreme Court as well as to the lower federal courts have now assumed paramount importance to the Republican party as well. Republican domination of national elections began in 1968 with Richard Nixon's bid for the White House and continued through the Reagan era and the presidencies of the Bushes, father and son. For Nixon, campaigning against the alleged liberal abuses of the Warren Court was a way to link middle America to the Republican party, and that theme, in one form or another, has resonated in every subsequent Republican campaign at the national, and at times local, level. By the turn of the century, the Republican coalition was anchored on one end by upper-income Americans favored by the party's tax and economic policies and on the other by lower-income southern whites and northern ethnics attracted by the "family values" and patriotism agenda promoted by the modern Republican party. Holding such an incongruent coalition together is a tricky endeavor, even in the fluid, sometimes surreal, world of American party politics. For the modern Republican party, a highly promoted campaign to alter the makeup of the Supreme Court as the first step in bringing forth a new conservative social agenda served to solidify the party's link with the New Right while at the same time focusing the attention of this important component of the Republican coalition away from the party's extended efforts to enact an economic program that served the interests of the most well-to-do segments of the electorate.

THE RISE OF THE NEW REPUBLICAN MAJORITY

Running against the Court

On the eve of the 1968 Republican National Convention, Richard Nixon addressed several southern delegations. In Washington the Fortas nomination was in jeopardy, and Nixon was asked his thoughts on the appointment of a new chief justice. "I don't know what the Senate is going to do," Nixon stated,

> but if I have the chance to appoint Justices to the Supreme Court, they will be the kind of men I want—and I want men who are strict constructionalists, men that try to interpret the law and don't try to make the law. I want men, for example, who are for civil rights, but who recognize that the first civil right of every American is to be free from domestic violence. That is the kind of men we are going to have, and I think we need that kind of balance in the courts.

Later that week, during his acceptance speech, Nixon restated a theme he would repeat throughout his campaign: "Let us always respect, as I do, our courts and those who serve on them, but let us also recognize that some of our courts in their dissents [*sic*] have gone too far in weakening the police forces against the criminal forces of this country."[1] The Nixon campaign had begun in earnest.

The task for Nixon was to develop a winning coalition out of the ashes of Goldwater's crushing defeat in 1964. The key components would be southern white defectors from the Democratic party and their northern counterparts. Kevin Phillips, then a young Nixon strategist, captured the spirit of the enterprise: "Who needs Manhattan when we can get the electoral votes of eleven Southern states? Put those together with the Farm Belt and the Rocky Mountains and we don't need the cities. We don't even

1. Quoted in Bruce Murphy, *Fortas* (New York: Morrow, 1988), 466–67.

want them. Sure Hubert [Humphrey] will carry Riverside Drive [in New York City] in November. La-de-dah. What will he do in Oklahoma?"[2] Nixon's Republican revival would be fueled by a powerful lower-middle-class populism. Angered by rising crime rates and welfare rolls and threatened by cultural upheaval, the "silent majority" would become the new Republican majority. The 1968 Nixon campaign did not invoke the traditional Republican images of wealth and economic privilege; it did not speak the language of Palm Beach or even of Wall Street. Instead, the question asked about any campaign strategy was soon "How will it play in Peoria?"[3]

Whereas the liberal establishment was fair game and could be attacked directly—running mate Spiro Agnew's specialty—race was a more subtle and difficult card to play. George Wallace's third-party candidacy was also directed at middle America, and his appeal was more overtly racial. In the long term the Wallace campaign furthered Republican interests by dislodging Democrats from the party; in the short run, however, Wallace might attract many potential Nixon votes and throw the election to Humphrey.[4] The tightrope Nixon walked in 1968 demanded that he publicly support civil rights while simultaneously con-

2. Quoted in Gary Wills, *Nixon Agonistes: The Crisis of the Self-Made Man* (New York: NAL, 1970), 248.

3. Or perhaps, better yet, "How will it play in Mobile?" The importance of the white South to Nixon is illustrated by the fact that in the thirty-nine states outside the South and the District of Columbia, Nixon lost to Humphrey by approximately 30,000 votes. In the eleven states of the South, Nixon led Humphrey by about 500,000 votes. William J. Keefe, *Parties, Politics and Public Policy in America* (New York: Holt, Rinehart and Winston, 1972), 34. Nixon received only 12 percent of the black vote, while 85 percent of the nonwhite voters cast their ballots for Hubert Humphrey.

4. While Nixon often contended that Wallace's appeal was racist, he was obsessed with the Wallace vote and the need to draw off a good deal of Wallace supporters if he was to win the election. One explanation for his choice of Spiro Agnew as running mate was Agnew's appeal to the Wallace constituency. See Stephen E. Ambrose, *Nixon: The Triumph of a Politician, 1962–1972* (New York: Simon & Schuster, 1989), 163–65. Wallace ultimately won 9.9 million votes (13.5 percent) and 46 electoral votes. Nixon received 31.79 million votes (43.4 percent) and 301 electoral votes, to Humphrey's 31.25 million votes (42.7 percent) and 191 electoral votes.

veying sympathy and understanding for the "forgotten Americans" attracted to Wallace. The federal judiciary, and in particular the Supreme Court, provided a handy foil for making this appeal. Nixon's typical stump speech, echoing his acceptance speech in Miami, often began with a short, respectful testimonial to judges and equality under the law. Very quickly, however, he would castigate the Court for any one of many constitutional decisions that in his view weakened the police in the battle against crime or substituted a judge's social values for those of the people and their elected representatives.

The Court became the metaphor that allowed Nixon to play on racial divisions without violating the standards of civility demanded by mainstream American politics of the day. In a television broadcast shown in twelve southern and border states, Nixon attacked the Warren Court for constitutionalizing the "social ideas" of some of its members.[5] In the waning days of the campaign, Nixon assured voters that his judges would not be tempted to view themselves as "super-legislators with a free hand to impose their social and political viewpoints upon the American people."[6] Nixon responded to a late Humphrey surge by reminding voters that throughout the campaign his opponent had steadfastly refused to criticize the Court. "Whenever I begin to discuss the Supreme Court, Mr. Humphrey acts like we're in church. Mr. Humphrey's respectful silence [on controversial Court decisions] may stem from the fact that he has spent four years in [LBJ's] obedience school." Humphrey had done nothing, Nixon scornfully concluded, "while watching the United States become a nation where 50 percent of American women are frightened to walk within a mile of their homes at night."[7] In the supercharged atmosphere of the 1968 presidential campaign, silence on the subject of the Warren Court was not without political risk.

5. "Social ideas," of course, was the polite way of referring to court-ordered racial integration. Quoted in *New York Times*, October 4, 1968, 50.

6. *New York Times*, November 3, 1968, 79.

7. Ambrose, *Nixon*, 202.

Richard Nixon: The Court as Scapegoat

The Nixon victory in 1968 began the Republican domination of the modern presidency. By eschewing the laissez-faire policies of earlier Republican administrations, Nixon hoped to transcend the image of the "party of privilege" and reinvent the Republican party as "the party of middle America." His economic program (particularly when contrasted with that of Reagan and both Bushes) was pragmatic and evidenced a frankly New Deal faith in government intervention and regulation.[8] In 1970, for example, Nixon proposed to reform the welfare system through a guaranteed annual income, and in 1971 he imposed wage and price controls throughout the United States. On social issues Nixon moved to the right. His policy on civil rights was, in the words of Thomas and Mary Edsall, to develop "a strategy of staying within the letter of the law, while making abundantly clear wherever possible his reluctance to aggressively enforce it."[9] Nixon's response to the social and cultural revolution that swept America during the 1960s, however, was far less subtle. To the men of the Nixon White House, the rebellion on the campuses and in the streets was the result of rule by a rich, effete, liberal establishment, and they countered with unremitting hostility and contempt. Pragmatic economic policies coupled with social conservatism united the Republican party with the silent majority. In the hands of Richard Nixon, Republican control of the White House became a fiercely middle-class affair.

8. Numerous commentators have noted that Nixon's economic policies could have become the nucleus of a progressive modern Republicanism. See, for example, E. J. Dionne, Jr., *Why Americans Hate Politics* (New York: Simon & Schuster, 1991), 193–200; Kevin Phillips, *The Politics of Rich and Poor: Wealth and the American Electorate in the Reagan Aftermath* (New York: Random House, 1990), 39–42. Of course, the economic populism in the essentially pragmatic approach taken by the administration in domestic affairs was undercut by the venality of both Nixon and the political thugs he brought to the White House. The Nixon years produced several important accomplishments—the opening to China, for instance—but the student of American politics faces the inescapable conclusion that Nixon was a crook.

9. Thomas Edsall and Mary Edsall, *Chain Reaction* (New York: Norton, 1991), 81.

An important step in binding the South to the new Republican majority was to make good on promises regarding the Supreme Court. Lyndon Johnson had accepted Earl Warren's resignation subject to the confirmation of his successor; after the Senate's failure to confirm Fortas, Warren agreed to continue as chief justice until Richard Nixon could name a replacement. During the spring of 1969, as the Nixon administration considered candidates to replace Warren, rumors spread throughout Washington that Justice Fortas had engaged in financial dealings with Louis E. Wolfson, a wealthy financier convicted of violating federal securities law. In early May, *Life* magazine ran its famous story outlining the Fortas-Wolfson connection, and within a few weeks Fortas resigned from the Court.[10] Less than six months into his presidency, Richard Nixon was blessed with the opportunity to fill two vacancies on the Court.

To replace Earl Warren, Nixon named Warren Burger, a law-and-order judge who had served on the Court of Appeals for the District of Columbia Circuit for thirteen years. In his judicial opinions and his off-the-bench writings and speeches, Burger had become a frequent, well-known critic of many Warren Court criminal process decisions, and his tough, at times strident views regarding the criminal process brought him to the attention of Nixon. Conservatives and southern Democrats in the Senate welcomed Burger with open arms. Robert Byrd, Democrat of West Virginia, for example, quoted with approval a 1967 Burger speech in which the soon-to-be chief justice questioned the sense of a criminal justice system that had as its primary goal the protection of citizens from police abuse rather than the protection of citizens from the criminal element.[11] Burger was easily confirmed, with only three senators registering negative votes.

To replace Fortas, Nixon sought a southern conservative; he nominated Clement F. Haynsworth, a court of appeals judge from South Carolina. "With this one," he was reported to have gloated,

10. The story of the Fortas resignation is detailed in Murphy, *Fortas*, chap. 24.

11. See Leonard Levy, *Against the Law: The Nixon Court and Criminal Justice* (New York: Harper & Row, 1974), 20–21, for a short description of the Burger hearings.

"we'd stick it to the liberal Ivy League clique who thought the
Court was their own private playground."[12] Unmoved by the
claims of civil rights organizations that Haynsworth was racially
biased, the Senate appeared disposed to confirm, until hearings
before the Senate Judiciary Committee revealed that Haynsworth
had, at best, ignored or, at worst, actively avoided conflict-of-
interest standards while ruling on several cases involving companies in which he held a financial interest. With memories of
Fortas in the minds of senators on both sides of the aisle,
Haynsworth was rejected by a vote of 55 to 45. Asserting that the
Senate's action was simply another example of anti-South preju-
dice, Nixon vowed to continue his campaign to transform the
Court. Although a setback to the administration, the rejection of
Haynsworth probably enhanced the Republican resurgence in the
South; nineteen Democratic senators, all from states below the
Mason-Dixon line, cast votes in support of the nominee.

The nomination of G. Harrold Carswell following the defeat
of Haynsworth showed—at least until Watergate, several years
later—the Nixon administration at its worst. Carswell, described
by Attorney General John Mitchell as "too good to be true," combined overt racism with marginal professional qualifications.[13]
During his tenure as U.S. attorney in Florida, for example, Carswell helped in the assignment of a municipal golf course to a private club. The transfer of the city-owned facility, accomplished
through a ninety-nine-year lease with rent of one dollar a year,
was designed to avoid Supreme Court decisions outlawing segregation in publicly owned facilities. Later, when students at
Columbia University Law School carefully reviewed Carswell's
judicial career, they discovered an extraordinary reversal rate

12. Quoted in Ambrose, *Nixon*, 296.
13. Earlier, Carswell had run for a seat in the Georgia Legislature proclaiming,
"I yield to no man . . . in the firm, vigorous belief in White Supremacy, and I shall
always be so governed." After his failed nomination, Carswell ran in the Florida senatorial primary. He was photographed during that campaign with the sign "Heah Come
de Judge" around his neck. Henry Abraham, *Justices and the President*, 3d ed. (New
York: Oxford Univ. Press, 1992), 18.

during his tenure as a trial judge. Distinguished legal scholars hammered away at the slender qualifications offered by the nominee.[14] On April 9, 1970, the Senate defeated the Carswell nomination by a six-vote margin. Again Nixon charged the Senate with "regional discrimination," maintaining that because of the Senate's intransigence he would be unable to name a southern conservative to the Court, and once again his administration gained stature and support in the South despite the defeat of the nominee.[15] Nixon's nomination of Harry Blackmun, a moderate conservative from Minnesota, was approved by a vote of 94 to 0.

The defeats of Haynsworth and Carswell (as well as that of Fortas) signaled a dramatic change in the politics of judicial confirmation and were pivotal events in the evolution of the modern Republican party. Richard Nixon's "southern strategy" was a calculated effort to hasten the passage of southern whites to the Republican party. Attacks on the Supreme Court, both rhetorical and through the appointment process, were important ingredients in that strategy. Notwithstanding Nixon's outrage, the Haynsworth and Carswell defeats did little damage to the party's long-range electoral strategy; indeed, the twin setbacks confirmed the administration's commitment to make the white South a part of the Republican party. The Nixon administration's spin was to blame the defeats on a liberal elite's zealous defense of the judiciary as the instrument for imposing unwelcome social policies on the nation. The Supreme Court as the bastion of liberal elit-

14. Provoking one of the most famous examples of senatorial idiocy on record. Roman Hruska, Republican of Nebraska, responded to the "mediocrity" claim of Carswell's critics by stating to a radio interviewer, "Even if he were mediocre, there are lot of mediocre judges and people and lawyers. They are entitled to a little representation, aren't they, and a little chance? We can't have all Brandeises and Frankfurters and Cardozos and stuff like that there." Quoted in Richard Harris, *Decision* (New York: Dutton, 1971), 110. This book remains one of the best case studies of the defeat of Carswell.

15. In subsequent elections one indirect result of the Haynsworth and Carswell votes became apparent. Democratic Senators Albert Gore of Tennessee and Joseph Tydings of Maryland were defeated by Republican opponents, and the liberal Democratic Senator Ralph Yarborough lost to a more conservative Democrat in the Texas party primary. Their votes against Carswell were seen as important factors in their defeats.

ism and the symbol of the retreat from fundamental American values, a metaphor artfully employed during the 1968 campaign, became Republican orthodoxy during the Nixon years and a powerful theme in the resurgence of the party.

Throughout Nixon's term in office, the judiciary remained a convenient scapegoat whenever the administration faced controversial policy choices. When, for example, intractable southern school districts continued to avoid the obligation to integrate, the Nixon White House chose lengthy court action rather than a speedy cutoff of federal funds (administered through the executive branch) as the appropriate federal response. Although leaders of the NAACP castigated Nixon for pursuing a policy of delay, the decision kept the administration within the confines of the law while refocusing southern attention on the courts and away from the executive branch. When Leon Panetta, then head of the Civil Rights Office in the Department of Health, Education, and Welfare, sought to answer the NAACP charges, John Ehrlichman of the White House staff told him to "cool it" and not challenge the NAACP interpretation of events. Panetta's conclusion was that the White House was not at all upset by the angry public reaction of the civil rights establishment.[16] The message to the white South was unmistakable: under the Republicans the executive branch would remain passive—and even encourage delay—in desegregating the South.

This strategic use of the federal courts to deflect the wrath of southern white voters proved quite successful. Among southern voters, Republican party registration increased along with expanded court-mandated integration. Southern politicians often went to great lengths to exonerate the executive branch and place responsibility on the Supreme Court for the changes in their constituents' lifestyles. After the executive branch joined the state of Mississippi in a futile attempt to delay the judicial implementation of a desegregation plan, Strom Thurmond announced, "The

---

16. A. James Reichley, *Conservatives in an Age of Change* (Washington, DC: Brookings Institution, 1981), 184.

Nixon administration stood with the South in this case, but the Court has chosen to override the state of Mississippi and the Department of Justice."[17] With the judiciary the institution responsible for the integration of the South, the Nixon administration could escape the political consequences of a white backlash. Southern white support could be secured for the GOP, without significantly altering the inevitability of integration, by having the president denounce busing and affirmative action and by making promises and determined efforts to transform the Court through the appointment power. The strategy was extremely successful, and, whatever his motives, Nixon produced a minor political miracle; in 1972, southern whites' identification with the Republican party peaked, even though the South was far more integrated at the conclusion of Nixon's first term than at its beginning. By Nixon's second term, making the Court a scapegoat had proved to be a surefire Republican strategy.

CAPITALISTS AND FUNDAMENTALISTS

From Nixon to Reagan

In politics, choosing one's enemies wisely often proves even more important than choosing one's allies carefully. In placing the responsibility for the ills of America on the Supreme Court, Nixon had found a villain without a voice of its own and with limited institutional capacity to defend itself and counter negative public opinion.[18] During a time of domestic upheaval and change,

---

17. Quoted in James Simon, *In His Own Image: The Supreme Court in Richard Nixon's America* (New York: David McKay, 1974), 128.

18. Historically, the federal judiciary has relied on presidential support to counter political attacks. More recently, the judiciary's linkages with powerful political groups—for example, the New Progressives—have increased its ability to withstand political retribution. In the late 1960s, the New Progressives lacked the organization and political clout they enjoy today, and the Court's defenders were centered mainly in the civil rights community, a constituency that Nixon had long written off. See, generally, Mark Silverstein and Benjamin Ginsberg, "The Supreme Court and the New Politics of Judicial Power," *Political Science Quarterly* 102 (1987): 371–88.

Nixon's unambiguous theme was that permissive judges had created a permissive society, and the message found a receptive audience. The Warren Court, at least in the view of its critics, was in the forefront of the dramatic changes sweeping America. Richard Nixon's message to middle America was that a change in the makeup of the Supreme Court was a necessary first step in reestablishing in the nation a respect for the sacred institutions and traditions of American life and that as president he could be counted on to wage the long battle to transform the Court.

Watergate cut short the Nixon romance with middle America, exposing the paranoia and the amorality at the core of the man and destroying his presidency. Nevertheless, although Watergate did pave the way for the election of Jimmy Carter in 1976, it did not permanently derail the Republican national majority. When Ronald Reagan regained the presidency for the GOP in 1980, however, the party had a distinctly new look.[19] The Republican coalition as envisioned by Nixon was anchored in middle America, with a profoundly middle-class social and economic outlook. Nixon's economic policy promoted state control and often drastically constricted the freedom of the markets; Kevin Phillips recalled that during the five years of the Nixon presidency there was little faith in the redemptive powers of unbridled capitalism.[20] It remained for Reagan to "unleash capitalism" and redirect national economic policy in favor of a capitalist elite. The 1980s became America's second Gilded Age; the rich got richer and the Reagan team dismantled the regulatory apparatus of the New Deal era, championing economic policies that advanced the concentration of wealth and ensured the victory of capital over labor. Upper-income taxpayers prospered, while lower-income Americans struggled to stay afloat and blue-collar

19. This distinction is forcefully developed by Phillips, *Politics of Rich and Poor*, in chap. 2.

20. Ibid., 35–36.

jobs disappeared. The middle-class economic populism of Nixon gave way to the "country club" economic elitism of Reagan.

In short order, Reagan's ascendancy undercut any hope of a broad-based Republican economic populism. Moreover, "Reaganomics" posed at least a theoretical threat to a Republican revival by rewarding one part of the coalition (the entrepreneurial economic elites) at the expense of another (Nixon's forgotten American). A mark of Reagan's political genius was his ability to close this potential fissure by combining an abiding faith in the power and fairness of the financial markets with an embrace of the social values of a new movement within the Republican ranks. And an important part of Reagan's political wizardry, like Nixon's, lay in his capacity deftly to employ promises of an enduring campaign to recast the makeup of the Supreme Court as the means of holding this most unlikely of coalitions together.

The New Right and the New South

Since the days of the New Deal, mainstream conservatives in the United States had stressed the twin themes of free enterprise on the domestic front and a strident anti-Communism in international affairs. By the 1960s this brand of conservative politics was increasingly out of touch with the needs and concerns of large numbers of American voters. In what amounted to a populist revolt against the blue-blood Republican establishment, a movement gathered force in the 1970s seeking to redirect conservative attention to "issues that people care about."[21] The New Right did not completely dismiss traditional Republican concerns, but the emphasis on the issues that people cared about—such as busing, abortion, pornography—and the skillful use of modern political

21. The words are those of Paul Weyrich, one of the foremost strategists of the New Right. Quoted in A. James Reichley, *Religion in American Public Life* (Washington, DC: Brookings Institution, 1985), 319. For an interesting essay comparing the New Right to the New Progressives, see Barbara Ehrenreich, "The New Right Attack on Social Welfare," in Fred Block et al., *The Mean Season: The Attack on the Welfare State* (New York: Pantheon, 1987).

technology connected these "new" conservatives with the blue-collar and ethnic American voter in ways that traditional conservatives could only imagine.

The coming of the New Right also coincided with the resurgence of the Republican party in America's southland. At mid-century, the Democratic party dominated national politics. From 1932 to 1972, Democrats won seven of the eleven presidential elections and controlled the House and the Senate for all but a few years, while also securing a sizeable majority of governorships. During this time, a significant majority of voters identified with the Democratic party, and the party dominated national politics. Central to Democratic hegemony was the fact that below the Mason-Dixon line, the only politics was Democratic politics. For generations, the continuation of white supremacy was the cornerstone of southern politics, and allegiance to the Democratic Party was deemed essential to the maintenance of the racial status quo. One-party rule assured the continued subjugation of former slaves and, when joined with memories of Reconstruction, produced a loyalty to "the party of our fathers" that equated a vote for the Republican party with outright treason.[22]

If the GOP was to become electorally competitive at the national level, the Democratic party's stranglehold on southern politics had to be broken. *Brown* v. *Board of Education* in 1954 provided an unexpected (and certainly unintended) step in that direction. Southern politics was, for the most part, racial politics, and the Court's landmark desegregation decision, coupled with the national Democratic party's increasing reliance on black votes and its embrace of a national civil rights agenda, wrenched white southerners from their reflexive support of local Democrats. The passage of the Civil Rights Act of 1964 not only placed the federal government inexorably behind the effort to desegregate southern schools and thus further distanced Democratic admin-

---

22. One of the very best analyses of the era of the solid south remains V. O. Key, *Southern Politics* (New York: Vintage, 1949).

istrations from southern whites, but also effectively heralded the eventual end of state-supported apartheid. A substantial number of white southerners, rather than accept integration in public education, eventually fled the public schools in favor of newly established private, all-white academies. In the decades following *Brown*, the correlation between the pace of public school desegregation and the growth of private, segregated academies was unambiguous.[23] In many cases, the organizing force behind the development of the private academies was the Evangelical Protestant church, and over time, the private, white academy morphed into the private, white, Christian academy.

Opposition to integration was not the only motivation compelling the creation of white Christian academies. A belief that public schools were infested with crime and drugs and had become bastions of "godlessness," for example, certainly contributed to the growth of the private Christian school movement. For white southerners, the discontent with the public school system led to a deepening hostility toward the Supreme Court and the lower federal courts. *Brown* and subsequent school busing decisions, coupled with *Engle* v. *Vitale* and *School District of Abington* v. *Schemp* soon produced "Impeach Earl Warren" signs throughout the region.[24] During the 1960s and 1970s, an ever-increasing number of conservative Christians abandoned public education for private academies, and quite rapidly the movement spread beyond the states of the old Confederacy. By 1985, over 1 million students attended Christian academies.[25] It is probably

23. John Jeffries and James Ryan, "A Political History of the Establishment Clause," *Michigan Law Review* 100 (2001): 331. Professors Jeffries and Ryan provide a short and incisive review of the rise of Christian academies in the South and the impact of this development on constitutional law and politics in general, and the discussion that follows borrows from their work.

24. *Engle* v. *Vitale*, 370 U.S. 421 (1962), struck down a prayer composed by the New York State Board of Regents and recited in many New York state schools at the beginning of the school day. *Abington* v. *Schemp*, 374 U.S. 203 (1963), held Pennsylvania's policy of state-mandated bible reading in public schools unconstitutional.

25. Jeffries and Ryan, "A Political History," 336.

safe to say that a substantial number of the families sending children to Christian academies would lay at least a portion of the blame for their disillusionment with public education on the Supreme Court of the United States.

The appearance of Christian academies in the South would play an important role in the resurgence of the modern Republican party. During the mid-1970s, the IRS began to scrutinize carefully the admission policies of not-for-profit private schools and proposed a rule that would deny tax-exempt status to private religious schools that discriminated on the basis of race. Fearing increased government control of their schools as well as the financial consequences of losing tax-exempt status, evangelicals and conservative Christians, who had previously avoided and disdained involvement in day-to-day politics, mobilized in opposition to the IRS regulations. The battles with the IRS over tax exemptions for their schools had the effect of thrusting previously apolitical evangelicals inexorably into the political arena. With the leadership of televangelists like Jerry Falwell and Pat Robertson, what had begun as a defense of segregated private religious schools from government regulation evolved into a nascent political force challenging the social change and secularization attributed to the Democratic party and its institutional partner, the federal judiciary.

Leaders of the New Right astutely recognized the electoral potential of these developments, characterizing the evangelical movement as the "sleeping giant" of American politics. At the urging of Paul Weyrich, Falwell formed the Moral Majority in 1979 to organize and direct further evangelical political action. Later, the Moral Majority would evolve into the Christian Coalition in the continuing effort to build a nationwide conservative political movement.[26] In the South, the politicization of evangelicals was a critical step in the resurgence of the Republican party and the demise of the Democratic solid South. Republican candidates and strategists quickly developed the skills and techniques to identify

---

26. The politicization of America's evangelicals is described in Kenneth Ward, *Religion and Politics in the United States* (New York: St. Martin's Press, 1987), chap. 7.

and manipulate the "wedge" social and cultural controversies that could be employed to rouse the sleeping giant. And, not surprisingly, inexorably linked to most of these controversies was the image of the Warren Court and an activist federal judiciary.

By the 1970s, students of American politics were well aware that the South could be a key to the revitalization of the Republican party, but the leaders of the New Right also understood that a focus on the issues people cared about (e.g., busing, abortion, prayer) could be the glue that bound together the secular New Right, Protestant evangelicals, and conservative, urban Catholics. A defense of Christian values and institutions fit easily into the agenda of the secular New Right, although it was ultimately a strident and uncompromising opposition to abortion rights that brought together the secular and religious movements. The organizational skills of the operatives of the New Right combined with the widespread appeal of television ministries to produce a potent political force, dedicated to mobilizing essentially blue-collar conservatives in a nationwide campaign to save the unborn, battle the moral relativism of modernity, and ensure the continued Republican hegemony in national politics.

In his drive to secure the Republican nomination in 1980, Reagan made an extended effort to court the New Right and link the evangelical movement to the Republican party. During the 1980 campaign the majority of fundamentalist leaders were outspoken champions of the Reagan candidacy, and polls showed that on election day born-again Christians supported Reagan against the deeply religious Carter by a two-to-one margin. Evangelical churches became, in effect, the political "clubs" that impelled a Republican resurgence in the rural South. In the 1984 election, white born-again Christians favored Reagan over Walter Mondale by a four-to-one margin.[27] Both the secular and the religious

27. It is important to remember that in the 1980 election Reagan's opponent was Jimmy Carter, a dedicated evangelical, who spoke publicly and sincerely of the importance of God in his public and private life. In the 1988 presidential election, George Bush, hardly one's image of a born-again fundamentalist, actually increased evangelical support for the Republican ticket.

components of the New Right played significant roles in Republican victories during the 1980s, and the success of Ronald Reagan was due, in no small measure, to the fact that he stepped forward as the secular voice of a growing rebellion against the iniquities of modern life, a rebellion that found vivid expression in the religious revivalism of the last twenty years.[28] Focusing on the issues people cared about—abortion, prayer in school, pornography, traditional family values—paid huge electoral dividends and permitted Reagan to forge a strong bond with middle America. That it was Ronald Reagan—divorcé, irregular churchgoer, and longtime Hollywood film actor—who became the herald of a return to traditional family values lends credence to the hackneyed observation that politics makes for strange bedfellows.[29]

Conservative positions on issues like abortion and prayer in school, combined with the effective manipulation of patriotic symbols, attracted to the GOP many lower-income voters severely bruised by Reagan's tax and income policy. The political scientists Benjamin Ginsberg and Martin Shefter have described a successful Republican strategy of transforming "workers to patriots" and "Southerners to evangelicals."[30] Republican anti-abortion rhetoric, for example, played equally well in rural, conservative Protestant churches and urban Roman Catholic districts; it permitted the party to "unite two forces—Catholics and Protestant

28. The political impact of this religious revival has been the subject of several perceptive essays. See, for example, Walter Dean Burnham, "The 1980 Earthquake: Realignment, Reaction, or What?" in Thomas Ferguson and Joel Rogers, eds., *The Hidden Election: Politics and Economics in the 180 Presidential Campaign* (New York: Random House, 1981): Alan Wolfe, "Cultural Sources of the Reagan Revolution: The Antimodern Legacy," in B. B. Kymlicka and Jean V. Matthews, eds., *The Reagan Revolution* (Chicago: Dorsey Press, 1988), 65–81.

29. This was not the only contradiction inherent in the Reagan revolution. Reagan gave political expression to evangelical religious values while, at the same time, proclaiming a ferociously secular activity like venture capitalism to be the highest form of human endeavor. E. J. Dionne, Jr., neatly captured another side of the contradiction: "Young investment bankers who looked kindly on cocaine and fundamentalist factory workers who saw a world full of sin and corruption could vote for Ronald Reagan with equal enthusiasm. And they did." Dionne, *Why Americans Hate Politics*, 242.

30. See Ginsberg and Shefter, *Politics by Other Means* (New York: Basic, 1990), chap. 4.

evangelicals—that have been bitter opponents through much of American history."[31] Republican strategists unabashedly manipulated patriotic and military symbols to erode the traditional Democratic ties of blue-collar workers and southern whites; during the 1988 presidential campaign the American flag effectively supplanted the elephant as the symbol of the Republican party.

Like the Democratic coalition it succeeded, the Republican electoral coalition of the 1980s involved an attraction of opposites; it was anchored, on the one end, by lower- and middle-income northern ethnics and white southerners attracted by the conservative social policies advocated by Republican candidates and, on the other, by an economic elite generously rewarded by Republican tax and economic policy. In the Republican party evangelical voters play a role that mirrors that of black voters in the Democratic party, in effect forcing Republican candidates to the right and demanding explicit positions on controversial social issues.[32] On the other hand, high income is more closely associated with liberal than with conservative social views, and, as a result, only a small percentage of the Republican economic elite shares the social agenda of the secular and religious New Right.[33] Republicans on the national level now face a perplexing quandary: to push effectively the social policy program of the New Right risks alienating the economic well-to-do; to fail to produce legislative gains on a conservative social agenda invites potential discord on the right.[34]

31. Benjamin Ginsberg, *The Captive Public: How Mass Opinion Promotes State Power* (New York: Basic, 1986), 112–13.

32. In 1988, white evangelicals made up approximately 9 percent of the electorate, and slightly over 81 percent cast their vote for the Republican ticket. Blacks constituted 10 percent of the 1988 electorate and voted just over 85 percent Democratic. See Martin B. Wattenberg, "From a Partisan to a Candidate-Centered Electorate," in King, *New American Political System*, 2d version, 139–74. From the Reagan era to the present, Republican presidential candidates have been able to count on approximately 80 percent of the evangelical white vote.

33. Ibid., 165.

34. The potency of a revolt from the right even to an incumbent Republican president is well illustrated by the discomfort Pat Buchanan caused George Bush during the early days of the 1992 primary season.

Reagan: The Court as Alibi

The Nixon success in 1968 set the stage for a scenario in which the Supreme Court played the heavy for countless Republican office seekers. Placing responsibility for the ills of modern America on the federal judiciary deflected voter anger from the governing regime and became a proven Republican campaign theme. During the Reagan-Bush years the Court played an equally important but slightly altered role. Although the Reagan coalition could agree on the virtue of freeing capitalism from the vice of government regulation, the social agenda championed by the New Right contained the seeds of political disaster. Once again, however, the Supreme Court indirectly allowed Republicans to escape their own internal contradictions. In the most sublime of ironies, precisely the same Court decisions so easily reviled on the campaign trail were the decisions that would protect Republican presidents and legislators from the potentially disastrous electoral consequences of their enacting the social policy agenda of the New Right. Whatever the intensity of the chief executive's opposition to abortion, as long as *Roe* v. *Wade* remained good law, abortion rights were beyond presidential control. Reagan might promise to do all he could to return prayer to the classroom, but until *Engel* v. *Vitale* was overruled, the support remained rhetorical.[35] Indeed, almost all the social agenda championed by the New Right was governed by Supreme Court precedent and thus removed from executive and legislative control.

The continuing force of many of the most controversial decisions of the Warren and Burger Courts permitted Reagan to retain the unquestioned loyalty of the right wing of his party through little more than a combination of pious rhetoric and promises to alter the makeup of the federal courts. Until a new conservative majority was installed on the Court, Republicans could hardly be held accountable for their failure to enact the new social agenda. Throughout the Reagan years, the attention of the New Right was

35. *Engel* v. *Vitale*, 370 U.S. 412 (1962).

focused on the staffing of the federal judiciary; this produced significant political benefits for the administration. On the one hand, it marginalized the influence of the radical Right on domestic policy matters; without major changes in the federal judiciary and, in particular, the Supreme Court, sweeping social change was impossible. Until the judiciary was transformed, administration support for a pro-family, Christian moral and social agenda would be mainly symbolic. On the other hand, economic elites could easily support a Reagan presidency, secure in the knowledge that Supreme Court rulings on a host of privacy and First Amendment issues precluded enactment of the New Right's agenda. Winking at the language of the devout was a tiny price to pay for a reduction in marginal tax rates.

Success in American electoral politics has never demanded a high degree of internal logic, and throughout the 1980s Republicans continued to campaign to transform the federal courts, even if the alliance that underwrote Republican victories could be maintained only so long as a active judiciary imposed a constitutional bar to the social radicalism of the New Right. During the Reagan years this occupation with judicial decisions and staffing kept the coalition together with little political cost. Although several leaders of the religious Right claimed that the administration failed to invest sufficient political capital in the battles to secure desired social legislation, evangelicals overwhelmingly supported Reagan's reelection in 1984. Jerry Falwell, of the Moral Majority, for example, closed the 1984 Republican convention with a benediction that heralded the party's candidates as "God's instruments in rebuilding America," and the campaign platform called for an end to abortion, defeat of the Equal Rights Amendment, and support of prayer in public schools.[36] Throughout the campaign and his final term in office, Reagan continued to speak the language of the pious, asserting that the Bible contained "all the answers to all the problems that face us today," but the energy

36. Wald, *Religion and Politics*, 194.

of his administration was directed to the overwhelmingly secular matters of tax cuts, deregulation, and a military buildup to challenge the Soviets.[37]

Judicial Politics in the Reagan Era

The administration did not, however, completely abandon the legislative agenda of the New Right, particularly when the proposed action was of little concern to the remainder of the Republican coalition. For many years fundamentalists had clashed with the IRS over the tax-exempt status of church schools that discriminated against racial minorities. In 1982, Treasury Department officials announced that the IRS policy of refusing tax-exempt status for these religious schools would be revoked. Because the issue was then before the Supreme Court (the Carter administration had successfully defended the policy in litigation with Bob Jones University and the Goldsboro Christian School, and the schools had appealed to the Supreme Court), the Reagan administration moved to withdraw from the case, asked the Supreme Court to dismiss, and announced that both schools would be granted the requested tax exemption. The religious Right hailed the action, but civil rights groups fought back and secured a federal court injunction preventing the IRS from granting the exemptions.

The Reagan Justice Department responded by withdrawing its request for the Court to dismiss the Bob Jones and Goldsboro cases but announced that the government would appear on behalf of the two schools and not defend the IRS policy. The Supreme Court appointed William Coleman, a prominent private attorney, to argue the IRS position, and the next year, in an 8-to-1 vote, it upheld the IRS regulations refusing tax exemptions to religious schools that practiced racial discrimination.[38] Although moder-

---

37. Quoted in Reichley, *Religion in American Public Life*, 325.
38. *Bob Jones University* v. *U.S.*, 461 U.S. 574 (1983). The deputy solicitor general who signed the government's brief in the case arguing on behalf of the two schools

ate Republicans may well have been embarrassed by the administration's heavy-handed efforts, the political cost was small, and, in the view of the New Right, Ronald Reagan had again fought the good fight against encroaching secular humanism and its champion—the U.S. Supreme Court.

To appease the New Right further and divert attention to the judiciary, the Reagan administration often demanded that government attorneys appearing before the Supreme Court urge upon the justices only the most conservative of legal positions. For example, during the 1984 term the Court confronted the issue of whether an Alabama statute setting aside one minute at the start of each school day for meditation or voluntary prayer violated the establishment clause of the First Amendment.[39] Attorney General Edwin Meese and other close Reagan advisers were reported to have pressured the solicitor general to urge upon the Court the proposition that the Bill of Rights did not apply to the states.[40] Such an argument, despite some historical validity and modern appeal to opponents of active judicial review, ran afoul of over fifty years of Supreme Court precedent and would not be accepted by the Court. Rex Lee, Reagan's first solicitor general, was placed in the uncomfortable position of having to refuse the administration's request to make the most extreme, doctrinaire arguments before the Court. "If I had done what was urged on me [by White House staff and Justice Department officials]," Lee said, "I would have lost those cases and the Justices wouldn't have taken me seriously in others. There has been this notion that my job is to press the Administration's policies at every turn and announce true conservative prin-

---

noted in a footnote that, although he was signing the brief, he personally believed that the contrary position was the correct one. The remainder of the government attorneys who worked on the government's brief refused to sign it. For the complete story see Lincoln Caplan, *The Tenth Justice: The Solicitor General and the Rule of Law* (New York: Vintage, 1987), chap. 5; Elder Witt, *A Differential Justice: Reagan and the Supreme Court* (Washington, DC: CQ Press, 1986), 107–8.

39. *Wallace v. Jaffre*, 472 U.S. 38 (1985).

40. See Witt, *Different Justice*, 133, which presents an interesting review of the Reagan administration's legal strategy and the response of the Supreme Court.

ciples through the pages of my briefs. It is not. I'm the Solicitor General, not the Pamphleteer General."[41]

Despite the harm it did to the solicitor general's credibility with the justices of the Supreme Court, the policy of urging the court to reverse years of constitutional precedent produced political dividends, permitting Reagan to solidify his position as the champion of the New Right's social agenda. Moreover, the Court's reluctance to acquiesce in these extreme arguments ultimately enhanced the political rewards by allowing Reagan to assume this position without jeopardizing the support of the remainder of the Republican coalition.[42]

Equally important in securing the support of the religious Right without seriously imperiling the Republican coalition was Reagan's effort to transform the federal judiciary. Although all modern presidents have paid lip service to the importance of appointments to the federal bench, before the Reagan presidency, executive scrutiny of potential nominees to lower federal courts was haphazard at best and limited by respect for senatorial patronage.[43] Under Reagan, however, the President's Committee on Federal Judicial Selection, consisting of key members of the White House staff and the Justice Department was formed to screen judicial appointments and allow the administration to apply a consistent ideological measure.[44] The Reagan Justice

41. Quoted in Caplan, *Tenth Justice*, 107. The solicitor general is appointed by the president and represents the government in cases before the Supreme Court. Because the United States is the most frequent party before the Court, the solicitor general occupies a unique position, representing the United States and yet serving almost as a "tenth justice," because the justices rely on the solicitor general's expertise and good faith.

42. The strategy may also have produced some anger on the part of at least three Reagan/Bush appointees to the Court. In *Planned Parenthood* v. *Casey*, 112 S. Ct. 2791 (1992), Justice O'Connor began her opinion, joined by Justices Souter and Kennedy, with the observation "The United States, as it has done in five other cases in the last decade, again asks us to overrule *Roe*." The tone of Justice O'Connor's opinion suggests a good deal of frustration with Republican administrations for continually pushing the divisive abortion issue on the Court.

43. The principal study being Sheldon Goldman, *Picking Federal Judges: Lower Court Selection from Roosevelt through Reagan* (New Haven: Yale Univ. Press, 1997).

44. Ibid., chap. 8.

Department conducted extensive interviews with prospective nominees to the federal bench, and the agenda of the New Right often formed the basis of the questioning. For example, Judith Whittaker, the associate general counsel to Hallmark Cards and highly rated by the American Bar Association, was rejected because she had supported the Equal Rights Amendment, and Andrew Frey, an assistant solicitor general, was turned down when his donations to Planned Parenthood and the National Coalition to Ban Handguns were discovered.[45] Although liberals and moderates complained that Reagan had introduced an "ideological litmus test" to the selection of judges, the New Right warmly endorsed the undertaking. The undeniable fact was that the Reagan administration had established the most comprehensive and effective process for recruiting and screening federal judges in the history of the American presidency.[46] And the minuscule political costs among mainstream Republicans were again more than offset by the political gains among the supporters of the New Right.

The campaign to change the ideological makeup of the Supreme Court was, of course, more visible. In naming the first woman to the Supreme Court, Reagan neutralized opposition from the Left but encountered some surprising opposition from the New Right. Sandra Day O'Connor was a moderate-to-conservative Arizona Republican, having served as a state legislator and appellate court judge. Warmly endorsed by many women's groups, O'Connor encountered New Right opposition when it was discovered that as a state legislator she had favored a bill that would have repealed Arizona's remaining abortion laws and supported the Equal Rights Amendment. Her failure to

45. See David M. O'Brien, "The Reagan Judges: His Most Enduring Legacy?" in Charles O. Jones, ed., *The Reagan Legacy: Promise and Performance* (New York: Chatham House, 1988), 69.

46. See Stephan J. Markman, "Judicial Selection The Reagan Years," in *Judicial Selection: Merit, Ideology and Politics* (Washington, DC: National Legal Center for the Public Interest, 1990), 33–48, for a sympathetic description of the Reagan process of judicial selection.

take an unequivocal stand against abortion rights caused New Right conservatives in the Senate, led by Jesse Helms of North Carolina, to express grave misgivings about O'Connor, but in the end the Senate confirmed Reagan's first appointment to the Court with little debate.[47]

The decision to elevate William Rehnquist to replace the retiring Chief Justice Burger in 1986 and then name D.C. Circuit Judge Antonin Scalia to Rehnquist's vacant associate justice seat was the result of a multifaceted political calculation. As the Reagan administration was acutely aware, the nomination of Rehnquist would most certainly result in Democratic opposition. Since assuming his seat as associate justice in 1972, Rehnquist had emerged as the Court's most influential conservative voice, and as a result, several administration officials expressed real concern over whether he would secure Senate approval.[48] On the other

47. The hearings before the Senate Judiciary Committee were another matter and provided some melodrama. Senator Jeremiah Denton, Republican of Alabama, a favorite of the evangelical Right, was frustrated in his attempts to prod O'Connor to engage in a discussion of her views on abortion and complained, "I do not feel I have made any progress personally in determining where you stand on the issue of abortion." His Republican colleague Senator East of North Carolina, another voice of the religious Right, agreed and suggested that O'Connor's failure to answer their questions forthrightly undercut the Senate's role in the confirmation process. See Witt, *Differential Justice*, 40–41. Of course, in politics, as in life, what goes around comes around. A few years later, during the Souter and Thomas confirmation hearings, Democratic members of the Judiciary Committee expressed the same frustrations and misgivings, while conservative Republicans argued that attempts to question prospective nominees regarding their positions on abortion "politicized" the entire nomination process. O'Connor's position on the "issues people cared about," particularly abortion, troubled some White House officials as well. At the very least, these members of the White House staff believed a nominee to the High Court should be subject to the same ideological scrutiny as lower court appointments. O'Connor's nomination, however, was championed by Attorney General William French Smith, and his office provided most of the background information on O'Connor. Professor David Yaloff has concluded that had the White House staff, particularly the White House Counsel's office, participated more directly in the background investigation of O'Connor, her at best ambiguous (and, for the New Right, potentially troubling) stand on abortion might have doomed her nomination. See David A. Yaloff, *Pursuit of Justice: Presidential Politics and the Selection of Supreme Court Nominees* (Chicago: Chicago Univ. Press, 1999), 135–42.

48. One concern was the reappearance of the "Jackson memorandum." After his graduation from Stanford Law School, Rehnquist had served as a law clerk to Justice Robert Jackson during the period of the school desegregation cases. While the Court

hand, Rehnquist was a sitting justice, and no one questioned his intellect or his relationship with the other members of the Court. In the final analysis, the administration made an educated bet that he could survive the expected liberal firestorm while at the same time deflecting liberal opposition from the Scalia appointment. It was an astute calculation. Rehnquist was confirmed after a long and acrimonious battle that produced thirty-three negative votes—the most ever for a successful nominee to the chief justiceship. With Rehnquist attracting the energy of liberal opposition, Scalia was confirmed with nary a single negative vote.[49]

Within a year, Democratic opposition would again be mobilized when Reagan nominated Robert Bork to replace the retiring Justice Lewis Powell. Bork possessed unquestioned professional and intellectual qualifications, as well as a judicial philosophy that squared neatly with conservative social views, and his appointment to the Court would have been the crowning achievement in the New Right's efforts to transform the Court.[50] So great was the New Right's rage over the defeat of his nomination that

---

was considering *Brown* v. *Board of Education*, Rehnquist authored a memorandum asserting that the justices could find segregated schools unconstitutional only by reading their own personal social and political views into the constitution. At his hearings in 1971, Rehnquist asserted that the memo was written at the behest of Jackson, and Rehnquist maintained the same position in 1986. Whether the memo reflected Rehnquist's position in 1953 (as seems likely) or the position of Justice Jackson, it resurfaced in both the Rehnquist confirmation proceedings and provided particular fuel to the fire of those opposing his appointments.

49. Years before, Rehnquist had provided a similar service for Lewis Powell during their confirmation hearings. As a Richmond, Virginia, lawyer during the period of massive resistance to the *Brown* decision, Powell had served as chair of the Richmond School Board and throughout the period of his service (1953–61) only two children of color attended school with white students. Although race played a role in the Powell confirmation hearings, the issue never really gained traction, in part because liberal opposition focused solely on the Rehnquist appointment. See John Jeffries, Jr., *Justice F. Lewis Powell, Jr.* (New York: Scribner's, 1994) for a discussion of Justice Powell's legal career and confirmation proceedings.

50. Those who maintained that the New Right may have lost the battle but ultimately won the war because Anthony Kennedy, the jurist confirmed in place of Bork, was equally conservative missed the significance of the Bork nomination and defeat. Bork's background, intellectual development, and personality suggested to many students of the Court that, once appointed, he would assume a leadership role on the

the anger even spilled over to taint Ronald Reagan for what many considered his lackluster and detached efforts on behalf of Bork.[51]

REPUBLICAN ARMAGEDDON

End Game

In the 1988 presidential campaign, George H. W. Bush promised a continuation of the Reagan policies, albeit in a more tempered and gentle manner. Ronald Reagan came to office with what was perceived as a powerful mandate for change and responded with bold initiatives that set the tone and tenor of his entire presidency. The Bush campaign of 1988, however, was lacking new ideas but steeped in the symbols of patriotism, race, and crime, and Bush entered the White House with neither a personal agenda nor a real electoral mandate for altering existing policies. A cautious politician by nature, Bush was uncomfortable with ideological rhetoric, and his initial years in office were marked by an obvious attempt to avoid (at least in the realm domestic affairs) major confrontations with the Democratic Congress. The most difficult problems facing the nation (escalating deficits, the cost and availability of health care, urban decay, and so on) were left untouched as the president pursued a risk-averse policy designed to lower the expectations of the electorate. In the aftermath of the Persian Gulf War, his popularity reached historic proportions. The epitaph for his presidency, however, might well be that in the last years of his term in office George Bush accomplished nothing with this popular mandate.

Court, exercising great influence on the development of constitutional law for several decades. Justice Kennedy is a competent jurist and *may* become a leader on the Court; Judge Bork, however, appeared *destined* to play such a role. Kennedy's refusal to vote to overrule *Roe* in *Planned Parenthood* v. *Casey*, 112 S. Ct. 2791 (1992), further vindicates the extraordinary effort of the New Progressives to defeat the Bork nomination.

51. See, for example, Patrick McGuigan and Dawn Weyrich, *Ninth Justice* (Washington, DC: Free Congress, 1990), 220–21.

His long-term electoral strategy was similar to that of Reagan: Keep in place Reagan tax and spending policies while courting the New Right through symbolic support of family values. The tangible rewards to the right wing of the party would be judicial appointments. The Reagan promise of transforming the federal courts through the appointment power would continue to be honored. The policy of appointing conservatives to the bench "was the greatest priority of conservatives who followed George Bush's election," noted Clint Black, a prominent New Right conservative who headed a group monitoring judicial appointments.[52] The two most important innovations during the Reagan era—the President's Committee on Federal Judicial Selection and the systematic screening of all potential nominees to the federal bench—were maintained by the Bush administration.[53] The profile of the typical Bush nominee to the federal bench was similar to that of the typical Reagan nominee. And the political impact of the appointments was to continue to fuse the Republican party's linkage with the New Right. "It's a very tasty morsel he gives to the rightwingers," said one judge (appointed during the Reagan-Bush era) of the Bush administration's efforts to appoint only the most conservative of jurists.[54]

During Bush's term in office the downside of this strategy became readily apparent. Throughout the 1980s Reagan skillfully used the staffing of the federal courts to quiet—and marginalize—the New Right. With the New Right preoccupied with the selection of judges, Reagan was free to go on in his secular quest to dismantle America's limited welfare state and erect Reaganomics as the centerpiece of a new entrepreneurial America. Until the judiciary was transformed, action on the politically

52. Quoted in Neil A. Lewis, "Selection of Conservative Judges Guards Part of Bush Legacy," *New York Times*, July 1, 1992, A13.
53. See Sheldon Goldman, "The Bush Imprint on the Judiciary: Carrying on a Tradition," *Judicature* 74 (1991): 294, for a review of the first two years of the Bush administration's record on judicial appointments.
54. Quoted in Lewis, "Selection of Conservative Judges."

divisive issues of school prayer, abortion, and racial integration could be postponed and energy and political capital concentrated on Reagan's economic program. By the time of the first Bush presidency, decades of Republican appointments to the Court *had* altered the federal judiciary, enhancing both the expectations of New Right and the fears of socially moderate elements of the party. In his final years in office, Bush confronted what Reagan had long managed to avoid: a belief on the part of both critical wings of the Republican party that the constitutional constraints on the promotion of a new social agenda would soon be gone.

In the summer of 1989, the Supreme Court announced its decision in *Webster* v. *Reproductive Health Services*.[55] *Webster* had assumed unusual significance because it promised the first opportunity for Justices Scalia and Kennedy to make clear their positions on the abortion issue and perhaps to provide Justice O'Connor with the occasion to amplify her position on *Roe* as well. The drama was enhanced when the Court waited until the final day of the 1988 term of the Court to announce the decision. Although no one opinion commanded a majority and only four justices specifically recorded a willingness to overrule *Roe*, the tenor of the *Webster* decision appeared to indicate that the Court had turned a corner in the abortion debate, returned to the individual states substantial authority to restrict abortions.

The political fallout from *Webster* was considerable. Leaders of the evangelical and secular Right proclaimed that *Webster* was the long-awaited major victory and that the crusade to save the unborn and to redeem America was fast approaching a glorious conclusion. Pro-choice activists were galvanized into action, mobilizing their constituencies with the warning that no longer could the Supreme Court be relived upon to protect abortion rights.[56] The political director of the National Abortion Rights Action League (NARAL) characterized the decision as "the smok-

55. 492 U.S. 490 (1989).

56. The reaction to *Webster* created a new abortion strategy. When the Supreme Court rendered the next long-awaited abortion decision, *Planned Parenthood of South-*

ing gun needed to mobilize our people."[57] Membership and contributions to pro-choice groups increased in the wake of *Webster*.
Of utmost significance was the fact that the appeal to protect abortion rights resonated loudly within the ranks of moderate Republicans. In the 1989 New Jersey gubernatorial election, James Florio,
pro-choice Democrat, soundly defeated Republican James Courtier,
an opponent of abortion rights, and in Virginia, Democrat Douglas Wilder became the first elected African American governor
in the nation's history. In the cases of Florio and Wilder and in a
host of other national, state, and local elections, exit polling indicated that the *Webster* decision and the intense political activity
in its aftermath had energized a pro-choice majority that drew
important support from segments of the Republican party.[58] In
the words of Republican Senator Bob Packwood, Republicans in
the 1989 elections "got the bejabbers beaten out of them because
of abortion."[59]

Throughout the 1992 election season George Bush struggled
to hold the Reagan coalition together. The religious Right, in the
form of the Christian Coalition, under the leadership of Pat
Robertson, supported Bush's reelection but warned that the fail-

---

eastern Pennsylvania v. *Casey*, 112 S. Ct. 2791 (1992), in which the Court again significantly cut back on *Roe* but pointedly refused to overrule that decision and return complete control of abortions to the states, both pro- and anti-abortion forces were quick
to proclaim the decision a major *defeat* as a means for rallying their supporters. See
Maralee Schwartz and Don Balz, "Preparing to Play Abandon Politics in an Election
Year," *Washington Post National Weekly Edition*, July 6–12, 1992, 8. Perhaps the real loser
was George H. W. Bush. New Progressives announced that once again it was apparent that the overturning of *Roe* was only one vote away and that was precisely what
the upcoming presidential election was about. Important leaders of the New Right,
characterizing the bloc of Justices O'Connor, Souter, and Kennedy that voted to retain
the core constitutional principle of *Roe* as the "wimp bloc," called these appointments
"an embarrassment to the presidents that appointed them." See Al Kamen, "Conservatives See a 'Wimp Bloc,'" ibid., 7–8.

57. Quoted in Barbara Craig and David O'Brien, *Abortion and American Politics*
(New York: Chatham House, 1993), 296.

58. See ibid., chaps. 8 and 9, and Laurence Tribe, *Abortion* (New York: Norton, 1990),
chap. 8, for a review of the impact of *Webster* on elections and on legislative politics.

59. Quoted in Craig and O'Brien, *Abortion and American Politics*, 299.

ure to deliver on social policies and judicial appointments might result in the religious Right's sitting out the 1992 election. The *Webster* decision, coupled with the Bush Supreme Court appointments of David Souter and Clarence Thomas (to replace Justices Brennan and Marshall, two of the strongest defenders of abortion rights on the Court), heightened the expectations of the religious and the secular Right. In an attempt to forestall even the hint of a rebellion from this part of the Republican coalition, Bush campaign advisers permitted the 1992 Republican National Convention to become a religious revival meeting, with the Bush-Quayle ticket anointed as God's champion in the battle against modernity and moral decay. From the more affluent and socially moderate members of the coalition, however, came the warning that the failure to temper the Republican party's conservative social agenda, particularly regarding abortion rights, would cost the party critical votes in key states such as California. In his struggle to hold the coalition together, Bush often appeared indecisive, without aim or direction. The New Right and the economic elites, always wary of each other, were equally uninspired by Bush, and a worsening economic situation and the candidacy of H. Ross Perot paved the way for Democratic victory.

The Loyal Opposition Once Again

A quarter of a century separates the fall of Abe Fortas from the tumult surrounding the Clarence Thomas appointment. During that period, the changes in the politics of judicial confirmations served as dramatic illustrations of the vicissitudes of modern American politics. For all its significance, the Fortas defeat, in retrospect, was a relatively quiet affair. Television played a minor role, and the American populace remained uninvolved. But the battle over Fortas heralded a new type of confirmation politics. By the mid-1980s, nominations to the federal bench often evoked the best and worst of modern American politics, as sophisticated media coverage and manipulation triggered mass participation in the selection of judges. In the midst of one of the most divisive Senate proceedings in modern memory, one participant described the process of Clarence Thomas's confirmation to the Supreme Court as "the worst kind of sleazy political operation."[60] Hyperbole aside, the description strikes home, if only because of the extraordinary participation of powerful groups of both political parties in a process often naïvely thought to be immune from politics as usual.

The election of Bill Clinton refocused the New Right's obsession with the staffing of the federal judiciary, and the shift to Republican control in Congress in 1994 further polarized the proceedings. New Right groups pledged to wage a continuing battle to deny Clinton the opportunity to "pack" the federal bench with "activist judges." Republican senators promised to employ all the powers of the majority party to make it as difficult as possible for Clinton to move his nominees to the bench. Republican Senators Kyl of Arizona and Gordon of Washington, for example, seriously proposed that Clinton cede half of the nominations for the federal courts to the Republican majority in the Senate as the price for confirmation of at least a certain proportion of his nominees.[61] Republican Orrin Hatch of Utah, the chair of the Senate Judiciary Committee, often simply refused to hold hearings on nominees, thus grinding the process of confirming federal judges to a virtual halt. Even when a nominee did clear the Judiciary Committee, "holds" were frequently placed on the nomination and a vote ultimately either delayed or denied.[62] Nor was the obsession with the federal judiciary limited to Senate Repub-

60. Senator John C. Danforth, Republican of Missouri, quoted in the *New York Times*, October 9, 1991, A20.

61. See Neil Lewis, "Clinton has Chance to Shape the Courts," *New York Times*, February 9, 1997, 30.

62. In the tradition of the filibuster, a "hold" is the power of one senator, either publicly or anonymously, to request that Senate action be blocked. For an interesting spin on the Republican use of "holds" on Clinton judicial nominees, see the press release from the office of Democratic Senator Patrick Leahy, "The Estrada Nomination: The Misquote of Senator Patrick Leahy on Filibusters," March 3, 2003.

licans. In 1997, then Republican House Majority Whip Tom DeLay announced that many sitting judges on the federal bench needed to be "intimidated," and he vowed to proceed via impeachment for those who committed the high crime and misdemeanor of "activism." If federal judges don't behave, DeLay proclaimed, "we are going after them in a big way."[63]

Republican promises to curb "Warren Court-type activism" and "legislating from the bench" resonated powerfully within an increasingly conservative Republican base. The Republican strategy of employing the Senate's many tools for obstruction and delay to deny Democratic appointments to the federal bench, even ideologically moderate Clinton nominees, paid significant political dividends in the party's continuing courtship of southern whites and evangelicals, as well as undercutting the links between the New Progressives and the federal judiciary. As David O'Brien has aptly noted, Clinton's goals for judicial recruitment were limited from the outset of his presidency.[64] After the 1994 elections, those goals became even more constrained, much to the consternation of many in the Democratic party. For President Clinton, satisfying the New Progressive's dream of a revitalized federal judiciary after years of Republican rule had to be measured against the demands of governing in a political universe where presidential power was defined by the ability to form the ever-shifting coalitions needed to win the next political battle. By the end of his two terms in office, Clinton's own indifference to judicial appointments, coupled with Republican intransigence, left New Progressives frustrated and fearful and the New Right spoiling for the next battle over the future of the federal judiciary.

63. Joan Biskupic, "Hill Republicans Target 'Judicial Activism'," *Washington Post*, September 14, 1997, A1.

64. David M. O'Brien, "Judicial Legacies: The Clinton Presidency and the Courts," in Colin Campbell and Bert A. Rockman, eds., *The Clinton Legacy* (New York: Chatham House, 2000), 116.

Chapter 5

THE SENATE: FROM MEN'S CLUB TO PUBLICITY MACHINE

The alteration of judicial power and the fragmentation of the governing coalitions shape the process of selecting and confirming the justices of the Supreme Court. These developments must also be placed in the context of the changes that have taken place in the U.S. Senate. The "advice and consent" of the Senate is the final step in the confirmation process, and the transformation of the Senate from a hierarchical, inner-directed chamber to a more responsive and effective institution for the articulation of group interests has had a profound impact on the selection of judges.

In the aftermath of World War II, the New Deal coalition was firmly in place, judicial restraint was the guiding principle of judicial liberalism, and the Senate was an insulated and conservative institution in which a handful of senior members dominated the distribution of resources, and widely accepted norms constrained behavior. These factors worked in concert to make the confirmation of a Supreme Court justice a low-key, predictable affair. In the 1960s, however, the Senate began a transformation as the accepted norms of Senate behavior lost their hold and the distribution of power and influence in the institution broadened. Individual senators became highly visible political actors, alive to the opportunity to champion the causes of citizens' groups with large, national constituencies. With the governing coalitions in disarray and the federal judiciary emerging as an important policymaking arena, the Senate provided a receptive forum for interests battling to control the shape and direction of the modern judiciary.

Today, however, a rising tide of partisanship and partisan conflict in the Senate has joined with the tradition of individual prerogative to alter the politics of confirmation. Conflict continues to mark the confirmation process, but in today's Senate, conflict is now defined by distinct ideological positions and party divisions, and the conclusion of any confirmation battle hinges not necessarily on the outcome of an up-or-down vote but rather on the minority party's willingness to use the rules and structure of the Senate to obstruct and delay the legislative process.

THE SENATE AT MIDCENTURY

The World's Greatest Deliberate Body

"[T]he Senate," wrote Alexis de Tocqueville, "contains within a small space a large proportion of the celebrated men of America. Scarcely an individual is to be seen in it who has not had an active and illustrious career. . . . "[1] His contempt for the more democratically elected House of Representatives, however, was unmistakable: "On entering the House of Representatives of Washington one is struck by the vulgar demeanor of the great assembly. Often there is not a distinguished man in the whole number. Its members are almost all obscure individuals, whose names bring no associations to mind. They are mostly village lawyers, men in trade or even persons belonging to the lower classes of society."[2] Tocqueville's aristocratic lineage and fear of a tyranny of the majority render his preference for the Senate hardly remarkable. Yet throughout a good deal of American history, even those without his aristocratic predilections have found

1. Alexis de Tocqueville, *Democracy in America*, vol. 1 (New York: Knopf, 1956), 204.
2. Ibid. A reason that Tocqueville considered the Senate the more worthy chamber was that senators were appointed by state legislatures and thus freed from a direct connection with the petty concerns of constituency. An observer with greater sympathy for modern mass democracy might easily conclude that the Seventeenth Amendment enhanced Senate power by providing senators the legitimacy conferred by direct election.

the Senate the more attractive chamber. There are many reasons for this preference, beginning with a senator's larger constituency and longer term in office. The disparity in the size of membership between the Senate and House, however, provides perhaps the most satisfying explanation. With over four times the membership of the Senate, the House utilizes strict rules limiting debate and equips its leadership with real authority over the prerogative of individual members. The greater the number in a legislative body, the more compelling the need for rules of organization and procedure. Although such rules presumably advance institutional goals, they do, at least in the House, sharply curtail the power of a single representative to alter the course of legislation.

The compactness of the Senate, however, demands less organization and permits greater independence for the individual legislator. Compared with those in the House, Senate leaders enjoy limited authority. A powerful Senate majority leader, for example, is nearly always a testimony to the leader's individual skills and personality, because the formal powers that attach to the post are minimal. Two former majority leaders, Robert Byrd, Democrat, and Robert Dole, Republican, used the word "slave" in describing their experiences in the position, and Senator Tom Daschle recently characterized the incentives at his disposal as majority leader to influence his colleagues as "a bushel full of carrots and a few twigs."[3] Moreover, few, if any, legislative assemblies in the world encourage individual autonomy and free debate to the extent the U.S. Senate does. The Senate, as an institution, venerates the prerogative of the individual senator and, because

3. Dole's predecessor as majority leader, Howard Baker, Republican of Tennessee, was less melodramatic when he characterized the leadership position as essentially "janitorial" in nature. See Roger Davidson, "The Senate: If Everyone Leads Who Follows?" in Lawrence C. Dodd and Bruce I. Oppenheimer, eds., *Congress Reconsidered*, 4th ed. (Washington, DC: CQ Press, 1989), 275–306; Holly Idelson, "Signs Point to Greater Loyalty on Both Sides of the Aisle," *CQ Weekly* December 19, 1992, 3849. The Daschle quote can be found in Theodore Lowi et al., *American Government: Power and Purpose*, 7th ed. (New York: Norton, 2002), 204.

of its permissive rules and flaccid organization, during the twentieth century emerged as the arena where the ambitious can make a difference and become figures of national repute and importance. It is therefore hardly surprising that promising members of the House usually harbor aspirations at one time or another of joining "the greatest deliberative body in the world."

The Folkways of the Senate

One might expect in an institution that proudly retains a tradition of unlimited debate, minimal formal leadership, and membership autonomy a good deal of conflict over matters as weighty and potentially divisive as appointments to the Supreme Court. For a substantial part of the twentieth century, however, conflict was the exception rather than the rule. Despite the long tradition of members' independence, throughout much of this period the Senate was a comparatively cohesive, self-contained, and efficient legislative body. The lack of strict procedural regulations led to a highly developed pattern of unwritten rules and norms that governed behavior in the institution and stifled the independence of members. "There is great pressure for conformity in the Senate," reported one of its influential members during the early 1950s; "it's just like living in a small town."[4] And in the small town that was the Senate of the 1950s, the unwritten but well-understood rules of conduct virtually guaranteed that such potentially polarizing issues as the appointment of judges would not be permitted to disrupt the orderly flow of Senate business.

In his pioneering study of the Senate of the 1950s, Donald Matthews stressed the significance of what he termed the "folkways of the Senate" in structuring behavior within an institution whose organization and formal rules exalted the unfettered

4. Quoted in Matthews, *U.S. Senators and Their World* (Chapel Hill: Univ. of North Carolina Press, 1960), 92.

autonomy of each of its members.[5] Matthews reported, for example, that every new senator was expected to serve a period of apprenticeship. The apprenticeship norm required younger members to remain subservient to their more experienced colleagues, postponing for a substantial period full participation in the legislative process while learning the ways of the Senate. Admonished not to appear too aggressive, newcomers thus often avoided engaging in floor debates during their initial years in the Senate. Slots on important committees went to senior members; newcomers had little control over their own fate, invariably serving the bulk of their apprenticeship on the least-desirable committees. The new arrival was expected to seek the advice of older senators and, with some luck, might become the protégé of a powerful colleague, hastening the end of the apprenticeship period and the junior member's ascent of the rigid hierarchy of the Senate. "Like children, we should be seen and not heard," observed one senator about the norm of apprenticeship.[6]

One consequence of the apprenticeship system was to diminish significantly the number of senators likely to play important roles in controversial matters. This effect was enhanced by the general expectation that the primary concern of a senator was to be the work of the Senate. Although the need for favorable publicity was acknowledged to be part of public life and thus unavoidable, the folkways of the Senate dictated that the quest for public acclaim always be kept secondary to the work of the institution. To showboat and to court unduly the attention and accolades of the press was to risk the disdain of one's peers. In stark contrast to the ethos of today's Senate, the norms of this era gave rise to an institution where the respect and influence accorded a senator by colleagues tended to vary inversely with the degree of media attention and publicity attracted by him or her.

5. Ibid., chap. 5. Much of the material that follows regarding the folkways of the Senate of the 1950s is drawn from this work.
    6. Ibid., 93.

Thus the most influential and important senators, in the view of their fellows, were those who developed areas of expertise and dedicated substantial time and effort to specializing in one sphere of legislative activity. By midcentury, the quantity of complex legislation confronting the Senate demanded a division of labor, and the committee system, buoyed by the norm of specialization, assured senators that, before reaching the Senate floor, proposed legislation had undergone the scrutiny of peers who had spent years becoming expert in the relevant policy areas. In this highly structured world a few senators might manage to acquire influence beyond their area of expertise (Richard Russell being the perfect example), but this unusual power invariably restored on a generally acknowledged base of specialization.[7] Although "playing to the galleries" by speaking out on a broad range of issues might gain a senator public attention, such behavior ran counter to well-established norms and was almost certain to earn the gadfly the contempt of his or her colleagues.

Professor Matthews described an institution in which reciprocity was a way of life. Senators were expected to aid their colleagues whenever possible, and a bargain struck was a bargain kept. By demanding deference to the decisions of the relevant committees, reciprocity reinforced the norm of specialization and made unruly floor fights rare events. Furthermore, reciprocity became the lubricant that prevented the antiquated gears of the Senate from sticking. The rules and traditions of the Senate entrusted to the individual member enormous power to bring the work of the chamber to a complete halt.[8] The spirit of reciprocity proscribed the exercise of that power in all but the most extraordinary cases. Any senator who pursued personal goals

7. Barbara Sinclair, *The Transformation of the U.S. Senate* (Baltimore: Johns Hopkins Univ. Press, 1989), 18.
8. Matthews suggested several examples of this power. The filibuster remains, of course, an obvious one. Much of the Senate work on the floor is done under unanimous-consent agreements, which supplement or substitute for the standing rules

through the use of these draconian powers would be breaking a widely accepted norm of behavior and inviting retaliation from other senators. When coupled with the convention of courtesy (for example, refraining from personal attacks, always complimenting colleagues, avoiding outward manifestations of partisanship) and institutional patriotism (always being protective of the Senate as an institution), these folkways formed a powerful check on the behavior of most of the members of the institution and provided the Senate with the coherence and structure necessary for the efficient operation of any lawmaking body.

The self-regulating effect of these norms was reinforced by the political makeup of the post–New Deal Senate. During the 1940s and 1950s membership in the Senate was divided almost equally between Democrats and Republicans; not until 1958 did the Democrats establish a lopsided majority. The equality of the parties produced a decidedly conservative Senate. Southern Democrats often teamed with Republicans to form a conservative majority that effectively controlled the operation of the institution. Southern states, with all-white Democratic electorates, repeatedly reelected Democratic senators, and Senate norms and the rules of seniority guaranteed these men positions of influence. Republicans of the era were always conservatives. Thus, no matter which party formed a narrow majority, the conservative coalition dominated the Senate, and a disproportionate share of power rested in the hands of conservative Senate elders. These men— Richard Russell and Everett Dirksen among them—profited the most by the general acceptance of the Senate norms and, not surprisingly, manipulated the resources of the institution to ensure their vitality. In the Senate at midcentury, a set of rules of behav-

---

and often are designed to limit debate and floor amendments. Unanimous-consent agreements can be adopted only if no senator objects; a single senator, simply by objecting to all unanimous-consent agreements, can bring proceedings in the Senate to a virtual halt. Furthermore, a single senator can sneak measures through by acting when few others are in attendance on the floor of the Senate. See Matthews, *U.S. Senators*, 100.

ior and control of the institution by a conservative oligarchy went hand in hand.

The norms of the Senate were also in basic harmony with the political world in which the typical senator lived and worked. Despite the general trend of the twentieth century toward the centralization of power in Washington, D.C., this process was (and continues to be) a gradual one, and for a good part of the century the jurisdiction of the national government was, by today's standards, limited. The narrow range of federal activity curbed the number and variety of private interests seeking to influence national lawmaking. Moreover, not long ago most states had a relatively homogeneous population, and the typical senator served a constituency with only a handful of major policy concerns. The broadcast media were in their infancy, and a senator had few opportunities to seize a highly visible issue and ride it to national prominence. Of necessity, and with few exceptions, senators responded to stimuli within the institution; the Senate of this era was, in the words of one prominent scholar, a "self-contained, self-regulating inward-looking institution."[9]

In such a political setting the cost to the individual member of following Senate norms was not great.[10] Committee assignments, for example, could be more easily tailored to constituency needs, and therefore specialization often aided and rarely hampered reelection. The narrow scope of federal legislation and the limited activity of organized interests provided little impetus for the typical senator to defy the unwritten rules of the Senate and seek fame and glory outside its confines. On the other side of the ledger, abiding by the norms promised a senator a satisfying career in a predictable and stable setting. Even the most junior of senators might be beguiled by the prospect of rising through the

9. Richard F. Fenno, "The Senate through the Looking Glass: The Debate over Television," in John Hibbing and John Peters, eds., *The Changing World of the U.S. Senate* (Berkeley, CA: IGS Press, 1990), 184–85.
10. See Sinclair, *Transformation of the U.S. Senate*, chap. 2, for an interesting discussion balancing the costs and advantages of adherence to the Senate norms.

hierarchy and someday assuming a leadership position, and this could be accomplished only by playing strictly according to the rules. Although the net effect of the Senate norms was virtually to guarantee that most senators toiled in relative obscurity, the benefits of maintaining the norms for most members far outweighed the cost of being a maverick.

The Cost of Being a Maverick: The Case of Hubert Humphrey

Nevertheless, the rules of conduct were not universally accepted; the Senate has always had its share of nonconformists. Professor Matthews identified several factors that limited the universality of the norms.[11] People who achieved political prominence in another setting before coming to the Senate, for example, inevitably had difficulty working within the constraints of the Senate folkways. Political ambition also weakened the force of the norms on some senators; those with dreams of the presidency typically sought greater national visibility than Senate norms allowed. Nonconformity was also more prevalent among senators who represented states with diverse, heterogeneous populations where fierce two-party competition made reelection a constant concern. Constituency pressure was particularly a problem for "liberal" or "progressive" senators. Elected to office by voters expecting dramatic legislative action, liberal senators confronted a conservative institution that demanded the postponement, if not the total surrender, of a personal legislative agenda. For obvious reasons, conservatives found the Senate a more hospitable environment.

The experience of Senator Hubert Humphrey during this period illustrates the difficulty of challenging the clubby atmosphere of the old Senate. A well-known progressive, Humphrey became a player in midwestern politics when he successfully negotiated the alliance between the militant Farmer-Labor party

11. Matthews, *U.S. Senators*, 102–17.

of Minnesota and the Democratic party. A lifelong advocate of activist government, Humphrey was one of labor's most forceful champions and a passionate supporter of civil rights policy. Elected mayor of Minneapolis in 1945, the dynamic Humphrey virtually dominated post–World War II politics in Minnesota. In 1948, while a candidate for a U.S. Senate seat, Humphrey addressed the Democratic National Convention in support of a minority resolution seeking to add a civil rights plank to the party platform. His speech—only eight minutes long—electrified the crowd, and, in a stunning upset, the resolution passed despite the opposition of southern delegates.[12] The convention speech catapulted Humphrey into the national limelight, with Democrats in the South castigating him as a dangerous demagogue and progressives welcoming the voice of a resurgent liberalism.

Humphrey's pre-Senate political experience was that of a dynamic, hands-on executive of a large city, and on the eve of his arrival in Washington he had already experienced the flush of national prominence. As the spokesman for the Democratic Left, he naturally expected to pursue his progressive agenda and his own political career in a national forum. Following his election to the Senate, for example, Humphrey accepted the chairmanship of Americans for Democratic Action. The ADA had been founded a few years earlier by liberal New Dealers who believed that the Democratic party was drifting to the right and becoming a party of reaction. The organization sought to influence national Democratic party politics, and Humphrey's willingness to head

12. Indeed, Humphrey's address to the Democratic convention, in hindsight, might be considered one of the more important moments of America's twentieth-century political history. It decisively placed the national Democratic party in support of civil rights. Following the speech, delegates from four southern states bolted the convention and later nominated Senator Strom Thurmond as the Dixiecrat candidate for president. From the moment of Humphrey's speech through the 1960s, the links between the Democratic party and the white supremacist South became increasingly tenuous, because, in the words of his biographer, "Humphrey's speech and the vote that followed nailed civil rights to the masthead of the Democratic party and set the nation, as well as his party, on a new course." Carl Solberg, *Hubert Humphrey: A Biography* (New York: Norton, 1984), 19.

the organization on the eve of his arrival in the Senate made him the spokesman for an organization with a broad national agenda. Today a similar position gains the neophyte senator prestige and national visibility; in 1948 it guaranteed the wrath of Senate elders.

With an abundant faith in the virtues of activist government and a burgeoning national reputation, Humphrey felt little inclination to adapt to the ways of the Senate. He considered himself competent to speak on a range of problems and did not hesitate to express his views on the floor of the Senate. When Senate leaders treated him like a newcomer, Humphrey responded by charging that too many Senate elders were too beholden to powerful interests. He directly challenged the Senate seniority system and scorned the norm of apprenticeship; during his first year in the Senate, he offered fifty-seven bills, spoke out on some 450 different topics, and filled the *Congressional Record* with insertions.[13] The Senate hierarchy did not take kindly to such assertiveness by a newcomer. Not one measure he introduced was enacted, and despite his national reputation, his dynamic style, and his boundless energy, Humphrey soon became an isolated figure in the Senate.

By 1950 he was so frustrated that he attacked Harry Byrd of Virginia, one of the Senate whales. Byrd, a conservative Democrat, headed the Joint Committee on Non-Essential Expenditures, a committee created primarily to permit Byrd to voice his contempt for government spending through a steady stream of press releases. A local Minnesota group, working with the Byrd committee, had gathered statistics vastly inflating the potential cost of measures proposed by Senator Humphrey and released the numbers to the Minnesota press. When Humphrey spoke out against Republican efforts to slash federal spending, Republicans sought to use the statistics to embarrass Humphrey and impeach his credibility on economic matters. Unwilling simply to refute the statistics, Humphrey counterattacked, describing the Byrd committee as a waste of taxpayers' money and a perfect exam-

13. Ibid., 143–45.

ple of the nonessential expenditure of federal funds. Although in private, few would have disagreed with this assessment, Humphrey's statement was taken as a personal attack on a powerful, senior member of the Senate. To make matters worse, not only had a freshman senator challenged a pet project of a Senate whale, but the attack had taken place while Byrd was out of town visiting a sick relative and unable to defend himself on the floor of the Senate.

A few days later Byrd responded to Humphrey. Following Byrd's remarks, the senior members of both parties each, in turn, castigated the upstart newcomer. The humiliation of Hubert Humphrey on the floor of the Senate lasted for over four hours. When Humphrey finally was recognized and rose to speak, the Senate whales marched out of the chamber. He had become, quite simply, a Senate untouchable. Bobby Baker, a longtime aide to Lyndon Johnson, described the event rather starkly: "Humphrey made a big mistake when he first got to the Senate. He got up and said that Senator Harry Byrd of Virginia was a no-good sonofabitch, and they almost kicked him out of the Senate for that."[14]

Later, one of Humphrey's aides reported that newly available information substantiated his charges against the Byrd committee, and he urged his boss to remain on the offensive. Humphrey declined; he had learned his lesson. "I found out where the power was in the Senate," Humphrey recounted in his autobiography," and I found out what you could expect when you challenge that power frontally."[15] The transformation of Hubert Humphrey into a highly effective member of the Senate was aided immeasurably by Lyndon Johnson. Although LBJ had arrived in the Senate the same year as Humphrey, he quickly developed an instinctive feel for the institution and its members.

---

14. Merle Miller, *Lyndon: An Oral Biography* (New York: Putnam, 1980), 154.

15. Hubert H. Humphrey, *The Education of a Public Man* (Garden City, NY: Doubleday, 1976), 130–31.

His basic message was simple; the path to power in the U.S. Senate was to do things "their" way. Influence and prestige coupled with the ability to move legislation could be attained only through an acceptance of the folkways of the Senate and not in defiance of them.[16] Johnson's willingness to help Humphrey was itself a lesson in the ways of the Senate; Johnson had designs on becoming the Senate Democratic leader, and by cultivating Humphrey he could establish a link to the small band of Democratic Senate liberals. As for Humphrey, with Johnson's tutelage, he became a more effective senator. "I've stopped kicking the wall," he said, with regard to his transition.[17]

The Old Senate and the Old Politics of Judicial Confirmations

The agonizing education of Hubert Humphrey as a U.S. senator not only sheds light on the Senate of the 1950s but also provides a powerful explanation for the high success rate enjoyed by presidents in obtaining Senate confirmation of Supreme Court nominees for two-thirds of the twentieth century.[18] During Humphrey's first years in the Senate, the surest path to influence

16. In the words of longtime political commentators Rowland Evans and Robert Novak, Johnson "gave Humphrey a short course on the Senate and how it really functioned. He explained the importance of knowing the strengths and weaknesses of every Senator, of concentrating on committee work and of mastering a specialty." Evans and Novak, "Lyndon B. Johnson: The Ascent to Leadership," in Norman Ornstein, ed., *Congress in Chicago: Evolution and Reform* (New York: Praeger, 1975), 128.

17. Quoted in Solberg, *Hubert Humphrey*, 164. Until his death in 1978, Humphrey pursued an extraordinary career in public service, with the Senate as a principal base of operations. In fact, Humphrey proved to be one of the first of a new breed of senator, combining a mastery of the inner workings of the Senate with a broad focus on national issues.

18. From 1900 to 1968, apart from the rejection of Judge Parker in 1930, the Senate confirmed every nominee. By way of contrast, during the nineteenth century the Senate rejected one out of three nominees to the Court. The Senate of that era was a more partisan institution. With senators appointed by state legislatures—the Seventeenth Amendment was ratified in 1913—powerful state party leaders often found their way to the Senate and used it to funnel patronage back to the state party organization. The typical senator of the nineteenth century had a secure local power base and little tolerance for institutional norms that constrained individual behavior.

and power in the institution was to gain the respect of colleagues. Much to Humphrey's discomfort, gaining it demanded submission to the folkways of the Senate; nonconformists might achieve a certain prominence (Humphrey's first, futile years in the Senate, for example, did not prevent him from continuing as a nationally recognized champion of liberal causes), but isolation in the institution and limited legislative effectiveness would inevitably be the costs. Political life always demands an appreciation of the costs and benefits of action; one of Humphrey's most important lessons was that influence in the Senate was a finite resource to be cultivated and conserved for the battles that might really matter.

In the Senate at midcentury, however, the confirmation of federal judges was often a battle that did not matter and thus presented senators with a relatively simple decision. With few exceptions, appointments to the Supreme Court were of little electoral import to senators. After the constitutional revolution of 1937, the attention of the New Deal coalition shifted from the judiciary to the administrative state, and, until the Warren Court revolution of the 1960s, the nature of judicial power did not make judicial appointments critical events for potent political forces. Rarely would an appointment even to the Supreme Court attract the attention of a senator's constituents; it is probably safe to say that from 1900 through 1967, not one senator's career was enhanced or cut short by constituent response to a confirmation vote.

In the self-contained world of the Senate, such freedom from electoral retribution yielded more rather than less conformity. For the typical senator of this era, pursuing an independent course on the consideration of a Supreme Court nominee presented few tangible benefits; conforming to the expectations of colleagues in the institution, however, would almost certainly further other personal and political goals. If the leaders of the Senate were satisfied with a judicial nominee, there was simply nothing for the average member to gain from challenging that conclusion.

Considered from this perspective, LBJ's strategy in the Fortas nomination made perfect sense.[19] He consulted with the appropriate Senate elders, and he used the extensive resources of the executive branch to cultivate these votes without public scrutiny or participation. The conduct of affairs within the Senate had always depended on informal, personal agreements made among the whales, and their ability to manipulate the resources of the Senate, coupled with the moderating effect of the Senate norms, always produced a stable and predictable pattern of behavior. It was unthinkable, for example, that a group of renegade young Republicans would defy Everett Dirksen, particularly on a matter of so little significance to constituents. In terms of the traditional Senate norms, such behavior made no sense. In the Senate of Lyndon Johnson, where formal norms protected the status quo and where members were continually encouraged to seek the approval of their peers and discouraged from pursuing undue national exposure, the odds overwhelmingly favored a president in the confirmation process.

THE MODERN SENATE

A New Political World

Commenting about life in the Senate during the 1980s, Arkansas Senator David Pryor quipped: "Being in the U.S. Senate is like getting stuck in an airport and having all your flights can-

---

19. One student of the confirmation process has concluded that Johnson mismanaged the Fortas nomination, stressing his decision to consult with only a few Senate elders and the resulting failure to accurately assess the mood of the Senate. See John Massaro, *Supremely Political: The Role of Ideology and Presidential Management in Unsuccessful Supreme Court Nominations* (Albany: SUNY Press, 1990), chap. 2. In retrospect, this conclusion appears unassailable. One might also conclude, however, that Johnson, lacking the wisdom provided by hindsight, conducted the Fortas nomination with an understanding of the well-established folkways of the Senate. The "mismanagement"— if that is the appropriate term—was the failure of Johnson in 1968 to grasp the extent to which new forces were undercutting the old norms and reshaping the Senate.

celed."[20] Pryor's reproach was echoed by many of his colleagues, although their criticisms often lacked his gentle, homespun touch. Whereas senators once spoke in reverential tones of "the world's greatest deliberative body," today's senator is more likely to describe chaos and anarchy and complain of the trivial nature of much of the work. The senator of an older generation often spoke warmly of his colleagues as "the best men in political life."[21] Nowadays, senators are more apt to agree with Warren Rudman's unsenatorial portrait of his colleagues: "One third of the members of the U.S. Senate know why they're here, know what they want to do, and how to do it. The second third know why they're here and what they want to do, but don't know how to do it. And that last third, I'm not sure why they're here."[22] The Senate norm of institutional patriotism, demanding that senators revere the institution and its personnel and champion both in the outside world, has obviously fallen upon hard times. In fact, few, if any, of the norms described by Professor Matthews in his study of the Senate of the 1950s compel the same allegiance today.[23] The erosion of these folksways has transformed the institution, producing a new Senate populated by a new type of senator. One consequence of this transformation has been to alter dramatically the politics of judicial confirmations.

20. Quoted in Hedrick Smith, *The Power Game* (New York: Ballantine, 1989), 26.

21. See Matthews, *U.S. Senators*, 102, for an example of how senators of the 1950s spoke of the institution and their colleagues.

22. Quoted in Smith, *Power Game*, 673. Rudman, expressing a frustration with the political process that carried well beyond the confines of the U.S. Senate, announced in 1992 that he would not seek reelection despite a highly favorable reputation among New Hampshire voters.

23. The best single discussion of the changes in the modern Senate appears in Sinclair, *Transformation of the U.S. Senate*. None of the discussion that follows is intended to suggest that senators never express allegiance to the old norms or that those norms are currently without effect. Rather, the norms today are simply more honored in the breach than in the observance. See Burdett A. Loomis, ed., *Esteemed Colleagues: Civility and Deliberations in the U.S. Senate* (Washington, DC: Brookings Institution Press, 2000) and Fred R. Harris, *Deadlock or Decision: The U.S. Senate and the Rise of National Politics* (New York: Oxford Univ. Press, 1993).

The first challenge to the inner-directed world of the Senate came from a profound change in membership. The late 1950s were difficult years for Republicans. In 1957, President Eisenhower suffered a stroke, and, despite his recovery, his health continued to haunt Republican politics. In 1958, scandal surfaced in the White House when Chief of Staff Sherman Adams accepted gifts from a businessman, Bernard Goldfine, and intervened with the Federal Trade Commission to discuss a case involving Goldfine. Marines were sent to Lebanon, and voters grew uneasy over the threat of another foreign war. A recession took a heavy toll on the prosperity of many Americans. The congressional elections of 1958 reflected the Republican decline. In the House, Democrats won a 283-to-153 majority; in the Senate, Democrats gained 13 seats, bringing their total to 64. Many of these new Democrats were liberal northerners; Edmund Muskie of Maine, Philip Hart of Michigan, Eugene McCarthy of Minnesota, and William Proxmire of Wisconsin were among the new Democrats in the Senate who would rise to prominence in the 1960s. Frustrated with the ways of the old Senate, the new liberal contingent set out to reform the institution. Although their initial efforts failed—in January of 1959, for example, southerners led by Richard Russell defeated attempts to liberalize cloture—the locus of power in the Senate began to shift.

The change in membership was symptomatic of other developments in the body politic that eventually converted the Senate from a tightly organized, self-regulating institution to a more fluid body, populated by members with an acute appreciation of the political world beyond the Senate chamber. The New Deal gave momentum to the centralizing forces in the American system, and by the 1960s, the expanded agenda of the national government produced a prodigious increase in the number of interests groups seeking access to national arenas of power. The growth was particularly evident in the number of citizen groups—those organizations open to all, regardless of occupation and status and concerned primarily with broad "quality of life" or public-interest issues.[24]

Although any interest group welcomes friendly voices in the Senate, the typical citizen group makes the Senate the focal point of its most intense lobbying efforts. "[I]ssues with national implications," writes Professor Ross Baker, "as opposed to more detailed and technical legislation [are] best pursued in the Senate. . . . If you can infuse one of the senators with passion for your cause and convince him or her that great policy consequences can be read in it, the senator can be an estimable catalyst and attract national attention."[25] The proliferation of citizen and public-interest groups undercut the inward-looking stability of the old Senate not merely by increasing the demands on senators but also by expanding greatly the opportunities for a senator to achieve national prominence outside the institutional confines of the Senate.

As Barbara Sinclair has noted, the Senate began its transformation in the 1960s, when the constellation of political forces rendered the old norms obsolete and provided senators with many new avenues to political success.[26] Chief among the new forces altering the world of the Senate was the rapid growth of the electronic media. It would be difficult to overstate the effect of the mass media on American politics; documenting this effect has become a veritable cottage industry for countless scholars and political commentators. Most of their efforts center on assessing the electoral repercussions of the media explosion. Whether the

---

24. Obvious examples of such groups include Common Cause, the Sierra Club, and the National Organization for Women. The links between many of these groups and the New Progressives are quite evident, and their prominence produced a reaction and countermobilization on the part of groups associated with the New Right. In addition, business interests responded to the success of citizen groups by increasing their presence in Washington, D.C. On the explosion of group interests, see, for example, Kay Lehman Schlozman and John T. Tierney, *Organized Interests and American Democracy* (New York: Harper & Row, 1986); Jeffrey Berry, *The Interest Group Society* (Boston: Little, Brown, 1984).

25. Ross Baker, *House and Senate* (New York: Norton, 1989), 166.

26. Sinclair, *Transformation of the U.S. Senate*, chaps. 4 and 5.

outcome of elections may be altered by media coverage or the manipulation of images by the candidates remains a subject of legitimate inquiry.[27] The conventional wisdom is that media coverage has a significant impact on who wins and who loses in American politics, and this perception creates its own reality.

As a consequence, the media do not merely report on modern politics but have become an integral part of the political process. Their impact is most easily observed in the modern presidency. A powerful explanation for the "imperial" presidency in the post-World War II era is that the presidency, centered on one individual, is far easier to package for the visual image than is an institution as large and diverse as the Congress. Television has also supplanted the political party as the primary link between the people and the politicians. Who needs a strong party organization to ring doorbells when an appearance on television will bypass the front door and put you in thousands of living rooms? The reality of the power of the media produced a new breed of legislator, skilled in the use of modern technology to enhance political power. A special telegenic charm and wit and the ability to speak in ten-, twenty-, or thirty-second sound bites are the qualities most cherished by a new generation of political leaders.

In the Senate increased media attention diluted the force of the traditional norms and encouraged a new style of behavior.[28]

27. See Doris Graber, *Mass Media and American Politics* (Washington, DC: CQ Press, 1989), for a review of the relationship between the media and politics. Thomas Patterson, *The Mass Media Election* (New York: Praeger, 1980), assesses the effect of the media on the 1976 presidential election.

28. See, for example, Gregg Easterbrook, "What's Wrong with Congress?" *Atlantic*, 1984, 26; Michael Robinson, "Three Faces of Congressional Media," in Thomas Mann and Norman Ornstein, eds., *The New Congress* (Washington, DC: American Enterprise Institute, 1981), 60–99. Stephen Hess, by contrast, concludes that the media focus on the small number of senators in leadership positions and therefore cannot be charged with producing the decentralization of power in the institution; Hess, *The Ultimate Insiders: U.S. Senators and the National Media* (Washington, DC: Brookings Institution, 1986). Even Hess's study confirms that senators (both junior and senior) with a flair for the media can become a presence on national television. A fascination with the *national* media, however, should not obscure the obvious growth of local news outlets and the obsession of officials in Washington with the need to have their words and faces beamed

At the core of the older Senate was the belief that prestige and power came to those who earned the respect of their colleagues in the institution. The established norms required senators who wished to achieve influence to conform to the expectations of other senators. The media explosion dramatically altered the Senate ideal, replacing the behind-the-scenes specialist with the highly visible, and quotable, generalist. The escalating costs of reelection campaigns reinforced this evolution, encouraging senators to attract out-of-state contributions by expanding, rather than narrowing, their scope of activities. Because national prominence is now an alternative path to power and influence in the Senate, enhancing the chances of reelection as well as a run for higher office, the modern, well-financed senator strives to achieve a public voice on a broad range of policy questions.

A classic example of such behavior took place in 1985 when the Senate Commerce Committee held hearings on the problem of "porn rock" and the advisability of compelling recording companies to provide warnings on the album covers of records containing violent or sexually explicit lyrics. Although the hearings featured appearances by Dee Snider (of the heavy metal band Twisted Sister) and rock icon Frank Zappa, the real star of the proceedings was Senator Paula Hawkins, first-term Republican of Florida. Neither a queen of rock nor a member of the Commerce Committee, Hawkins nevertheless requested the opportunity to testify, and she came equipped with her own television monitor to show rock videos (including Van Halen's "Hot for Teacher") as well as blowups of "explicit" album covers. Hawkins's multimedia performance caught the attention of the networks, and portions of her testimony appeared on two of the national nightly

---

back to the folks at home. Although not as dramatic as an appearance on *60 Minutes*, favorable local coverage is considered absolutely necessary for reelection. The technological advances that expand the breadth and sophistication of local media coverage intrude on the traditionally insular nature of the Senate and alter the behavior of its members.

news programs. Not so long ago, newcomers to the Senate would not even have dared to dream of such wide exposure.[29]

The Minnows Have Swallowed the Whales

Television has dramatically altered the folkways of the Senate. At midcentury, the limited concerns of constituency and the jurisdiction of committee defined a senator's policy agenda. Today pervasive electronic media coverage makes highly visible activities like contesting the nomination of a Supreme Court nominee a normal—and often necessary—event in a senator's life. One casualty of the seemingly endless effort by senators to be heard on a wide range of issues is the primacy of the committee system. Although committees remain a vital arena of legislative activity, committee assignments can no longer even pretend to exhaust the modern senator's policy interests. Because more senators wish to be heard on a substantial number of issues, debates on the floor of the Senate, rather than behind-the-scenes work in committee and subcommittee, increasingly dominate the lawmaking process. Amendments from the floor, for example, are now frequent and expected, and they often come from junior senators who are not even members of the committee that originally reported the legislation.[30]

The norms and Senate rules that relegated junior senators to a marginal Senate role have largely been abandoned. Today the Senate newcomer enters the chamber with a complete legislative agenda and fully expects to be involved directly in the legislative process. A minor skirmish during Pennsylvania Republican Arlen Specter's first term in office illustrates this development.[31] In his

29. Smith, *Power Game*, 119–21. In addition to her appearance on the national news, Hawkins, who was involved in a tough reelection campaign, made sure of local coverage by "feeding" the tapes of her performance to thirty local Florida stations through a satellite hookup provided by the Senate Republican Conference.

30. Sinclair, *Transformation of the U.S. Senate*, 80–84, quantifies this development.

31. Richard Fenno, *Learning to Legislate: The Senate Education of Arlen Specter* (Washington, DC: CQ Press, 1991).

second year in office Specter sponsored a nonbinding resolution requesting the president to convene a summit meeting with the Soviets in the hopes of limiting the arms buildup.[32] Senate elders on both the Foreign Relations Committee and the Armed Services Committee opposed the resolution. When Specter, despite his freshman status, refused to defer to the leadership, Republican John Tower, the powerful chair of the Armed Services Committee, enlisted senior members of the committee as well as the White House to pressure the upstart. Before the Senate vote, Tower announced to the members that both the Armed Services Committee and the Foreign Relations Committee were opposed to the resolution. Specter refused to back off, demanding that the secretary of the Senate check the precedents for similar informal statements of committee position and challenging Tower on the Senate floor about whether it was actually he or the committee that opposed the resolution (Tower admitted the former). Privately, Specter lobbied his younger colleagues for their votes, in effect championing the new individualistic ethic of the younger senators against the traditional powers of the Senate whales. The effort paid substantial dividends, though the resolution, which did pass, had no substantive effect on policy. In the eyes of his colleagues and the press, Specter had effectively "beaten" the powerful John Tower and, in so doing, enhanced his image both inside and outside the Senate.

In the old Senate, the brazen defiance of elders by a newcomer was not tolerated. Today, however, the norms that often stifled independence and cast senators like Hubert Humphrey in the role of mavericks have marginal influence. The qualities displayed by Senator Specter during the skirmish over the summit

32. "This kind of nonbinding resolution is a favorite of individual senators who want to convert a personal opinion of some sort into an opinion of a Senate majority, hoping to focus interest, attract publicity, and, if possible, influence behavior. The resolution is merely an expression of opinion; it requires no action by any committee; it cuts across the normal flow of legislative business; its passage forces no implementation and no official need act on it. Because it is an opinion, however, and because it often disrupts normal procedures, it may stir controversy." Ibid., 80.

resolution are hardly unique; independence, assertiveness, and a willingness to defy the Senate leadership are characteristics found today in many senators. In the contemporary Senate, leaders rarely express surprise when a junior member takes center stage or when colleagues are deeply involved in issues that fall outside the jurisdiction of their committees. The Senate's traditional, hierarchical structure at midcentury was no more.

Even the formal rules governing the structure of the Senate reflect these developments and now disperse power throughout the institution. Reforms instituted during the past forty years permit senators to serve on only one of the more prestigious committees (Appropriations, Armed Services, Finance, and Foreign Relations); as a result, 80 percent of the members now hold a seat on one of these committees. The limit on the number of committees a senator may chair and the increase in the number of subcommittees give more senators the opportunity for committee and subcommittee leadership. Both parties have modified the previously inflexible rule of seniority in the selection of committee chairmen, and within the committee the autocratic power of the chairmen has been tempered. That most meetings must now be open to the public, coupled with the ever-expanding television coverage of C-Span, makes it easier for even the most junior senator to become a public personality while pursuing policy goals.

In addition, the huge growth in personal and committee staff permits individual senators to spread themselves continually thinner, delegating responsibilities and relying on the expertise of staff members across a wide range of policy areas. Highly trained lawyers and policy analysts on Senate staffs render the specialization norm passé. There is little to be gained in spending years in Senate solitude on a quest for knowledge and experience when expertise is easily hired and senators are left free to pursue more visible, career-enhancing activities. The erosion of the specialization norm further weakens the committee system; the advent of the generalist not only challenges the primacy and exclusive authority of the appropriate standing committee but also directs attention away from the committee to the more egalitarian forum of the Senate floor. In sum, the ability to influence legislation is distributed evenly throughout the Senate, no longer correlated with longevity and formal position in the institution.

Other norms that were significant merely a generation or two ago also play a diminished role. Because the new generalist seeks to exert influence on a wide range of legislation, the Senate floor has become a critical playing field in the policy game. With activity on the floor thrust into the spotlight, the norm of courtesy and civility has suffered. Invective and thinly disguised personal insult often mark debate in the modern Senate.[33] Institutional patriotism has given way to a rash of critiques of both the institution and fellow senators; self-promotion and the quest for personal advancement are not easily compatible with strong institutional loyalty.

THE MODERN POLITICS OF JUDICIAL CONFIRMATION

A New Ball Game on a New Playing Field

The Senate of the 1950s was stable, predictable, and, for the most part, sheltered from the winds of change that might batter a more democratic institution. Not surprisingly, judicial confirmations of the same era were often uneventful and unaffected by partisan politics. The tradition of seniority, the explicit division of labor, and the disproportionate distribution of resources were combined with the folkways of the institution to guarantee the White House

---

33. Consider this exchange during the floor debate over the nomination of Clarence Thomas to the Supreme Court. Senator Edward Kennedy, responding to claims that Anita Hill perjured herself while testifying against Thomas, asserted, "There is no proof that she has perjured herself and shame on anyone who suggests she has." Senator Orrin Hatch responded, "Anybody who believes that, I know a bridge up in Massachusetts that I'll be happy to sell them." Hatch was obviously attempting to embarrass Kennedy by referring to the car accident at Chappaquiddick in 1969.

that any nomination would be contested on a playing field screened from public view, the number of important players would be small, the rules of the game rigid and strictly enforced, and the outcome reasonably predictable.

With members' attention directed inward to the institution, the Senate promoted efficiency by curtailing the number of influential actors on any policy matter and, not coincidentally, closing off the world's foremost deliberative body from many of the nation's most pressing concerns. (Witness, for example, Richard Russell's famed ability to keep civil rights legislation from coming to a floor vote.) The influential few were inevitably institutional conservatives, dedicated to maintaining the ways and norms of the Senate and ready to manipulate the allocation of resources to reward the conformist and punish the heretic. In such a setting, Senate elders were often able to deliver votes, and the cultivation of a few important senators, along with an abiding respect for the ways of the institution, formed the core of a successful strategy to manage any Senate vote.

The Senate of the 1970s presented a distinctly different picture.[34] The norms of an earlier era no longer reined in the behavior of individual senators; the result was a far less stable, more outward-looking institution and a more complicated process of securing the Senate's consent to a judicial nomination. Increased media coverage and the constant search for campaign funds invited independent action and encouraged senators to become visible players in matters of national interest. Televised committee hearings lessened the ability of the leadership control the proceedings, making the outcome far less predictable to friend and foe alike.

---

34. Norms in an institution such as the Senate always develop and influence behavior, and the modern senator thus is not totally free from their constraints, a point emphasized by Fred Harris in *Deadlock or Decision*, especially chap 4. Although the scholarly and journalistic inclination to underscore the conformity of the Senate of the 1950s and the individualism of the Senate of the 1980s might result in some exaggeration, the fact remains that change is a repeated theme in the literature discussing the modern Senate.

Beginning in the late 1960s, the dynamics of party politics and the changing nature of judicial power combined to make appointments to the Supreme Court very significant to powerful political forces. At the same time, the Senate became a more open and visible forum for the expression of diverse interests than it was even a generation ago. Activists in both political parties found important and vocal allies in the Senate; the New Progressives and the New Right have proved equally adept at cultivating senators to champion their respective causes. For the typical senator, identification with national issues that transcend state or regional boundaries became the cornerstone around which a triumphant senatorial career could be built, assuring the senator prestige in the institution, visibility among the folks back home, and, perhaps, a national following. For example, Senator Robert Griffin of Michigan was a little-known first-term Republican senator when he defied Everett Dirksen and led the insurgent Republicans against the Fortas nomination. Following his successful challenge to Fortas, Griffin was elected to a Senate leadership position and quickly emerged as a national spokesperson for an independent federal judiciary. During the Haynsworth nomination fight, Griffin was a key player, assiduously courted by both sides. After deciding to cast his vote against Haynsworth, he was characterized by several prominent observers, including the *New York Times*, as among the most influential opponents of the nominee.[35]

It made equally good sense for groups engaged in the policy process to court influence with senators. Interests broadly identified with the New Progressives or the New Right, for instance, favored a senator over a member of the House of Representatives as the "symbol" or "spokesperson" of the group not simply because of the Senate's constitutional role in the confirmation process but because senators tend to attract greater media

---

35. John Frank, *Clement Haynsworth, the Senate, and the Supreme Court* (Charlottesville: Univ. of Virginia Press, 1991), 89.

attention. In the 1970s, the Senate became the most accessible institution for those seeking to influence the national political agenda, with a membership acutely sensitive to the concerns of outside groups that champion causes with a national appeal. In terms of the confirmation of a Supreme Court justice, the changes in the nature of the Senate practically guaranteed that the proponents and opponents of any nominee were certain to find willing advocates in the Senate.

A New Political Calculus

The fact that politically powerful groups were willing to invest substantial time and resources in the battle to control the judiciary, coupled with the erosion of the old Senate norms and the appearance of a new Senate style, altered the political calculus for every senator confronting a vote on a nominee to the federal bench. Throughout much of the twentieth century, a senator could simply conform to the expectations of peers and accept the president's choice. The nomination of even a Supreme Court justice was of no electoral consequence, and thus the safest vote, in terms of the expectations of Senate leadership and presidential patronage, was usually a yes vote. In the Senate of the 1980s, however, to be counted for or against a particular nominee was often a decision of immense electoral significance, and each senator was keenly conscious of the potential consequences of such highly visible activities.

In 1969, when Abe Fortas resigned from the Court following the *Life* magazine article detailing his connection with the financier Louis Wolfson, Richard Nixon delivered on his "southern strategy" by nominating Clement Haynsworth, a native of South Carolina and a judge on the Court of Appeals for the Fourth Circuit.[36] Opposed from the outset by labor and civil rights groups, Haynsworth nevertheless presented solid legal credentials and

36. See chapter 1, n. 22.

appeared a safe bet for confirmation until the Judiciary Committee hearings revealed the conflict-of-interest improprieties that doomed the nominee. The opposition seized on the alleged improprieties to capture media coverage and focus public attention on the proceedings. Significantly, the opposition was led by Birch Bayh, Democrat of Indiana, a little-known second-term senator who, as a direct result of his efforts to defeat Haynsworth, established a national reputation as a leader in the civil rights and labor movements. Once the public interest was engaged, senators on both sides of the aisle were forced to reassess their original reflexive support for the nominee and measure their position against the expectations of constituents and important interest groups.

The White House responded with heavy-handed attempts to mobilize public support for Haynsworth and to increase pressure on recalcitrant senators. Southern state Republican leaders were asked to generate letter-writing campaigns stressing that Haynsworth was being attacked because of his ties to the South, and the White House lobbied large campaign contributors of key senators.[37] When the administration's letter-writing campaign appeared to be faltering, Nixon directed his staff to get in touch with Gerald Ford (then the House minority leader) to try to begin impeachment proceedings against William Douglas, the most liberal member of the Court. The obvious message to liberals was that Justice Douglas would be the price to be paid if Haynsworth were defeated.[38] The Nixon White House in this way raised the perceived stakes for each senator by injecting a still larger dose of politics into the process while publicly castigating opponents

37. John Anthony Maltese, "The Selling of Clement Haynsworth: Politics and the Confirmation of Supreme Court Justices," *Judicature* 72 (1989): 338.

38. Stephen E. Ambrose, *Nixon: The Triumph of a Politician, 1962–1972* (New York: Simon & Schuster, 1989), 315. The investigation of Douglas evolved around his connections with a foundation from which he received $12,000 a year as well as around his "radical" writings. The House Judiciary Committee actually investigated the matter, and it came to nothing. See William O. Douglas, *The Court Years: The Autobiography of William O. Douglas* (New York: Random House, 1980), chap. 15.

of the nomination for employing similar tactics. In the end, the efforts of groups opposed to Haynsworth to shape public opinion were successful, and Richard Nixon, still fresh from his presidential victory a year earlier, was unable to control the vote of seventeen Republicans. The nomination was defeated by a vote of 55 to 45.

In the years since the Fortas and Haynsworth confirmation fights, the politics of judicial confirmations have grown ever more complex. Consider, for example, the political calculations of southern Democrats in the Senate during the Bork proceedings. At the outset, many of these conservative Democrats appeared to welcome the nomination of Bork to the Court. At a minimum, Bork was an unrelenting critic of the judicial activism that had been anathema to the white South since the days of the *Brown* decision. Furthermore, the religious Right overwhelmingly supported Bork, and evangelicals constitute a powerful electoral force in southern elections. Few observers of the political scene, therefore, were exactly thunderstruck when Richard Shelby, a newly elected Democratic senator from Alabama, enthusiastically supported Richard Bork, commenting that if Ted Kennedy was against the nomination "a lot of us southern Democrats will have to be in bed with Bork."[39]

Shelby's ardor for Judge Bork, however, quickly cooled. As a member of the House of Representatives, Shelby had developed a reputation as a conservative on racial issues, voting, for example, against an extension of the Voting Rights Act and against the proposed Martin Luther King holiday. Stepping up to run for the Senate in 1986, he needed substantial black support to defeat the reactionary Republican incumbent, Jeremiah Denton, in a closely contested election. The approximately 90 percent of the black vote that Shelby received was, no doubt, attributable only to the notoriety of his opponent; the newly elected Senator Shelby could not expect similar black majorities in future campaigns against more

39. Ethan Bronner, *Battle for Justice* (New York: Norton, 1989), 285–88.

moderate opposition unless he tempered his own voting record. Three months of intense lobbying and polling data indicating a good deal of black opposition to Bork apparently convinced Shelby that a vote for the conservative Bork might considerably shorten his own Senate career.

Other southern Democratic senators experienced a similar conversion. The resurgence of the Republican party in the South makes Democratic electoral success often dependent on the black vote. In the battle over Bork, southern Democrats in the Senate were sensitive to the lobbying efforts of black organizations and aware that polls showed substantial African American hostility to the nomination. The result was that southern Senate Democrats formed a solid bloc (save for Ernest Hollings of South Carolina) voting against confirmation. Republicans, on the other hand, saw the Bork vote as an opportunity to solidify support among southern whites. In the days preceding the Senate confirmation vote, the question arose whether Bork should withdraw his name and avoid a crushing defeat on the Senate floor. Several key Senate Republicans (including Republican leader Robert Dole) urged him to stand firm, forcing Democrats like Shelby to cast a vote against Bork. The Republican leadership thought that the cost of such a vote to southern Democrats among white voters would more than offset the possible gain among black constituents.[40] The lesson of the Bork battle was not lost on the strategists of the Bush presidency. Intent on placing a New Right conservative on the Court, the White House settled on Clarence Thomas as part of a strategy to gain the votes of southern Democratic senators by marshaling the support of black voters.[41]

---

40. See Mark Gitenstein, *Matters of Principle* (New York: Simon & Schuster, 1992), 301.

41. The strategy worked. As was noted, only one southern Democrat, Ernest Hollings, voted for Bork. In the case of Thomas, Hollings was joined by John Breaux and John Johnston of Louisiana, Sam Nunn of Georgia, Charles Robb of Virginia, and Shelby of Alabama. Given the 52-to-48 margin of victory, the votes of these senators were of obvious significance. Prior to Anita Hill's allegations of sexual harassment,

By 1991, estimating the potential electoral consequences of the Clarence Thomas confirmation vote demanded a calculation of political variables so complex that even the most experienced and electorally secure senators were often unable to chart the politically wise (as well as safe) course. This was not always true. In 1916, following the confirmation of Justice Brandeis, the incumbent Woodrow Wilson faced Charles Evan Hughes (who had resigned from the Court to accept the Republican nomination) in a hard-fought presidential election battle. The confirmation battle played no visible role in the presidential campaign, and there is no evidence that senators on either side of the nomination battle faced significant voter recrimination. Seventy-five years later, however, the Clarence Thomas proceedings seriously damaged George Bush's reelection bid. More significant, perhaps, in terms of the Senate's understanding of the electoral impact of Supreme Court confirmations, was the primary defeat of a Democratic incumbent senator, Alan Dixon of Illinois, by a virtual political unknown, Carol Moseley Braun. Braun, the Cook County recorder of deeds, decided to enter the Democratic primary after Dixon voted to confirm Thomas, and voter discontent with the Dixon vote powered her campaign. In Pennsylvania, Arlen Specter, the leader of the Republican counterattack against Anita Hill, faced a potent reelection challenge by Lynn Yeakel, another political unknown inspired to run against a powerful incumbent by the Thomas hearings. Although Specter survived the challenge, the experiences of Specter and Dixon remain stark reminders to every senator of the potential electoral consequences of modern confirmation battles.

Thomas's key backer in the Senate, John Danforth of Missouri, predicted that sixty or so senators would vote to confirm (which, of course, would still have been a narrow margin of victory). Without the complications of the Hill testimony, more southern Democrats would have supported Thomas. For example, Senator Robert Byrd of West Virginia, who gave an impassioned speech on the Senate floor opposing Thomas, inserted into the record the speech supporting Thomas he would have given had he not believed Hill's allegations.

Individualism and Partisanship

In 1985, Democratic Senator Thomas Eagleton of Missouri declared the Senate to be "in a state of incipient anarchy."[42] By the mid-1990s, however, Senate "anarchy" had taken a new turn as the out-of-control individualism that prompted the Eagleton comment merged with a new stage in the evolution of the modern Senate—a rising tide of partisanship—to alter the politics of the confirmation process yet again. For decades, party loyalty was at best a sporadic concern for the typical senator; individual prerogative inevitably trumped any sense of obligation to party and party discipline. In the early 1960s and 1970s, for example, roll call votes in the Senate were only occasionally defined by party; during that period only one of three votes on average had a majority of Republicans opposing a majority of Democrats. The coming of the new millennium, however, has brought an increased ideological conflict to the U.S. Senate that triggers constant partisan divisions within the institution and a substantial increase in party voting among the senators. Party has become a defining feature of the legislative process, and senators today identify their career and legislative aspirations with those of relatively partisan, homogeneous parties.[43] Consequently, the policy areas where Republicans and Democrats might find common ground has diminished dramatically; during the Reagan years, Democratic Congressman Leon Panetta lamented the fact that the political center in Congress had shrunk to perhaps 100 Republicans and Democrats; today that estimate could easily be halved.[44] Ide-

42. Eagleton's remark was challenged by his Republican colleague from Missouri, John Danforth. Danforth apparently would have preferred "fully developed" in place of "incipient." See Ross Baker, *House and Senate*, 2d ed. (New York: Norton, 1995), 188.

43. See for example, Barbara Sinclair, "Individualism, Partisanship, and Cooperation in the Senate," in Burdett A. Loomis, ed., *Esteemed Colleagues: Civility and Deliberation in the U.S. Senate* (Washington, DC: Brookings Institution, 2000); and Conference Report, "The Polarization of American Politics: Myth or Reality," Center for the Study of Democratic Politics, Princeton University, December 3–4, 2004, www.princeton.edu/~cdsp/events/pdfs/Polarizationfinal.pdf.

44. Carl Cannon, "State of Our Disunion," *National Journal*, January 20, 2006.

ological polarization, moreover, presents particular problems for an institution such as the U.S. Senate, where individual senators and the minority party enjoy extraordinary opportunities to disrupt the orderly business of the institution.[45]

Several explanations may help to account for the rise of partisanship in the Senate. Students of politics generally agree that the appearance of the primary election as the principal method for choosing candidates for office produces more partisan officeholders. Because the most motivated (i.e., ideological) voters dominate in the traditionally low-turnout primary, the candidate must pay substantial heed to this active (and inevitably extreme) part of the electorate to win the nomination and, as senator, to forestall potential primary challenges in subsequent elections. Put simply, it now makes excellent electoral sense for the typical senator to cater to the activist core of his or her party. The Republican resurgence in the South has also worked to alter substantially the ideological balance within the Senate. By the 1990s, conservative southern Democrats, who had previous served as a bridge between liberal Democrats and Republicans, had virtually disappeared from the Senate, replaced by conservative Republicans.

Although gerrymandering to create safe districts for both parties can explain partisanship only in the House, the Senate may be in the process of being altered by a redistricting of a different nature; a more mobile society may well be segregating itself into red and blue states as people seek out areas of the nation where they feel politically and ideologically comfortable. (The so-called red and blue states got their names from the colored maps used by NBC and CNN during election-night coverage in 2000:

45. Partisanship is not necessarily a bad thing; cohesive, ideologically charged, responsible parties present distinct choices to the electorate and the organization and discipline to carry out the party's agenda following electoral success. Considered from this perspective, polarization could provide the means for making the Madisonian construct a far more efficient governing system, similar to a parliamentary form of governing. On the other hand, the Senate is not structurally designed to accommodate party government.

red states were in the Republican camp and blue states in the Democratic.) One indication of this demographic trend, suggested by Mark Tushnet, is the marked decrease in the number of states sending a "mixed" delegation to the Senate.[46] Thus the senator of the early twenty-first century typically represents a state in which political activists provide the core support necessary to win primaries as well as low-turnout general elections and polarize into ideologically distinct parties. This in turn produces a Senate in which Republicans are inevitably more conservative than the most moderate of Democrats and where the ideological gulf between the two parties is deep and wide. The modern senator occupies a more extreme ideological position than his or her predecessors, and as a result, the political center has less leverage than ever before.

Partisanship plays a unique role in the Senate, where individual members retain extraordinary prerogatives and hence the minority party has a substantial array of potential weapons in its arsenal to hinder the smooth operation of the legislative process. Consider the filibuster. The filibuster was once used almost exclusively for the rare high-voltage issue that often cut across party lines; at midcentury, for example, the filibuster was used most frequently by southern conservative Democrats (joined by an occasional Republican) to battle proposed civil rights measures. The filibuster is now employed (or its use threatened) most often by the minority party as a potent weapon to frustrate majority policy initiatives. Hence, during the 1980s, senators were frequently heard complaining that the filibuster was being invoked "promiscuously" in response to "piddly little issues."[47] During the first two years of the Clinton presidency, Republicans effectively employed the filibuster to kill several major administration-

46. Mark Tushnet, *The New Constitutional Order* (Princeton: Princeton University Press, 2003), 15. In 1976, twenty-seven states had senators with different party affiliations; in 2006 the number dropped to fourteen, including Vermont, with Senator Leahy, a Democrat, and Senator Jeffords, an independent.

47. The words are those of senators Robert Byrd and Charles Grassley, respectively. See Robert W. Merry, "Essay: Senate and Sensibility," *CQ Weekly*, May 9, 2005, 1092.

sponsored measures, since the Democratic majority lacked the votes to invoke cloture and end debate. Significantly, the Republican minority in the Senate encountered few normative restraints in this calculated and organized effort to obstruct the majority's legislative program, and with Democrats unable to secure the bipartisan support needed to invoke cloture, the mere threat of a potential filibuster soon was sufficient to doom legislation.[48]

Writing of the legislative process, Barbara Sinclair has noted that sustaining the conditions necessary for the Senate to function "is a delicate enterprise."[49] The Senate of the last fifty years has proved to be neither a particularly influential arena for deliberation and debate nor an efficient legislative body, and a Senate now sharply divided along partisan lines devoid of a moderate center presents particular difficulties. From within and without the institution comes the constant complaint that rampant partisanship and individualism have now undone the very intricate balance of cooperation and comity necessary for the Senate to continue its unique position in the American political process. During the Clinton years, a Republican Senate minority and then a majority overtly sought to delay and deny Democratic judicial selections. While contentious, the partisan use of Senate rules and procedures on judicial nominations remained at best a secondary political issue, due in no small measure to Clinton's basic indifference to judicial nominations and his unwillingness to risk any political capital in battles over the staffing of the federal courts. The election of 2000, however, brought a new administration to power and the potential for far more visible and contentious Senate battles over judicial confirmations.

48. In Clinton's first two years in office, nearly half of the major measures introduced in Congress were eventually subject to either a filibuster or a significant threat of extended debate. See Barbara Sinclair, *Unorthodox Lawmaking* (Washington, DC: CQ Press, 1997). So frequent was the use of the filibuster that the Senate developed procedures through unanimous consent agreements to continue Senate business. "Double-tracking" allows Senate leadership temporarily to shelve a bill that is under a filibuster while other business is conducted.

49. Sinclair, "Individualism, Partisanship and Cooperation," 75–76.

Chapter 6

THE SECOND BUSH PRESIDENCY: IDEOLOGY AND CONFRONTATION

Throughout his 2000 presidential election campaign, George W. Bush characterized himself as a "compassionate conservative" and a "uniter, not a divider." Nevertheless, after securing his disputed victory, President Bush steered clear of any suggestion that he govern from the middle and followed an agenda that was designed to please the religious and social conservatives who made up a substantial core of his support. This was particularly the case with his judicial appointments. Unlike President Clinton, who sought unsuccessfully to defuse the confrontational politics of confirmation through the nomination of judicial moderates, the new president did not hesitate to push ideologically charged nominees to the federal courts. Evoking yet again the image of the evils of the Warren Court and the vice of activist judges, the president energized the activist core of his support while Democrats in the Senate employed every tactic available to the minority party to preserve the judiciary from Republican control.

Against the backdrop of September 11 and the war on terror, it was the confirmation of federal judges that provoked the partisan warfare that threatened the very institutional integrity of the Senate. That the Senate appeared about to implode over the confirmation of any one of several appointments, not to the Supreme Court but to the lower courts, would have dumbfounded the senators of the 1950s and 1960s. The same forces, however, that had set in motion the confrontational politics of Supreme Court confirmations for an earlier generation of sen-

*ators now also shaped the appointment of judges to the intermediate
appellate courts of the United States.*

*By the spring of 2006, President Bush had successfully named two
new Supreme Court justices. His eventual victory in that endeavor,
however, cannot conceal the daunting challenges that a vacancy on the
high court currently presents to a modern president. The appointments
of Chief Justice Roberts and Justice Alito could well be the crowning
achievements in the long Republican campaign to transform the
Supreme Court. The president's failed nomination of Harriet Miers to
succeed the retiring Justice O'Connor, however, may prove of even
greater significance. For the first time in modern history, a nomination
to the high court was crushed by the sustained and organized opposition of core elements within the president's own party. In the evolution
of the politics of Supreme Court confirmations, the Harriet Miers nomination may prove to be a seminal moment.*

THE WAR ON TERROR

Annus Horribilis

It had to rank as one of the worst weeks in presidential history.
To be sure, 2005 had not been a particularly good year for President George W. Bush. His legislative agenda was in disarray. A
much-ballyhooed plan for revamping Social Security was destined
for oblivion despite a month-long presidential barnstorming
effort, and the long-standing promise to permanently end the
estate tax appeared to share a similar fate. Ethics investigations of
important Republican legislators on Capitol Hill were gaining
momentum, and throughout the year, central members of the president's team, including his key adviser, Karl Rove, had been the
subject of a special prosecutor's investigation regarding the leak
of an undercover CIA agent's identity to the syndicated colum-
nist Robert Novak. Vice President Cheney and President Bush had
been formally interviewed as part of the inquiry. Hastily arranged

presidential trips to the Gulf Coast did little to erase from the nation's collective memory the horror of bodies floating down the flooded streets of New Orleans and thousands of impoverished black Americans stranded in the wake of the destruction caused by Hurricane Katrina, crying out for food and water as the president joshed with Michael Brown, the head of the Federal Emergency Management Administration, about a job well done. And, despite continual assurances by high-ranking administration officials that the end was in sight, the ill-fated war in Iraq continued.

But the last week in October of 2005 had to rank as the nadir of George W. Bush's "annus horribilis." At the outset, the military grimly noted the two thousandth American combat death in Iraq, as a war that had been set in motion on the basis of flawed (or worse, manufactured) intelligence was now approaching its third year. Promised a quick and decisive—indeed practically bloodless—engagement to excise "weapons of mass destruction" from Iraq, the American people now faced a body count of two thousand Americans and countless deaths among those we had come to liberate. That same week, the special prosecutor in the CIA leak investigation announced the indictment of Vice President Dick Cheney's chief of staff, Lewis "Scooter" Libby on charges that included perjury and obstruction of justice. Although Karl Rove escaped formal charges, the indictment of Libby left President Bush facing the prospect of prolonged legal proceedings destined to keep the administration's blemished use of intelligence data in the public spotlight. And then, on the morning of October 27, Harriet Miers, White House counsel and the president's nominee to succeed the retiring Justice O'Connor, formally withdrew her nomination. Just weeks earlier, Republicans had eagerly anticipated a new nominee to the Court in the expectation of not only solidifying the conservative transformation of the judiciary, but rallying the party as well. The Miers nomination, however, failed on both counts. Battered for weeks regarding her questionable qualifications for the job (qualifications, it must be said, not considerably weaker than those presented by Justice

O'Connor at the time of her nomination in 1980), Miers was ultimately done in by the hard-line conservatives of the Republican party, who challenged her ideological commitment to their social and political agenda. Justice O'Connor's position as the swing vote on many important issues made this a most significant appointment to social and religious conservatives in their continuing effort to reshape the Supreme Court, and they were wary of any nominee who was not cut in the mold of Scalia or Thomas. "They had been burnt on so many ones before," commented Senator Sam Brownback of Kansas. "They wanted to really know."[1] It was perhaps the unkindest cut of all—a president who had so enthusiastically hitched his presidency to the wars on both terrorism and relativism, undone by those whose agenda he had so faithfully promoted. As the week drew to a close, the President faced the selection of a new nominee for the O'Connor seat with the core of his party determined to accept only a "true" conservative, and Democrats, vitalized by the president's political woes, vowing to wage the mother of all confirmation battles.

The Commander in Chief

George W. Bush lost the popular vote in the 2000 election by over half a million votes, but won the presidency by one vote in the United States Supreme Court and thus became the first president since 1888 to assume the presidency without even a plausible claim to a popular mandate.[2] The 2000 presidential election engaged Americans in a riveting case study of the constitutional provisions governing presidential selection as well as the most arcane details of Florida election law; it most certainly failed to provide the ulti-

1. Robin Toner et al., "Weeks of Erosion in Support for the Nomination," *New York Times*, October 28, 2005, A16.

2. In the 1888 election, the Democratic incumbent, Grover Cleveland, won the popular vote but was defeated by Republican Benjamin Harrison in the Electoral College. Twelve years earlier, Rutherford Hayes defeated Samuel Tilden in the Electoral College after having lost the popular vote.

mate winner the momentum to govern confidently in the afterglow of a successful national popular victory. The advice to the president-elect from the political pundits was just about unanimous; the proper move for the newly elected, albeit faintly illegitimate, president was to the middle, honoring his campaign pledge to govern as a "compassionate conservative," appointing Democrats to his cabinet, and making moderation and bipartisanship the watchwords of his new presidency.[3] In short, the conventional wisdom was that Bush must follow his father's model of a predictable, moderate, mainline Republican presidency.

That Bush chose not to govern from the middle but instead assumed a far more partisan, radical posture remains one of the most distinctive features of his presidency and a decision that would have a profound impact on the politics of judicial nomination and confirmation. In the aftermath of the disputed 2000 election, the President employed a confrontational style of governing that endeared him to the right wing of his party, produced some surprising victories (e.g., a $1.35 trillion tax cut), and alienated Democrats. The decision to play to his conservative base was particularly unexpected given the thin majorities enjoyed by Republicans in both houses of Congress. When, however, Republican Senator James Jeffords of Vermont announced that because an increasingly conservative Republican Party had abandoned the moderation that had been its core for over one hundred years he was leaving Republican ranks to become the Senate's only independent, the Bush style of governing suddenly seemed distinctly inapt.[4] In a partisan age, divided government tends to humble the most audacious of presidents, and the Senate in the

3. No less a pundit than Vice President–elect Cheney was quoted as reminding observers that Bush's decisions in the early days of his administration would be "influenced by the fact that it was a very close election." Quoted in Joel D. Aberbach, "The State of the Contemporary American Presidency," in Colin Campbell and Bert A. Rockman, *The George W. Bush Presidency: Appraisals and Prospects* (Washington DC: CQ Press, 2004), 51.

4. Following the 2000 election, Republicans controlled both houses of Congress. The Senate was divided 50–50, but with Vice President Cheney empowered to cast the deciding vote, Republicans controlled the Senate. With Senator Jeffords's announcement in May of 2001, the Democrats regained the Senate.

hands of the opposition effectively neutralized Bush's ambitious conservative agenda. Moreover the president's ability to sell the electorate on his brand of conservative activism was questionable under the best of circumstances. Gallup polls placed the president's approval ratings at a lackluster 50 percent, but the percentage of those surveyed expressing disapproval of his job performance was on the rise, and this trend would continue throughout the summer of 2001. By September 2001, the prospects for a dynamic Bush presidency leading a conservative revival seemed dim indeed.

The events of September 11, 2001, transformed a nation, but also revitalized the presidency of George W. Bush. In the days following the terrorist attacks, the President's overall approval ratings approached 90 percent. He was always a favorite among the Republican faithful, but after September 11, his standing among Democrats rose dramatically. A PEW Research survey conducted in mid-September showed 8 of 10 Democrats expressing approval of the president's handling of his job.[5] Anger, fear and a profound national grief merged with surging patriotism to hand President Bush record levels of popular support. His stature at least temporarily enhanced, George W. Bush—who, together with many of his closest advisers, had managed to avoid service during the Vietnam War—assumed the mantle of commander in chief in the war against terrorism. Ultimately, al-Qaeda soon provided Bush what the national election of 2000 had not—the groundswell of popular support that cut across party lines and operated, at least temporarily, to unify a divided system.

In the days and months following the attacks on the Pentagon and the World Trade Center, the war on terror and the Bush presidency merged. He was never particularly articulate or adept at public discourse; the president's greatest personal asset in the months before 9/11 appeared to be a genial "just one of the plain

---

5. For a quick review of the impact of September 11, 2001, on Bush's approval ratings, see Michael A. Dimock, "Bush and Public Opinion," in Gary L. Gregg and Mark J. Rozell, eds., *Considering the Bush Presidency* (New York: Oxford Univ. Press, 2004).

folks" persona that held a certain appeal for many Americans.[6] After the September attacks, the president was recast as the cold steel warrior in the crusade against America's enemies. The invasion of Afghanistan to destroy al-Qaeda and Osama bin Laden was followed by the Iraq war to rid the world of Saddam Hussein and weapons of mass destruction. With the president unequivocally portraying the war on terrorism as the moral equivalent of World War II, the administration offered no apologies for measures that violated the most fundamental tenets of American law. To question the incarceration of so-called "enemy combatants" without formal charges or judicial proceedings was to question America's campaign against terrorism. Unprecedented domestic surveillance of citizens was defended as a "vital tool in our war against terrorists."[7] No rhetoric was too bellicose and no claim to executive power and prerogative too extreme. The war on terror garnered President Bush extraordinary approval ratings; during the six months following 9/11, the president's ratings were at a record 80 percent, and in the 2002 congressional elections, Republicans regained the Senate and increased their control of the House.

THE SENATE ON THE BRINK

The Federalist Society

In 1987, following his failed nomination to the Supreme Court, Robert Bork predicted that a new generation of conservative

---

6. The fact that George W. Bush was born to privilege and wealth and had employed family money and contacts to further his business and political careers never intruded on this "down home" image. Of course, the fact that it did not may be the ultimate testimony to Bush's skill as a politician.

7. In December 2005, the *New York Times* revealed that the Bush administration had ordered the National Security Agency to begin spying on U.S. citizen. See James Risen and Eric Lichtblau, "Bush Lets U.S. Spy on Callers without Courts," *New York Times,* December 16, 2005, A1. Within days, President Bush admitted that he had secretly signed the order years earlier for this domestic surveillance, contended that it was a vital tool in the battle against terrorism, and asserted that those who challenged his

lawyers "often associated with the Federalist Society" will "sweep the elegant, erudite, pretentious and toxic detritus" of liberal jurisprudence out to sea.[8] Putting aside Judge Bork's typical verbal excess, this prediction may prove to be one of his most accurate; the development of the Federalist Society would prove to have profound implications for the modern politics of judicial confirmations.

Founded in 1982, the Federalist Society has grown into an organization of over 35,000 with chapters in almost every law school and major American city. Dedicated to basic conservative legal and social principles, it counts among its members Supreme Court justices, United States senators, and respected professors at many of America's most prestigious law schools. Generously funded by conservative organizations such as the John M. Olin and Scaife foundations, the society's real influence can be found in the well-established and powerful network it provides to link conservative lawyers in the political, judicial, and academic worlds. For the young lawyer seeking employment in a Republican administration, for example, the ideal career pattern would be membership in the Federalist Society at a prominent law school such as the University of Chicago followed by a clerkship with an appellate judge with connections to the Federalist Society (Judge Michael Luttig of the Fourth Circuit or Laurence Silberman of the D.C. Circuit would be the ideal). A short stint at a private law firm such as Kirkland & Ellis (where Kenneth Starr, Federalist Society luminary and Whitewater Independent Counsel investigating President Clinton, ran the appellate department) would be quite advantageous. In the Bush administration, getting a plum job in the Justice Department without a similar pedigree would be next to impossible.[9] Inside the Department of

---

efforts were "endangering" the lives of Americans. See David E. Sanger, "In Address Bush Says He Ordered Domestic Spying," *New York Times*, December 18, 2005, 1.

8. Quoted in Gail Russell Chaddock, "A Judicial Think Tank—or a Plot?" *Christian Science Monitor*, August 4, 2005, 1.

9. See Vanessa Blum, "How to Get a Job at Justice," *Legal Times*, April 25, 2005, 1.

Justice, high-level appointments inevitably had a link to the Federalist Society.[10] And perhaps most significant, the Federalist Society cultivated the nomination of several of its most prominent young members to the federal appellate bench and, in so doing, established a supply of young, conservative, vetted jurists whenever coveted openings would arise at the level of the United States Supreme Court.

Since the twilight of the Warren Court era, Republican presidents have made judicial appointments a gift to the most conservative components of the Republican coalition. In the Reagan years, appointments to the federal courts glued the religious right to the Republican Party. During the reign of George W. Bush, this strategy, with the active assistance of the Federalist Society, outstripped the efforts of even the Reagan administration. Within the Department of Justice, the Office of Legal Policy was reinstituted, whose chief responsibility was selecting potential nominees to the federal bench. Assistant Attorney General for Legal Policy Viet Dingh, a Federalist Society member, was placed in charge of the OLP, and most of the lawyers working under his direction were affiliated with the Society. The impact was immediate. At least six of Bush's first eleven nominees to the court of appeals had ties to the Federalist Society, and by 2005, approximately fifteen of the forty-one Bush court of appeals judges confirmed by the Senate had identified themselves as members of the Society.[11] President Clinton had expended little if any political capital on his appointments to the federal judiciary. President Bush, on the other hand, remained committed to the idea that focusing time and effort on the ideological makeup of the federal judiciary, even

10. Among the society's members in the Bush Department of Justice were Attorney General John Ashcroft, Deputy Attorney General Larry Thompson, Solicitor General Ted Olsen, Deputy Solicitor General Paul Clement, and Associate Deputy Attorney General R. Ted Cruz. Similar staffing decisions were made in the White House Office of Legal Counsel.

11. Jason DeParle, "Nomination for Supreme Court Stirs Debate on Influence of Federalist Society," *New York Times*, August 1, 2005, 12. Needless to say, a rather high percentage of those nominees who had not been confirmed were also members.

at the district and appellate court levels, would continue to pay political dividends. With the active and effective assistance of the Federalist Society, the Bush administration proved willing to do what the Clinton White House had not: expend time, effort, and political resources in the effort to transform the federal bench.[12]

The president's readiness to push the ideological envelope on judicial appointments, coupled with Democratic control of an increasingly partisan Senate and a lingering suspicion on the part of many Democrats that the conservatives on the Supreme Court had stolen the 2000 election, proved to be a combustible combination. The Democrats on the Judiciary Committee blocked several of Bush's most conservative nominees for the federal appellate courts, and rhetoric on both sides of the aisle quickly escalated. Senator Rick Santorum, Republican from Pennsylvania, charged the Democrats on the committee with engaging in "McCarthyism" by denying confirmation to anyone who had "ever been a conservative or a member of a conservative organization."[13] For their part, the Democrats vowed to continue their efforts to protect the federal courts from a "radical" conservative takeover. The conflict over the staffing of the federal courts intensified, and during extensive campaigning prior to the 2002 midterm elections, President Bush and social conservatives labored mightily to return the Senate to Republican control in part to break the Democrats' domination of the confirmation process.[14]

12. And at least from an ideological perspective, it did pay dividends. See Kenneth L. Manning and Robert A. Carp, "The Decision-Making Ideology of George W. Bush's Judicial Appointees: An Update," paper presented at the 2004 Annual Meeting of the American Political Science Association, Chicago, September 2–5, which concludes that Bush's judicial appointments evidence the most conservative voting patterns in generations.

13. Quoted in David M. O'Brien, "Ironies and Disappointments: Bush and Federal Judgeships," in Colin Campbell and Bert Rockman, eds., *The George W. Bush Presidency* (Washington DC: CQ Press, 2004), 144.

14. For example, Phyllis Schlafly exhorted social conservatives to recognize that "the most important issue of the election of November 5th is whether or not to elect enough U.S. Senators to confirm constitutionalist judges." *The Phyllis Schlafly Report*, 30 (October 2002).

The 2002 election produced a Republican gain of six seats in the House and, more important, two in the Senate. If the president had been unwilling to compromise on judgeships during the period of divided government, he certainly was in no mood to do so after his unprecedented midterm victory and the return to unified Republican control. Several of the delayed Bush nominations were cleared and confirmed by the Senate almost instantly following the election results.[15] The president, however, enraged Democrats by resubmitting a number of controversial nominees previously rejected by the Judiciary Committee. No longer able to control proceedings at the committee stage, the Democratic leadership immediately threatened a filibuster on the floor of the Senate, while the president charged Democrats with playing politics and urged the American people to demand an up-or-down vote (to bring a bill or candidate directly out of committee to a floor vote) for his judicial nominees. In the spring of 2003, when the nomination of Miguel Estrada to the D.C. Circuit Court of Appeals reached the Senate floor, the Democrats made good on their filibuster threat.[16] Estrada's confirmation ordeal continued

15. Michael McConnell, for example, was nominated to the Tenth Circuit Court of Appeals on September 9, 2001. McConnell had been a professor at the University of Chicago Law School from 1985 to 1996 before joining the faculty at the University of Utah Law School. A former clerk to Justice William Brennan, McConnell was an acknowledged expert on the religion clauses of the First Amendment, had argued several cases before the United States Supreme Court, and was a prominent member of the Federalist Society. The Judiciary Committee kept back the McConnell nomination for over a year before holding hearings. Following the 2002 election, his nomination was sent to the full Senate and he was confirmed on November 15, 2002.

16. Miguel Estrada grew up in Honduras and came to the United States at seventeen to live with his mother and study at Columbia University. Graduating with honors, he attended Harvard Law School, clerked for Justice Kennedy, and worked in prestigious private law firms, the attorney general's office, and with the solicitor general. A member of the Federalist Society, he was among President Bush's first nominees to the federal bench in 2001 and appeared before the Judiciary Committee in September 2002. Democrats on the Committee complained that Estrada was unresponsive to their questions, and the administration refused to turn over documents from Estrada's days in the solicitor general's office. The committee did not act on his nomination, and the President renominated him in January 2003; his nomination was sent to the full Senate following a 10-to-9 party line vote. Considered a potential nom-

for another six months and included six failed cloture votes before he finally withdrew his name from consideration in September 2003.

Perhaps because Estrada was often mentioned as a potential nominee to the Supreme Court and because a seat on the D.C. Circuit Court had in the past been the first judicial appointment for several Supreme Court justices, the Estrada nomination became the most visible flashpoint in the battle over the staffing of the lower courts that raged throughout 2003–2004. For the remainder of Bush's first term in office and continuing after victory in the 2004 election, however, Bush and his fellow Republicans continued to push high-visibility, ideologically charged nominees for court of appeals vacancies, while Democrats held fast to their announced intention to resist the most conservative of President Bush's judicial picks. The Democratic caucus position was that if the Democrats on the Judiciary Committee unanimously opposed a nominee, then a filibuster would be threatened when the nomination reached the floor of the Senate. By early 2005, an organized Democratic minority had successfully denied confirmation to at least ten of the president's nominees to the federal bench. Because each had sufficient Republican votes to win an up-or-down vote, Democratic obstruction produced, in the words of Republican Senator Orrin Hatch, "a tremendous amount of angst."[17] Republican angst, inflamed rhetoric, and intransigence on the part of both Democrats and Republicans made the appointment of lower court judges the stuff of high political drama. Stated most simply, the new politics of judicial confirmations had migrated down to the level of lower court judges.

---

inee for any Supreme Court vacancy, Estrada was opposed by several Latino organizations who feared his conservative views on civil rights, while Republicans were enthralled with his conservative positions, his Horatio Alger history, and, most significant, the fact that Republicans would be appointing the first Hispanic to the important D.C. Circuit Court of Appeals.

17. Quoted in Jeffrey Toobin, "Blowing Up the Senate," *New Yorker*, March 7, 2005.

The Nuclear Option

The filibuster may be the single procedure that defines the unique quality of the United States Senate as an institution where cooperation and compromise have shaped, by and large, the lawmaking process. In an era when governing is often akin to trench warfare, the filibuster guards what remains of a tradition of courtesy and respect for the views and integrity of fellow senators. With sixty votes necessary for cloture (and a two-thirds vote necessary to alter the rules governing the filibuster), the majority party can ill afford the arrogance of power, and legislative success often depends on a frank appreciation of the importance of collegiality, civility, and cooperation. The distinctiveness of the Senate, for better or worse, lies in the fact that historically it has been the legislative institution that has stood most often as a bulwark against the political passions of the time. And at the center of that hedge against majority rule has been the filibuster.[18]

Whatever its value to the legislative process, in the days following the November 2004 election (an election in which not only was the president reelected but Republicans increased the size of their majorities in both houses of Congress), one would have been hard pressed to find any Republicans singing the praises of the filibuster. Although rejuvenated by a victory that reaffirmed their majority status, Senate Republicans were acutely aware that they lacked the sixty votes necessary to control debate and end the filibuster of judicial appointments. Early in 2005, President Bush placed two of his more controversial nominees on the appellate courts via the recess appointment route, but other high-visibility nominees remained stalled by Democrats' delaying tactics.[19] Frustration inevitably led to Republican ruminations

18. For a wonderful essay on the history and importance of the filibuster, see Robert W. Merry, "Essay: Senate and Sensibility," *CQ Weekly*, May 9, 2005, 1188.

19. Article 11, Section 2 of the Constitution permits the President to make appointments for a vacant position when Congress is in recess without first obtaining the advice and consent of the Senate. The appointment expires at the conclusion of the current session of the Senate, when the nominee must obtain Senate approval before

about end runs around the filibuster dilemma. A direct attempt to change Senate rules requires a two-thirds vote, but Republicans began to consider the possibilities of a motion to declare extended debate to be out of order. Such a motion would, in turn, trigger a ruling by the presiding officer (the vice president) to sustain the point of order. Any challenge by Democrats to a ruling by the presiding officer could be defeated by a simple majority vote, and, as long as a sufficient number of Republicans held firm, the Senate would proceed to a vote on the contested confirmation. In the view of those who found Democratic obstruction intolerable, the virtue of this parliamentary maneuver would be to establish a new precedent governing majority control of filibusters of judicial nominees.[20] The downside, however, was that even its most passionate advocates understood that undercutting the way the Senate traditionally conducted business would be contentious in the extreme; Republican Senator Trent Lott of Mississippi aptly named it "the nuclear option."

---

continuing in the position. President Bush's two recess appointments to the federal bench following the 2004 election were Charles Pickering to the Fifth Circuit Court of Appeals and William Pryor to the Eleventh Circuit. Pickering, a federal district court judge in Mississippi, had been appointed by George H. W. Bush in 1990 and was nominated to be elevated to the Court of Appeals by George W. Bush in 2002. Opposed by numerous civil rights groups, his nomination was defeated by a Democratic majority in the Judiciary Committee. Following the 2002 election, Bush renominated Pickering, and Democrats filibustered the nomination on the floor of the Senate. A cloture vote fell six votes short and Pickering's nomination languished until the recess appointment. At the conclusion of the congressional term, Pickering tendered his resignation rather than face the confirmation process once again. William Pryor, the former Attorney General of Alabama, was opposed by numerous civil rights organizations, women's groups, labor unions, and gay and lesbian activists. Pryor was first nominated in April of 2003, and his confirmation was filibustered by Senate Democrats until the recess appointment in 2004. Pryor was eventually confirmed in June 2005, following a Senate compromise described below.

20. See Martin B. Gold and Dimple Gupta, "The Constitutional Option to Change Senate Rules and Procedures: A Majoritarian Means to Overcome the Filibuster," *Harvard Journal of Law and Public Policy* 28 (Fall, 2004). Throughout the spring of 2005, various scenarios were proposed that were keyed to a ruling by the vice president—as the president of the Senate—that permitted either changing the rules or cutting off debate by majority vote.

By May of 2005, the lines appeared clearly drawn. The White House showed no indication of backing down on any of the stalled nominees. Senate Democrats, seething over various slights, including the memory of many Clinton judicial nominees held hostage, remained resolute. The politics of appointment and confirmation of judges had evolved into a high-stakes game of political chicken. The issue was no longer whether there would be a "nuclear" explosion but over which appointment this legislative form of Armageddon would come to pass. Attention soon focused on the nomination of Priscilla Owen to the Fifth Circuit Court of Appeals. A commercial lawyer in Houston, Texas, for most of her career and a member of the Federalist Society, Owen was elected to the Texas Supreme Court (Karl Rove had served as her campaign consultant) in 1994 and quickly gained the reputation of being one of the most conservative justices on a very conservative court.[21] Owen had been one of the original Bush nominees to the federal bench in 2001 and was rejected by the Senate Judiciary Committee in 2002. Nominated again in 2003, she had been subject to a continuing filibuster—four cloture votes had failed—and Democratic opposition as an "ideologue on the bench." With the Owen nomination percolating in the background, the Senate leadership continued to escalate the rhetoric. Senate Minority Leader Harry Reid asserted that the threatened

21. She served on the Texas Supreme Court with current Attorney General, Alberto Gonzales. In an abortion case involving the question of whether a college-bound high school senior could obtain an abortion without notifying her parents under the Texas abortion statute, Owen was among the dissenters asserting that exceptions to the notification requirement should be very rare and subject to the highest measure of proof. Writing for the majority, Gonzales was moved to charge the dissenters with an "unconscionable act of judicial activism" in construing the Texas statute in a manner that negated the legislature's procedures for bypassing parental notification. *In re Jane Doe*, 19 SW3d 346 (Texas, 2000). Gonzales was often at odds with Owens while both served on the Texas court. The fact that the Bush favorite Gonzales had criticized Owen was not lost on liberal groups opposing her nomination to the federal bench. On the other hand, Gonzales was often mentioned as a possible Bush pick for the U.S. Supreme Court, and his seemingly moderate rulings while on the Texas Supreme Court triggered suspicion on the part of social conservatives that he might not be tough enough on abortion.

move by Republicans to halt the filibuster was a "power grab" by an overbearing majority, while Majority Leader Bill Frist contended that he and fellow Republicans were simply carrying out a "constitutional obligation" to advise and consent by holding an up-or-down vote.[22] Frist vowed to call for a vote to cut off debate on the Owen nomination and, should cloture fail, to invoke the nuclear option.

Thus, during the spring of 2005, a Senate dominated by intense partisan disagreement appeared on the verge of implosion over the confirmation of lower court judges. Democrats made clear their intention—should the Republicans invoke the nuclear option—to retaliate with every means available to the minority party to delay and obstruct.[23] In early May, Arlen Specter, the chair of the Senate Judiciary Committee, came to the floor of the Senate to warn of the dire consequences if calm could not be restored. "It's up to us to save the Senate" was his final message, and no one accused him of hyperbole.[24] For a time, Majority Leader Frist and Minority Leader Reid sought a way out, but by mid-May they were no longer negotiating, and returned to their respective corners to prepare for the upcoming combat as interests on both sides urged their champions to accept no compromise.

At this point, an extraordinary event took place in the modern Senate. What remained of the moderates and institutionalists on both sides of the aisle came together and brokered a deal. Seven Republicans and seven Democrats—quickly named "the Gang of 14"—eventually reached an agreement for the seven Republicans to vote against any proposed change in the filibuster rules as long as the seven Democrats agreed not to prevent votes

22. See John Cochran and Keith Perine, "The Senate's Point of No Return," *CQ Weekly*, May 20, 2005, 01372.

23. For example, the Senate runs on unanimous consent (see chapter 5, n. 8) but any individual senator can refuse "consent" and thus force each bill to be read, every procedural vote to be taken, etc., etc. Objecting to unanimous consent agreements would, in effect, bring the Senate to a halt.

24. Quoted in Cochran and Perine, "The Senate's Point of No Return," 01372.

on judicial nominees save for "extraordinary circumstances." As part of the deal, Democrats agreed to clear Owen, Pryor, and Janice Rogers Brown for a vote, and all were confirmed within a month.[25] Conventional wisdom had once again been turned upside down in the often bizarre world of the politics of modern judicial confirmations; the "nonexistent" center in the Senate had, for a moment, been reborn and asserted itself by denying the leadership the opportunity to lead their respective parties in all-out partisan warfare. Group interests on both sides that considered the appointment of judges a "no-compromise" issue castigated the maverick senators. Social conservatives were particularly incensed that years of active campaigning for Republican candidates had produced a solid majority in the Senate but frustrating delays in the transformation of the judiciary. James Dotson of Focus on the Family characterized the seven Republicans as a "cabal" that had sold out conservative interests, and Kay Day of the Coalition for a Fair Judiciary vowed that the seven Republicans would "rue the day" they signed on to the compromise.[26]

Precisely what role the Gang of 14 would play in subsequent nominations remained undecided, and the crucial words "extraordinary circumstances" were conveniently undefined. Moderates and institutionalists in the Senate had emerged from the darkness simply because the implications of altering the age-old filibuster by means of a majority vote were beyond anyone's capacity to forecast. The consensus among the fourteen, however, would soon be sorely tested. On July 1, 2006, Justice Sandra Day O'Connor announced her retirement from the Court. The O'Connor announcement, coupled with the fact that Chief Justice

25. Janice Rogers Brown was a associate justice on the California Supreme Court. She was nominated by President Bush for a spot on the D.C. Circuit in 2003 and was subjected to continual filibuster based on her libertarian views and opposition to civil rights, particularly affirmative action. She was confirmed in June 2005 by a 56-to-43 vote. The two nominees specifically exempted from the deal were William G. Meyers (Ninth Circuit) and Henry W. Saad (Sixth Circuit).

26. Quoted in David Nather, "Centrists Strike Back in Senate," *CQ Weekly*, May 30, 2005, 1420.

Rehnquist was gravely ill with cancer and expected to retire soon, placed the unity of the Gang of 14 squarely on a collision course with the forces gearing up for what promised to be a divisive battle over the future of the Supreme Court.

A NEW SUPREME COURT

The New Chief

George W. Bush's announcement that John G. Roberts would be his nominee to replace the retiring Justice O'Connor was met with enthusiastic approval by Republicans, while Democrats reserved judgment for an individual they conceded had impeccable legal credentials. A graduate of Harvard University Law School, where he served as editor of the law review, Roberts after graduation had worked as a law clerk for Judge Henry Friendly on the Court of Appeals for the Second Circuit and then moved to the Supreme Court to clerk for Justice Rehnquist. He had then joined the Reagan administration in the White House counsel's office. After a stint with a prestigious Washington, D.C., law firm, Roberts returned to government service as the principal deputy solicitor general under Kenneth Starr and was nominated to the D.C. Circuit by George H. W. Bush. When his nomination died in a Democratic-controlled Senate, Roberts returned to private practice. In 2001, President George W. Bush again nominated him for the D.C. Circuit, and the nomination was once again blocked by Democrats in the Judiciary Committee. Roberts was renominated in 2003 and was eventually approved by the Senate without a roll call vote. During his two years on the D.C. Circuit, he was considered a personable, easygoing, but certainly conservative jurist, and, while Democrats remained cautious in their initial assessment, the conventional wisdom on the Hill was that it would be an extraordinarily difficult task to demonize Judge Roberts.

Although the Roberts nomination never produced the expected firestorm, it did highlight an interesting split between Democratic senators and New Progressive activists. The latter found much to challenge in Judge Robert's service in the Reagan and Bush administrations. Senate Democrats, however, stung by defeat in the 2004 election and determined to avoid charges of excessive partisanship, praised the credentials of the nominee and appeared to accept, albeit somewhat grudgingly, the inevitability of confirmation. "Why do we have to fight?" asked a Democratic staff person. "Just to fight?"[27] Many New Progressives, of course, would consider the answer all too obvious.[28] The Roberts nomination thus exacerbated the classic tension between party regulars, whose instinct after the party's failure in the 2004 election was to move to the center and to appear reasonable and conciliatory when faced with a nominee as personable and qualified as Roberts, and party activists, who had come to understand nominations to the Supreme Court as a call to battle and a means for firing up grassroots support. For Democrats, consideration of the Roberts nomination thus quietly morphed into a touchy family dispute over the appropriate role for the opposition party. The much-anticipated battle supreme between the parties over the first appointment to the Court in over a decade, however, was quickly evolving into little more than a minor skirmish.

On September 3, 2005, while the Senate was considering the Roberts nomination, the nation learned of the death of Chief Justice Rehnquist. After fourteen years as an associate justice and nineteen as chief justice, Rehnquist would be remembered as the architect of the modern Supreme Court's move to the right and probably as one of the great chief justices in American history. His death, however, took the Roberts confirmation in an unan-

---

27. Quoted in T. R. Goldman, "Liberal Lobbyists on Sideline of Roberts Nomination," *Legal Times*, July 29, 2005.

28. Or, as Ben Brandzel, advocacy director for MoveOn.org, put it: "Our credibility is not about getting the Senate to do our bidding. Our credibility comes from fighting for things our people believe in." Ibid.

ticipated direction. Seemingly within hours of the chief justice's demise, President Bush announced that he was withdrawing the nomination of Roberts to succeed the retiring Justice O'Connor and was now nominating Roberts for chief justice. In shifting the conservative Roberts to assume the seat of the conservative Rehnquist (as opposed to that of the more moderate O'Connor), the president removed whatever partisan heat remained in the Roberts confirmation hearings and redirected it to the future proceedings over the as yet undisclosed choice to replace O'Connor. The real discord that emerged from the Roberts hearings and vote (he was confirmed by a vote of 78-to-22) actually came from social conservatives and the religious right. During his hearings before the Judiciary Committee, Roberts acknowledged a right to privacy in the due process clause of the Fourteenth Amendment and characterized the Constitution as a living document that must adapt to a changing America. That testimony set off alarms among social conservatives who feared another moderate when they had been promised a real conservative.[29] But the rumblings remained muted, and the new chief justice easily assumed his seat in time for the beginning of the Court's term.

Harriet Who?

President Bush's announcement on October 3 that his White House counsel, Harriet M. Miers, would be his nominee to succeed Justice O'Connor was met with what initially can only be described as stunned silence. Miers, a graduate of S.M.U. Law School, had been a commercial lawyer in Dallas before serving as counsel to George Bush's 1994 Texas gubernatorial campaign. She followed Bush to the White House, first serving as staff secretary and then White House counsel. Active in both the Dallas and Texas bar associations (she had served as the first woman

---

29. See Charlie Savage, "Roberts's Testimony Alarms Conservatives," *Boston Globe*, September 15, 2005, A1.

president of both), she spent her private legal career with Dallas law firms representing corporate interests. Her public career was defined by service to her patron, George W. Bush. Miers's positions on the hot-button sociolegal and moral issues of the day were completely unknown. She had no background or practical experience in constitutional and civil rights law. There was nothing in her professional life that appeared to place her ahead of more prominent conservative jurists waiting in the wings for a vacancy on the Court. Stated bluntly, Harriet Miers was no John Roberts.

The most plausible explanation for the Miers nomination was that the Bush White House was governing with a diminishing supply of political capital. In choosing a nominee with absolutely no paper trail and no record on the socially divisive issues of the day, the Bush plan was to avoid a disruptive and costly confirmation battle. To add fuel to the fire, the administration, on the grounds of separation of powers, resisted making public any of Miers's memos written while she was White House counsel. As for the nominee's conservative credentials, the president was simply asking committed conservatives to trust his judgment. From the outset, however, those conservatives expressed a good deal of skepticism regarding the nominee's ideological purity and professional stature. Recalling the last time the right had trusted a Bush on an unknown nominee to the Court, Republican Senator George Allen spoke for many fellow conservatives when he announced that he "want[ed] to be assured that she is not going to be another Souter."[30] It quickly became apparent that the most potent and dedicated opposition to the Miers nomination would be found within the president's own party.

By mid-October, it was evident to all that the Miers nomination was a disaster. Leaders in both parties on the Judiciary

---

30. Quoted in David D. Kirkpatrick, "New Questions from the Right on Court Pick," *New York Times*, October 6, 2005, A1.

Committee united in asking Miers to resubmit her responses to the questionnaire provided by the Committee because members had found the answers "inadequate," "insulting," and "insufficient."[31] Arlen Specter, the Republican chairman of the Judiciary Committee, warned that Miers would need "a crash course in constitutional law" to navigate successfully the hearings before the Senate Judiciary Committee.[32] The White House devoted substantial time and effort to a public relations campaign to sell Miers to conservative groups and, at times, these efforts included backdoor contacts between administration officials and conservative religious leaders. James Dobson, founder of the evangelical group Focus on the Family, reported on his radio show that Karl Rove had privately assured him that Miers was an evangelical Christian and a member of a pro-life conservative evangelical church. What amounted to a White House advertising campaign featuring Miers's religious faith quickly evoked criticism across the political spectrum.[33] Americans for Better Justice, another conservative Republican group, ratcheted the opposition to the Miers nomination still higher when it purchased $250,000 worth of time on the Fox News Channel to pressure the president to withdraw the nomination.

The Miers nomination also produced high anxiety for senators of both parties. Republicans found themselves faced with a painful, difficult choice in the age of increased partisanship. On the one hand, they could swallow hard and simply support the Miers nomination out of loyalty to the president—the obvious choice for an earlier generation of senators. Or they could align with the conservative, activist base of the party and oppose her

31. See David D. Kirkpatrick, "Miers Is Asked to Redo Reply to Questions," *New York Times*, October 20, 2005, A1. Mr. Kirkpatrick reported that no one could recall a previous instance when the committee returned a questionnaire due to incomplete or insufficient answers.

32. Quoted in Sheryl Gay Stolberg, "Bush Addresses G.O.P. Unease over Nominee," *New York Times*, October 9, 2005, A1.

33. Elisabeth Bumiller, "Bush Criticized over Emphasis on Religion of Nominee," *New York Times*, October 13, 2005, A23.

confirmation on ideological and competence grounds—a choice that reflected the realities of the new partisan, individualistic Senate. Democrats had an equally puzzling choice. They could support the nominee precisely because she was not an outspoken conservative and might indeed turn out to be something of a moderate. Then again, they could join with conservatives and hand the Bush administration a most embarrassing bipartisan political setback. Making the computation even more complicated was forecasting how President Bush would react to the defeat of his nominee. Would he move to the middle and nominate a well-known moderate or return to his campaign promise and seek a nominee in the image of Justices Scalia and Thomas?

The Mother of All Confirmation Battles That Wasn't

It was over by October 27, a little more than three weeks after it began. In a letter to the president, Miers withdrew as nominee, citing the impasse over the Judiciary Committee's request for documents produced during her service in the White House. The constitutional argument over separation of powers was, of course, a smokescreen. The demise of the Miers nomination was of far greater long-term significance, stark testimony to the new politics of judicial appointments and the democratization of the confirmation process. Miers's withdrawal was produced not by the exposure of scandals or misdeeds from her past, nor was it the result of revelations of racism or sexism or some other "ism" that would disqualify her from service on the high court. There was no paper trail that linked her to controversial or unpopular positions on the issues of the day. No senator took the floor of the Senate to eloquently galvanize popular opposition to her appointment. Her qualifications for the position were admittedly modest, and she certainly lacked gravitas, but the same could easily have been said of Justice O'Connor or Justice Thomas at the time of their nominations. In fact, Miers was overwhelmed by the latest manifestation of the new politics of judicial confirmations—

i.e., an intractable grassroots opposition continually fueled by Internet blogs, talk radio, televangelists, talking heads, and cable television outlets that united important and powerful conservative interests in opposition to their president's choice on essentially ideological grounds. The ultimate irony was that Miers almost certainly had sufficient bipartisan votes for confirmation had her nomination reached the floor of the Senate. Social and religious conservatives, however, had dealt the president a harsh and totally unexpected setback. The lesson for President Bush (as it had been to a lesser degree for President Clinton) was that within the new politics of judicial confirmations, a president's most potent opposition can often be found within his own party.

If the Miers nomination drew the ire of the conservatives, the president's choice of Samuel Alito as the new nominee played to rave reviews on the right. A judge on the Third Circuit Court of Appeals, Alito not only had solid academic and professional credentials, but his fifteen years as a federal judge had produced the paper trail of a firmly conservative constitutional jurisprudence.[34] Alito was one of a handful of jurists enthusiastically championed by the Federalist Society, and his was a name readily familiar to religious and social conservatives. Moreover, with a Republican majority of fifty-five in the Senate, Alito could secure confirmation even allowing for a Republican defection or two. On the other hand, the forty-four Democrats (forty-five if the independent Jeffords was counted with the Democrats) had the votes to sustain a filibuster and prevent a confirmation vote. With the swing seat of Justice O'Connor hanging in the balance, the potential for a confirmation fight of epic proportions seemed clear.

34. A graduate of Princeton and Yale Law School, Alito held several posts in the Reagan Justice Department before being appointed United States attorney for the District of New Jersey. Appointed to the federal bench in 1990, Alito developed a reputation as a conservative jurist of the first order. A member of the Federalist Society, Alito, because of his Italian heritage and conservative rulings, was often derided as the clone of Justice Scalia and became known as "Scalito" to his critics.

The again, if the deal struck months earlier by the Gang of 14 held, Alito might be confirmed in relative calm. Everything appeared to hinge on that undefined phrase "extraordinary circumstances" that governed the Democrats' right to filibuster judicial nominees. For New Progressive activists, the nomination of an avowed ideological conservative to replace the moderate O'Connor on the Supreme Court was precisely the circumstance permitting (demanding?) a filibuster.[35] For the moderates and institutionalists making up the Gang of 14, however, Alito, albeit a conservative, was not the extremist, "in-your-face" conservative ideologue that President Bush might have selected. It quickly became apparent that as long as the collective mindset of the Gang of 14 regarded Alito as an "acceptable" conservative, then his confirmation, for all intents and purposes, was a done deal.

Nevertheless, New Progressives and Democratic allies did their best. From the moment his name was announced, liberal groups aggressively portrayed Alito as a dangerous enemy of abortion rights. In 1985, when he sought a position in the Reagan administration as an assistant attorney general, Alito's application spelled out his antiabortion, anti–affirmative action views while pointing with pride to his efforts to overturn *Roe* v. *Wade* during his days in the solicitor general's office. In the same document he listed his 1972 membership in the Concerned Alumni of Princeton, an organization that opposed the admission of women and minorities to the university.[36] Liberals and conservatives bickered throughout the winter of 2005 over the significance of this document, with Democrats demanding amplification and explanations and Alito's supporters dismissing the significance of a twenty-year-old job application.

---

35. "The point of the deal was to preserve the filibuster for a bad Supreme Court nominee. We are at that point now." Kim Gandy, president of the National Organization for Women, quoted in James Kuhnhenn, "Gang of 14 Set Stage for Alito's Possible Nomination," Knight Ridder/Tribune News Service, January 22, 2006.

36. See Dale Russakoff, "Alito Disavows Controversial Group," *Washington Post*, January 12, 2006, A06.

The Alito hearings before the Judiciary Committee can only be described as deadly dull. Try as they might, the Democratic members of the committee were never able to engage Alito in anything approaching an extended discussion. A rather quiet, unassuming man to begin with, Alito was extremely cautious in his replies to even the most innocuous of questions. Writing in *The New Yorker*, Janet Malcolm likened Samuel Alito before the Judiciary Committee to "an accountant patiently explaining why the figures on a tax return are correct," a description that, to those who viewed the proceedings, may have seemed patently unfair to accountants.[37] But Alito did well enough. The Democrats on the Gang of 14 remained united in the determination that the Alito nomination did not present an "extraordinary circumstance" and were unwilling to support a filibuster.[38] Lacking even a credible filibuster threat, Democrats were left with casting futile "no" votes. Alito passed the Judiciary Committee in a straight party-line vote of 10-to-8 and, by the end of January, the full Senate confirmed the nomination 58-to-42, making Alito only the second justice in the last 100 years to be confirmed with more than forty negative votes.[39]

37. Janet Malcolm, "The Art of Testifying," *New Yorker*, March 13, 2006, 75. Following the Alito hearings, Senator Joe Biden proposed that confirmation hearings be abolished simply because no nominee is currently willing to be sufficiently forthcoming, and hence the hearings are now of limited value in assessing a vote on a judicial nominee.

38. At the last moment, Senator John Kerry of Massachusetts urged his fellow Democrats to filibuster the nomination. Democrats were almost unanimous in opposing Alito, but a filibuster without the support of the seven Democrats on the Gang of 14 was an empty threat. A cloture vote produced seventy-two votes, far more than necessary to cut off debate. Charlie Savage, "Alito Filibuster Effort Falls Short," *Boston Globe*, January 31, 2006.

39. Justice Thomas's victory in 1991 was 52-to-48. Thomas, however, received the support of eleven Democrats. In testimony to the new partisan Senate, only four Democrats broke ranks to support Alito.

CONCLUSION:
THE DEMOCRATIZATION OF
THE CONFIRMATION PROCESS

In January of 1993, Justice Thurgood Marshall, who had retired in 1991, died of heart failure at the age of eighty-four, and America paid final tribute to an extraordinary man of the twentieth century. He reached the very pinnacle of power in the United States and yet, unlike many in public life today, never forgot where he came from. Justice Marshall was also possibly the last of a succession of justices whose appointment to the Court followed a long and distinguished career in public service. It would scarcely be a disservice to the memory of Justice Marshall to suggest that his greatest contributions came well before his appointment to the Court, during his years as the attorney for the NAACP leading the historic legal campaign to end apartheid in America. In the twilight of the twentieth century, we can look back and say with confidence that Marshall was America's greatest public lawyer. Had he never attained a seat on the Supreme Court, his place in history would still be secure.

The twentieth century has seen others like Marshall who accomplished much before ascending to the high court. Oliver Wendell Homes, Jr., wrote over one thousand opinions as a judge on the Supreme Judicial Court of Massachusetts, published the classic *The Common Law*, and emerged as America's foremost legal thinker before his appointment to the Court at age sixty-one.

Although he served for thirty years as associate justice, the case could be made that Holmes did his finest work prior to his years on the Supreme Court. His friend and colleague Louis Brandeis was considered by many to be America's foremost lawyer before his appointment to the Court in 1916, achieving almost mythical status as "the people's attorney" and the champion of progressive causes.

Charles Evans Hughes came to the Court in 1910, after serving as governor of New York. He resigned in 1916 to run for the presidency, losing that year's presidential election to Woodrow Wilson by a mere twenty-three electoral votes. He later served as U.S. secretary of state before his appointment as chief justice in 1930. William Howard Taft, of course, was president of the United States before achieving in 1921 the position he coveted—the chief justiceship. Benjamin Cardozo was America's most respected state court judge before his appointment, and his successor, Felix Frankfurter, while still a professor at the Harvard Law School, was described in 1936 by *Fortune* magazine as "the single most influential individual in the United States." Earl Warren was both governor and attorney general of California and Thomas Dewey's running mate in the 1948 election before he was tapped to be chief justice by President Eisenhower. Harlan Fiske Stone, William O. Douglas, Robert Jackson, and Abe Fortas also could be counted among the twentieth century's best-known nominees to the Court.

These men, irrespective of personal politics or judicial philosophy, were among the best and brightest of their generations. They came to the Court with unquestioned personal stature and achievement and amid widespread public anticipation that they would have a profound impact on the development of American constitutional law. Their appointments were the outcomes of a predictable and stable process controlled, for the most part, by legal and political elites. Today, however, the system of judicial confirmations is a far more democratic process, shaped by extraordinary public participation and media coverage, and one

might do well to ponder whether such a process is likely to produce appointees of similar talent and distinction. On occasion,
those of limited experience or parochial background may, while
serving on the Court, grow into giants of American law, just as
a nominee of great standing may prove a disappointment. Nevertheless, the conclusion that must be drawn from the preceding
pages is that the contemporary confirmation process is not
configured to favor nominees to the Court with the stature of
Frankfurter or Holmes or the legendary experience of Brandeis
or Thurgood Marshall.

A half century ago, the process was predictable and stable,
controlled by insiders and cut off from public participation. Gaining the support of a few key actors all but guaranteed confirmation. In such a setting, deals could be cut and votes traded to
secure the confirmation of an eminent nominee, no matter the
long paper trail and abundance of political enemies associated
with a career in public affairs. By the same token, similar deals
could be cut to elevate political hacks and cronies. For every
Brandeis and Frankfurter, the process also brought forth a
McReynolds or a Whittaker.[1] From the turn of the century
through 1968, the staffing of the Court depended on the good
will, vision, and political acumen of a small handful of men, and

---

1. James McReynolds was appointed by Woodrow Wilson in 1914 and served
for twenty-seven years. He was a reactionary, a misogynist, a racist, and an anti-Semite.
He often would leave the conference room when Brandeis spoke, and he read a newspaper during the swearing-in ceremony for Cardozo while muttering "another one."
See Henry Abraham, *Justices and Presidents*, 3d ed. (New York: Oxford Univ. Press,
1992), 178–79. Charles Whittaker, appointed by Eisenhower in 1957, served five undistinguished years on the Court. He was paralyzed by indecision, and the resulting anxiety led to a nervous breakdown and his resignation from the Court. William Douglas
recounted the tale of a case in which Whittaker was assigned the majority opinion and
Douglas voiced a dissent. Unable to decide how to proceed, Whittaker sought Douglas's advice. Not one to be constrained by convention, Douglas agreed to draft a majority opinion as well as write his own dissent, and within the hour the draft was on
Whittaker's desk. This was one of the few times, Douglas caustically noted in his autobiography, "in which the majority and minority opinions were written by the same
man." Douglas, *The Court Years, 1939–1975* (New York: Random House, 1980), 173–74.

the lack of public participation produced nominees that ran the gamut from the truly inspirational to the simply wretched.

In 1968, the defeat of Abe Fortas stunned many astute observers of the Washington political scene and was, in retrospect, the first sign that the constellation of political forces in the process of selecting and confirming Supreme Court justices was undergoing realignment. The end of the Roosevelt coalition split the Democratic party between old-line party regulars and the New Progressives. During the last quarter century, the federal judiciary has become an important ally of the New Progressives in securing and protecting policy victories, particularly the lifestyle issues of exceptional importance to an educated, upper-middle-class, professional elite. The litigation victories of the New Progressives in turn hastened the emergence of the New Right in the Republican party and gave rise to intense scrutiny of judicial appointments by powerful forces in both parties. The changes in the nature of judicial power over the past four decades ratcheted the stakes still higher by making the federal judiciary amenable to a wider range of litigants and claims than ever before in its institutional history. Changes in the formal rules and institutional folkways of the Senate enhanced the influence of individual senators at the expense of institutional cohesion and leadership control. By the late 1960s, these developments converged, making public battles over staffing the Supreme Court almost inevitable.

Like many Republican presidential candidates in the modern age, George W. Bush throughout his campaigns found the promise to bring social and legal conservatives to the federal courts a dependable rhetorical device for energizing his most conservative supporters. Once in office, President Bush ultimately made good on that promise by placing two acknowledged, well-known conservatives on the high court with remarkable ease despite the organized and determined opposition of New Progressives. At the same time, President Bush suffered a stunning setback when important supporters forced the president to back down from the Harriet Miers nomination. Thus, within six months, a president with extraordinarily low approval ratings, saddled with a disastrous war and stalled domestic policy initiatives, supported by a congressional party publicly charged with serious ethical transgressions, placed on the Court with little difficulty two self-described conservatives who, in the minds of many, championed a radical constitutional ideology that posed a direct threat to core Supreme Court decisions cherished by New Progressives. At the same time, he was soundly rebuffed when he offered up a relatively unknown nominee with no paper trail and no public record on the hot-button issues of the day and who probably would have been ultimately confirmed with at least the lukewarm support of a fair number of Democrats. To place even these extraordinary events in perspective requires an appreciation of the ever-evolving politics of judicial confirmations.

Democratic Representative Rahm Emanuel offers one explanation for the current state of judicial confirmations: "George Bush won the election. If you don't like it, you better win elections."[2] At least in terms of the selection of unelected and unrepresentative judges, elections ironically do matter more today than perhaps thirty years ago, because in a period when extreme partisanship and ideological division shape the Senate, there is no critical mass of centrists and moderates whose votes are up for grabs during confirmation proceedings.[3] With unified partisan control of the Senate and the presidency, the prospects for confirmation of a presidential choice are overwhelmingly favorable unless the minority party can successfully mount (or reasonably threaten) a filibuster. For precisely that reason, the emergence of the Gang of 14 was an unexpected and yet significant development. Leaving the "extraordinary circumstances" in which the Democrats in the gang could engage in a filibuster undefined made excellent sense in the effort to forge an agreement and avert

2. Quoted in Adam Nagourney, "Glum Democrats Can't See Halting Bush on Courts," *New York Times*, January 15, 2006, A1.

3. Ben Ginsburg and Alan Stone, eds., *Do Elections Matter?* 2d ed. (Armonk, NY: Sharpe, 1990).

the nuclear showdown. In this era of partisan divide, however, the only credible power for the minority party in a confirmation battle is obstruction and delay, and after Roberts and Alito one would be hard pressed to contend that a conservative judicial philosophy (unless that philosophy is, for lack of a better term, simply "over the top") constitutes an "extraordinary circumstance." Considered from the perspective of the New Progressives, the Gang of 14 agreement proved a costly deal, because as long as the accord holds, avowed conservative jurists with appropriate legal credentials and gravitas are certain of appointment even if they believe (but don't shout from the rooftops) that *Roe* v. *Wade* was wrongly decided.[4]

Moreover, the Roberts and Alito confirmations appear to affirm a growing impression that Republicans simply have become far more effective at the politics of Supreme Court confirmations than the Democrats. Over twenty-five years ago, the Reagan administration recognized that altering the makeup of the federal judiciary would be an important step in the development of a modern, socially conservative Republican party. Evoking the image of the Warren Court and the evils of a host of "liberal" Supreme Court decisions was a potent tool in forging this new Republican majority. For many of the new recruits to the Republican party, the struggle to alter the federal judiciary became nothing less than a continuing battle for the salvation of America, and the time, energy, and money they devoted to this crusade soon exceeded that of their opponents. What's more, Republicans now appear better prepared for these confirmation battles. Conservative public interest law firms abound, and the quality of their constitutional legal representation certainly matches that of legendary liberal advocates such as the ACLU and the NAACP Legal Defense Fund. Conservative donors have been extraordinarily

4. Of course, religious and social conservatives sharply criticized the Republican senators who joined in the Gang of 14. It does appear, however, that they got the better part of the deal.

generous in funding sophisticated, grassroots organizations skilled at using modern media outlets to extol the necessity of transforming the federal judiciary. Television evangelists effectively exhort the laity to political action on behalf of judicial nominees.

For its part, the Federalist Society has not only elevated conservative jurisprudence to a position of real respectability in the academy but it has also labored mightily to recruit "the best and brightest" among its members for careers in the Justice Department and the federal judiciary. Conservatives can now point to a number of committed conservative lawyers and judges with impeccable legal credentials and experience in the public arena, and, thanks to the efforts of Federalist Society and related organizations, there is a nucleus of legal strategists, media experts, and organizers who are familiar with these rising legal stars and are ready to mobilize on their behalf at a moment's notice.[5] The Republican Party, with the aid of the Federalist Society, in effect has produced an extraordinary judicial minor-league farm system dedicated to developing qualified young jurists ready to step up to the highest level whenever a vacancy appears, and the significance of this grooming of potential Supreme Court nominees cannot be overstated. The nomination of Harriet Miers, for example, failed in no small measure because the president simply could not explain to his conservative base why he had skipped over any one of a number of the Federalist Society's superstars in favor of an essentially unknown nominee.

The Democrats and the New Progressives have simply not kept up with these efforts. New Progressives, of course, can be counted on to rise to the defense of a liberal judiciary, but the triumphant moments of the earlier political and judicial campaigns on behalf of civil rights and personal liberties belong to the past,

---

5. For example, during the Roberts confirmation proceedings, the Federalist Society hired a public relations firm to place members on television shows and help train them on how best to present the case for Roberts to the public. See Jason DeParle, "Nomination Stirs a Debate on Federalists' Sway," *New York Times*, August 1, 2005, A1.

and the themes of personal freedom and individual choice that had galvanized so many on the left thirty years ago simply failed to resonate this time around. Perhaps decades of living with *Roe* has produced a certain complacency on the part of America's liberals. Early on, New Progressives recognized the significance of a sympathetic judiciary and developed the techniques of grassroots mobilization that expanded the democratization of the process of nominating and confirming Supreme Court justices and ultimately produced the prodigious effort to defeat Robert Bork. It was a defining moment for many activists on the left. Decades later the same techniques have been refined and enhanced by the New Right in support of sharply conservative jurists. This cyclical pattern is frequently encountered in American politics, but for the moment, at least with respect to the politics of Supreme Court confirmations, the pendulum has swung decidedly to the right.

The appointment of Roberts and Alito may prove decisive in the conservative campaign to transform the American judiciary, but there is, nonetheless, a lingering suspicion that it is the failed Meirs nomination that may come to represent a turning point in the evolution of the new politics of judicial confirmations. Traditionally, presidents cherished vacancies on the Supreme Court as a "no lose" opportunity to exercise presidential prerogative and to influence the development of American law for years to come. And, throughout a good portion of the twentieth century, there was little reason to question this conventional understanding. Presidents would consult with Senate leaders and perhaps strike a necessary behind-the-scenes deal, but to a remarkable degree, presidential choice with respect to Supreme Court appointments was honored. Beginning with the Fortas affair, however, the task of filling Supreme Court vacancies became significantly more difficult as presidents confronted a new politics of judicial confirmations. For modern presidents, a vacancy on the Supreme Court demands an intricate and high-stakes political calculation of the costs and benefits of any appointment. Bill Clinton, for example, found the potential cost of confirmation battles to be sufficiently high to risk disappointing his own supporters through the nomination of acknowledged moderates. Years later, when President Bush tried a similar tactic (and admittedly Miers lacked a track record as well as the superior legal qualifications of the Clinton choices), he confronted not simply the disappointment and discontent of core supporters but outright rebellion.

The failed Miers appointment now stands as a startling example of how successfully the new politics of judicial confirmations has worked to narrow and constrain presidential options. For generations, presidents could expect confirmation proceedings to be low-key, insider affairs, and serious opposition to presidential choice was an extraordinary event. The coming of the new politics of confirmation, however, increased the likelihood of opposition and narrowed presidential alternatives. In the years following Fortas, it became readily apparent that the nomination of a well-known individual with broad political experience, no matter how favored by a particular president, was certain to trigger potent opposition, while the appointment of experienced, competent, albeit invisible and seemingly apolitical judges was politically a far safer alternative. By the Clinton years, even this presidential option was showing signs of obsolescence, and the conservative backlash against the Miers nomination confirmed that a president is almost certain to face organized opposition regardless of the nature of the nominee. Today there appears to be no politically safe choice within the new politics of Supreme Court confirmations. Considered from this perspective, the Miers nomination may well mark the point in recent history at which vacancies on the Supreme Court, once cherished as political assets for any president, evolved into potential political liabilities.

Whether an asset or a liability, it is quite certain that the selection of new Supreme Court justices will remain highly visible, contentious affairs. It is in this often unseemly clash of interests that the modern liberal-democratic state seeks to achieve rough consensus on its most pressing and divisive issues, and it can hardly be surprising that a similar democratic struggle now defines the selection of our judges. The harsh reality that modern interest-group and media politics dominate the nomination process as well as the confirmation process has provoked a good deal of concern, and calls for the reform of the process are frequent.[6] Substantial reform, however, is perhaps unlikely—the stakes are too high for too many interests—and perhaps even ill-advised. Certainly, the apparent decorum that marked the process of the distant past was achieved at the expense of public participation and accountability. One may decry the demise of civility, but judges today are important policymakers, and public participation in both their nomination and confirmation may be the principal mechanism for ensuring a measure of public accountability. That a politicized system of selecting and confirming our judges may circumscribe presidential prerogative and preclude the appointment of people of stature—a Marshall, a Warren, or a Brandeis—is perhaps one unfortunate consequence of a nonetheless thoroughly democratic process.

6. See, for example, *Obstacle Course: Report of the Task Force on the Presidential Appointment and Senate Confirmation Process* (New York: Century Foundation Press, 1996).

INDEX

abortion, 72, 79*n*, 120–21, 208*n*
  Alito's record, 218
  the New Right and, 137, 141, 142,
    144, 148*n*, 149–50, 154, 156
  Planned Parenthood v. *Casey*, 148*n*,
    152*n*, 154*n*–55*n*
  reform of state laws, 68–69
  Roe v. *Wade*, 68–71, 106, 107, 121,
    144, 152*n*, 154, 155*n*, 225, 227
  Justice Ginsburg on, 80*n*, 117, 118
  Webster v. *Reproductive Health
    Services*, 154–55, 156
abstention doctrine, 59, 61
Acheson, Dean, 57*n*
activism, judicial, *see* judicial
  activism
Adams, Sherman, 175
affirmative action, 74, 98, 135, 218
  in the federal judiciary, 101*n*
African Americans, 187–88
  civil rights, *see* civil rights and
    civil liberties
  Democratic party and, 87, 89–90,
    91, 138
  slavery, 37
Agger, Carolyn, 14
Agnew, Spiro, 128
Alito, Justice Samuel, 5, 195, 217–19,
  223–24, 225, 227
Allen, George, 214
Alliance for Justice, 103*n*, 112
al-Qaeda, 199
American Association of University
  Women, 72

American Bar Association, 149
  Brandeis confirmation battle
    and, 3
American Civil Liberties Union
  (ACLU), 16, 72, 115*n*, 225
  Frankfurter and, 88
  Womens' Rights Project, 116
American Nurses Association, 74
Americans for Better Justice, 215
Americans for Democratic Action,
  105, 168–69
Americans United for Life, 72
amicus curiae (friend of the court)
  briefs, 73–74
Anderson, John, 101
Arnold, Fortas, and Porter, 14
Arnold, Judge Richard, 120–21
Arnold, Thurman, 13
Arnold & Fortas, 13
Aron, Nan, 112
Ashcroft, John, 202*n*
Ashwander v. *TVA*, 45–46, 59, 62
Association of Flight Attendants,
  107
Atherton Mills v. *Johnston*, 43–45, 59
Atlantic Monthly, 88*n*
Audubon Society, 77

Babbitt, Bruce, 115, 120
Baird, Zoë, 111
Baker, Bobby, 170
Baker, Howard, 161*n*
Baker, Ross, 176
Baker v. *Carr*, 54, 56–57, 57, 59, 64–65

Bakke case, 74
Bauer, Gary, 79*n*
Bayh, Birch, 186
Benton v. *Maryland,* 52*n*
Bickel, Alexander, 61–62
Biden, Joseph, 119–20
Black, Clint, 153
Black, Justice Hugo, 12
  credentials of, 88
  judicial activism in protection of
    individual rights and, 49, 58
  retirement of, 70
Blackmun, Justice Harry
  confirmation as associate justice,
    68, 133
  retirement of, 118
  Roe v. *Wade* and, 70–71, 121
blacks, *see* African Americans
Bob Jones University, 146
Bolick, Clint, 119
Borah, William, 2
Bork, Robert, 113–14
  confirmation battle, 4, 5, 9, 75–79,
    79, 103*n*, 105–7, 108, 151–52,
    187–88, 227
  credentials of, 9, 76, 79
  Federalist Society and, 200–201
  judicial activism, opposition to, 9,
    76, 105, 187
born-again Christians, 141
Brandeis, Judge Louis, 4, 67*n*, 69,
    190, 221, 222*n*
  confirmation battle, 3
  judicial restraint and, 43–46, 56,
    59, 62
Brandzel, Ben, 212*n*
Braun, Carol Moseley, 190
Breaux, John, 188*n*
Brennan, Justice William, 23*n*, 56–57
  retirement of, 108, 156
  Roe v. *Wade* and, 71
Breyer, Justice Stephen, 80, 82, 116,
    121–22
Brown, Judge Janice Rogers, 210
Brown, Michael, 196

Brownback, Sam, 197
Brown v. *Board of Education,* 21, 24,
    33, 51, 52, 54, 138, 139
Buchanan, Pat, 143*n*
Burger, Chief Justice Warren E.
  nomination and confirmation as
    chief justice, 66, 68, 131
  retirement of, 150
  Roe v. *Wade* and, 70
Burger Court, 66–75
Bush, George H. W., 103, 152–56,
    211
  presidential election of 1988, 90,
    107, 141*n*, 143, 152
  presidential election of 1992,
    155–56
  Supreme Court appointments
    David Souter, 108–9, 156
    Clarence Thomas, 79, 156, 188,
      190
Bush, George W., 194–200
  approval ratings, 199, 200
  constituency of, and style of
    governing, 194, 198–99
  domestic surveillance and, 200
  Iraq war and, 196, 200
  judicial appointments, 104*n*,
    194–95, 202–19
    Samuel Alito, 195, 217–19,
      223–24, 225, 227
    Harriet Miers nomination, 5,
      196–97, 213–17, 223–24, 226,
      228
    John Roberts, 195, 211–13,
      223–24, 225, 227
  presidential election of 2000,
    82–83, 194, 197–98
  September 11 and war on terror,
    199–200
Bush v. *Gore,* 82–83
business interests, 73
  Brandeis confirmation battle and,
    3
  Fortas and, 16, 20
  government regulation of, 38, 39

judicial activism on behalf of, 33,
    36–38, 39, 40, 43, 47
busing, 135, 137, 139, 140
Byrd, Harry, 169–70
Byrd, Robert, 131, 161, 189*n*

Cabranes, Jose, 119
California welfare system, 75
capitalist interests, *see* business
    interests
Capital Legal Foundation, 75
Cardozo, *Justice* Benjamin, 108–9,
    221
    appointment to the Supreme
        Court, 1–2
    reputation as a progressive, 1
Carnes, Edward, 105*n*
Carswell, G. Harrold, failure of
        Senate to confirm, as
        Supreme Court justice, 4, 68,
        132–33
Carter, Jimmy, 80, 96, 98, 100–101,
    116, 117, 136, 141, 146
Casals, Pablo, 16
Catholic Conference, 103*n*
Catholics
    Democratic party and, 87, 91
    the New Right and, 141, 142–43
    Republican party and, 101
Census Bureau, U.S., 37
Center for Law and Social Policy, 98
Central Intelligence Agency (CIA),
    195, 196
Charles River Bridge v. *Warren Bridge*,
    37*n*
Cheney, Dick, 195, 196, 198*n*, 207*n*
Chicago Democratic National
        Convention of 1968, 10, 93
child labor, 43–44
Children's Defense Fund, 102, 115*n*
Christian Coalition, 79, 140, 155–56
Christian private school movement,
    139–40
    tax-exempt status of, controversy
        over, 140, 146–47

Circuit Court Nominating
    Commission, 100*n*–101*n*
citizen groups, *see* interest groups
Citizens for Decent Literature, 27
Civil Rights Act of 1964, 18, 19, 21,
    138
civil rights and civil liberties, 94, 183
    class action suits, 61
    Democratic party and, 90, 91,
        138–39, 168*n*
    Humphrey as advocate of, 168
    Nixon administration and, 128,
        130, 134–35
    Warren Court and, 10, 24, 50–65
civil rights movement, 92–93, 96*n*
Clancy, James, 27
Clark, Ramsey, 19n
class action suits, 61
Clement, Paul, 202*n*
Cleveland, Grover, 197*n*
Clifford, Clark, 22n
Clinton, Bill, 110–25
    judicial appointments, 111–25,
        193, 194, 228
        to federal courts, 111–12,
            123–24, 125, 157–58, 202
        to the Supreme Court, 80,
            114–22, 124–25, 228
    1994 midterm elections and, 122,
        123
    partisanship in the Senate and
        agenda of, 192–93
    presidential election of 1992, 96,
        110
    Whitewater and, 121, 123, 201
Coalition for a Fair Judiciary, 210
Coalition for Traditional Values, 79*n*
Colegrove v. Green, 55, 57
Coleman, William, 146
Columbia Broadcasting System, 75
Columbia University Law School,
    132–33
Common Cause, 98, 103, 176*n*
Common Law, The (Holmes), 220
Concerned Alumni of Princeton, 218

Concerned Women for America, 79*n*
confirmation process
    for federal judges, *see* federal
        judges, nomination and
        confirmation of
    for Supreme Court justices, *see*
        history of the confirmation
        process to the Supreme
        Court; Senate confirmation
        of judicial appointments
Congress, U.S., *see* House of
    Representatives, U.S.; Senate,
    U.S.
conservatives, 137, 225–26
    Federalist Society and, *see*
        Federalist Society
    Miers nomination and, 5, 195, 197,
        214–17, 223, 226, 228
    New Right, *see* New Right
    public-interest law firms and legal
        foundations of, 74–75, 225
    the Senate at midcentury, 165–66,
        167, 183
Constitution, U.S.
    amendments to, *see individual
        amendments*
    powers of the judiciary, 35
consumer protection groups, 67, 73,
    100*n*
Consumers Union, 102
Courtier, James, 155
crime, 94, 111, 128
    party affiliation and attitudes
        toward, 94*n*–95*n*
criminal law and rights of the
        accused
    Fortas and, 10
    Warren Court and, 10, 24–27, 52,
        52*n*–53*n*, 62–64, 65, 68, 127,
        129
Cruz, R. Ted, 202*n*
C-Span, 181
Cuomo, Mario, 114

Danforth, John, 189*n*
Daschle, Tom, 161

Davis, John W., 42*n*
Day, Kay, 210
Days, Drew, 119
Deadlock or Decision (Harris), 183*n*
DeLay, Tom, 158
Democratic National Conventions
    1968, 10, 93
    1972, 93–94
    changes in guidelines for delegate
        selection, 93
Democratic party, 85–125, 168
    civil rights and, 90, 91, 138–39,
        168*n*
    legacy of the New Deal, 85–89
    New Deal liberals, *see* New Deal
        liberals
    New Progressives, *see* New
        Progressives
    1958 congressional elections, 175
    in the South, 11*n*, 19, 20–21, 30, 31,
        87, 90–91, 127, 138–39, 165,
        168*n*, 187–88
democratization of the confirmation
        process, 216–17, 220–29
Denton, Jeremiah, 150*n*, 187
Department of Interior, U.S., 13
deregulation, 146
desegregation, 64, 138–39
    Brown v. *Board of Education*, 21, 24,
        33, 51, 52, 54, 138, 139
    Nixon administration and, 134–35
Dewey, John, 42
Dewey, Thomas, 221
Dewey, Tom, 50*n*
Dingh, Viet, 202
Dionne, E. J., Jr., 100*n*, 142*n*
Dirksen, Everett, 19, 20, 29, 32, 165,
        173, 184
Dixon, Alan, 190
Dobson, James, 215
Doe v. *Bolton*, 70
Dole, Robert, 116, 161, 188
Dotson, James, 210
Douglas, Justice William O., 13, 186,
        222*n*
    credentials of, 88, 221

judicial activism and, 58
Roe v. *Wade* and, 71
Dred Scott v. *Sandford*, 37
Dukakis, Michael, 90, 107
Duncan v. *Louisiana*, 52*n*

Eagle Forum, 79*n*
Eagleton, Thomas, 190
East, John P., 150*n*
Eastland, James, 23
economic inequality, 37, 38
Economic Opportunity Act, 18
Edelman, Marian Wright, 114, 115*n*
Edsall, Mary, 130
Edsall, Thomas, 130
Ehrlichman, John, 134
Eighth Amendment, 52
Eisenhower, Dwight D., 31, 50*n*,
    175
    New Deal legacy and, 86–87
    Supreme Court appointments, 89,
        221
Emanuel, Rahm, 224
Engle v. *Vitale*, 139, 144
environmentalists, 67, 73, 100*n*
Equal Employment Opportunity
    Commission, 78
Equal Protection Clause, 53, 56, 82,
    83
Equal Rights Amendment (ERA), 98,
    149
Ervin, Sam, 24
Estrada, Miguel, 204–5
evangelicals, Protestant, 139, 140–41,
    142–43, 145, 155–56, 158, 187
Evans, Rowland, 171*n*
executive branch
    congressional challenges to the
        power of, 35
    New Deal liberalism and, 48

Falwell, Jerry, 140, 144
Family Research Council, 79*n*
family values, 126, 142, 153
Farm-Labor party of Minnesota,
    167–68

federal courts
    judicial activism, *see* judicial
        activism
    judicial restraint, *see* judicial
        restraint
    New Progressives and, 97–100,
        223
    the New Right and, *see* New
        Right, the judiciary and
    Nixon administration, as
        scapegoat of, 131–35
    Warren Court, 10, 26, 126, 127,
        129, 136
    relaxation of strict rules of access
        to, 7, 65–66, 72–73, 84, 223
    class action suits, 61
    jurisdiction, rules of, 53, 59, 61
    political-question doctrine,
        54–55, 56, 57, 65
    standing-to-sue doctrine, 30–31,
        34, 59–61, 65, 69, 76
Federalist Society, 200–203, 204*n*,
    208, 217, 226
federal judges, nomination and
    confirmation of, 6, 31
    George W. Bush administration
        and, 194–95, 202–10, 211
    George H. W. Bush administration
        and, 153–54, 211
    Clinton administration and,
        111–12, 123–24, 125, 228
    Federalist Society and, 200–202
    increased importance of a
        senator's voting record,
        104–5
    interest groups involved in, 75–76
    New Progressives and, 98, 100–10
    New Right and, 108, 148–49,
        153–54
    political patronage and, 98,
        112–13, 148, 171*n*, 202
    recess appointments, 206
Federal Rules of Civil Procedure,
    Rule 23 (class action suits), 61
Federal Trade Commission, 175
Field, Marshall, 37

Fifth Amendment, 52
filibuster, *see* Senate, U.S., filibuster
    and the cloture rule
First Amendment rights, 81
    establishment clause, 147
    Warren Court and, 52–53, 64
Flaming Creatures, 27
Florida Supreme Court, 82
Florio, James, 155
Focus on the Family, 210, 215
Ford, Gerald, 101n, 186
Fortas, Justice Abe, 10–28, 13
    business interests and, 16
    civil liberties and, 16
    credentials of, 12–13, 221
    friendship with Johnson, 12, 13,
        15
    as Johnson's adviser, 13–14,
        16–17, 24, 28
    Johnson's senate race of 1948 and,
        12
    nomination and confirmation as
        associate justice, 11, 14–16, 58
    nomination as chief justice, 10, 11,
        17, 127
        failure of Senate to confirm, 4,
            10, 11, 27–28, 29–30, 58, 65,
            66, 156, 184, 223, 227
        Judiciary Committee hearings,
            22–27, 30
    public-interest law and, 13
    resignation from the Supreme
        Court, financial dealings
        and, 11, 28n, 68, 131, 185
Fortune magazine, 221
Fourteenth Amendment
    due process clause, 38, 41, 213
    Equal Protection Clause, 53, 56,
        82, 83
Fourth Amendment, 52
    exclusionary rule and, 81
Fox News Channel, 215
Frankfurter, Justice Felix, 55, 60, 67n
    Colegrove v. *Green*, 55
    credentials of, 88, 221

divisions in the Roosevelt Court
    and, 49
judicial restraint, as advocate of,
    39–41, 49, 56, 57, 58, 68, 80–81
retirement of, 57–58
Sacco and Vanzetti case and, 88n
Frey, Andrew, 149
Friendly, Judge Henry, 211
Frist, Bill, 209
Fulbright, J. William, 18n

Gaertner, Gary, 112–13
Gallup polls, 199
Gandy, Kim, 218n
gays in the military, 111
gender discrimination, 98–99
Gideon, Clarence Earl, 13
Gideon v. *Wainwright*, 13, 53n
Ginsberg, Benjamin, 142
Ginsburg, Justice Ruth Bader, 80, 82,
    116–18, 121–22
Glazer, Nathan, 6n
Goldberg, Justice Arthur, 14, 58, 116
Goldfine, Bernard, 175
Goldsboro Christian School, 146
Goldwater, Barry, 25n, 87
Gonzales, Alberto, 208n
Gordon, Senator, 157
Gore, Albert, 133n
Gorton, Slade, 104
Grassley, Charles, 118
Griffin, Robert, 19, 184
Griswold, Erwin, 116–17
Griswold v. *Connecticut*, 60, 106

Hammer v. *Dagenhart*, 43
Harlan, Justice John, 58n, 70
Harriman, W. Averell, 14n
Harris, Fred, 183n
Harrison, Benjamin, 197n
Harrison v. *NAACP*, 59n
Hart, Philip, 175
Hatch, Orrin, 115, 116, 120, 157,
    182n, 205
Hawkins, Paula, 178–79

Hayden, Carl T., 20
Hayes, Rutherford, 197*n*
Haynsworth, Clement, 4, 68, 131–32, 133, 184, 185–87
Helms, Jesse, 150
Herblock (cartoonist), 15
Hess, Stephen, 177*n*
Hill, Anita, 79, 110, 182*n*, 188*n*, 189*n*, 190
history of the confirmation process to the Supreme Court, 1–6, 108–9, 171–73
  candidates denied confirmation, 3, 4
    Robert Bork, *see* Bork, Robert
    Harrold G. Carswell, 4, 68
    Abe Fortas, *see* Fortas, Justice Abe
    Clement Haynesworth, 4, 68
    James J. Parker, 3
  democratization of the confirmation process, 216–17, 220–29
  modern politics of judicial confirmation, 182–93, 194–95, 200–19, 227–29
  the nineteenth century, 4*n*, 171*n*
  from 1900 to 1968, 1–4, 32, 87, 88, 89, 171–73, 182–83, 185, 189
  1968 as turning point in, 4, 11, 28–32, 68, 89, 156, 223, 227
  see also names of individuals nominated to the Court
Hollings, Ernest, 188
Holmes, Justice Oliver Wendell, 1, 41–43, 56, 220–21
Hoover, Herbert, 108
  Cardozo nomination and, 1–2
House of Representatives, U.S.
  compared to the Senate, 160–62
  interest groups and, 184
  malapportioned congressional districts, 54, 55
  1958 congressional elections, 175
  Republican control of, 122

Tocqueville on, 160
2002 congressional elections, 204
2004 congressional elections, 206
Hruska, Roman, 133*n*
Hughes, Chief Justice Charles Evans, 3*n*, 190, 221
Humphrey, Hubert
  folkways of the Senate and, 167–71, 172, 180
  presidential election of 1968, 89, 128, 129
  presidential election of 1972, 94*n*
Hurricane Katrina, 196

Ickes, Harold, 13
individual rights, *see* civil rights and civil liberties
Industrial Revolution, 37
integration, *see* desegregation
interest groups
  cultivating of senators, 184–85
  increase in number and power of, in 1960s, 175–76
  judicial confirmation process, involvement in, 75–79, 84, 229
  use of the judiciary to achieve their goals, 67, 72–75, 81, 84
  see also individual groups
Internal Revenue Service (IRS), 139, 146–47
Iraq, war in, 196, 200

Jackson, Justice Robert, 150*n*, 221
Jeffords, James, 198
Jews
  Democratic party and, 87
  Supreme Court justices, 1, 3, 118
John Birch Society, 103
Johnson, Lyndon B., 64
  as congressman, 11, 12
  decision not to seek a second term, 17
  Fortas as adviser to, 13–14, 16–17, 24, 28

Johnson, Lyndon B. (*continued*)
  Fortas nomination as associate
      justice and, 14–15, 58
  Fortas nomination as chief justice
      and, 10, 11, 17, 58, 131
  understanding of the Senate
      and, 17–22, 29, 31, 173
  withdrawal of, 27–28
  friendship with Fortas, 12, 13, 15
  Great Society, 51
  Humphrey and, 170–71
  legislative record as president, 18,
      19
  as majority leader of the Senate,
      18*n*, 19
  Senate races, 11–12
  understanding of the Senate,
      17–22, 29, 31, 170–71, 173
Johnston, John, 188*n*
Jones, Paula, 123
judicial activism, 6, 47
  Bork as critic of, 9, 76, 105, 187
  civil liberties, to protect, 49
  criminal procedures and, 10
  of John Marshall, 35–36, 50
  political right's opposition to, 34
  progressives' opposition to,
      39–41, 42–49
  to protect business interests, *see*
      business interests, judicial
      activism on behalf of
  of Rehnquist Court, 81–83
  Taney Court and, 36–37
  of Warren Court, *see* Warren
      Court, judicial activism of
judicial confirmations, *see* federal
      judges, nomination and
      confirmation of; Senate
      confirmation of judicial
      appointments
judicial remedies, new and
      innovative forms of, 7, 30, 34,
      65–66, 67, 84
  Warren Court and, 62–64
judicial restraint, 80

Frankfurter and, 39–41, 46, 56, 57,
      58, 68, 80–81
  the New Deal liberals and, 41–49,
      51–52, 53, 55–56, 57, 58, 59,
      61–62, 89, 159
  post-New Deal, 50
Judicial Selection Monitoring
      Project, 113
Judicial Selection Project, 102–3, 107
judiciary, changing nature of the
      power of the, 33–84
  Constitutional powers, 35
  judicial activism, *see* judicial
      activism
  judicial review
      Marshall's establishment of the
          power of, 35–36
      proposals for formally
          restricting the power of, 40–41
      New Deal liberals and judicial
          self-restraint, 41–49, 51–53,
          55–56, 57, 58, 59, 61–62, 65,
          72, 159
      the progressives, *see* progressives
      Taney Court, 36–37
jurisdiction, rules of, 53
  abstention doctrine, 59, 61
Justice Department, U.S., 14
  Federalist Society and, 201–2, 226
  Office of Legal Policy, 202
  Reagan, 146, 148–49
justiciability, standards of, 45, 46, 53,
      61, 65, 66*n*, 67
  see also jurisdiction, rules of;
      political-question doctrine;
      standing-to-sue doctrine

Katrina, Hurricane, 196
Keck, Thomas, 81
Kennedy, Justice Anthony, 82, 148*n*,
      151*n*–52*n*, 154, 155*n*
Kennedy, Edward, 98, 182*n*, 187
Kennedy, John F., 57, 64, 114*n*
  New Frontier, 51
  Supreme Court nominees, 58

Kennedy, Robert F., 57
    assassination of, 9, 10
    resignation as attorney general, 14
Kerry, John, 219*n*
King, Martin Luther, Jr., 9
Kirkland & Ellis, 201
Kirkpatrick, Jeane, 93, 94, 95*n*
Klopfer v. *North Carolina*, 53*n*
Ku Klux Klan, 88
Kurland, Professor, 51
Kyl, Jon, 157

labor
    confirmation of Supreme Court
        nominees and, 3, 185
    Democratic party and, 87, 91–92
    Humphrey as champion of, 168
LaHaye, Beverly, 79*n*
Leadership Conference on Civil
        Rights (LCCR), 102–3, 107
League of Women Voters, 72
Lear, Norman, 103
Lee, Rex, 75*n*, 147–48
Lerner, Max, 36
Lewinsky, Monica, 123
Lewis, Ann, 105
Libby, Lewis "Scooter," 196
Life magazine, 28*n*, 131, 185
Lippmann, Walter, 38–39
Lombardi, Marianne, 113
Lott, Trent, 207
Luttig, Judge Michael, 201

McCarthy, Eugene, 175
McCarthyism, 13
McConnell, Michael, 204*n*
McFadden, Monica, 107
McGovern, George, 95, 96
McReynolds, Justice James, 222
Malcolm, Janet, 219
Mallory v. *United States*, 25–26, 27
Malloy v. *Hogan*, 52*n*
Manion, Daniel, 103, 104
Mapp v. *Ohio*, 52*n*
Marbury v. *Madison*, 35–36

Marshall, Chief Justice John, 33, 50,
        220
    distinguished career in public
        service, 220
    power of judicial review
        established by, 35–36, 50
    retirement of, 109, 156
Marshall, Justice Thurgood, 71, 80
mass media, 92, 156–57
    as part of the political process,
        177–78
    power of the, 96*n*
    the Senate and, *see* Senate, U.S.,
        mass media and
    Senate judicial confirmation
        hearings covered by, 156–57,
        183, 186, 221, 229
Matthews, Donald, 162–63, 164, 167,
        174
media, *see* mass media
Medicare, 18
Meese, Edwin, 147
Metzenbaum, Howard, 121
Miers, Harriet, 5, 195, 196–97,
        213–17, 223–24, 226, 227, 228
minimum-wage laws, state, 87
Miranda, Ernesto, 62
Miranda v. *Arizona*, 62–63, 65
Mitchell, George, 118–19
Mitchell, John, 132
Mondale, Walter, 141
mootness, 69, 70, 71
Moral Majority, 140, 144
Morris, Dick, 123
Mountain States Legal Foundation,
        75
MoveOn.org, 212*n*
Muskie, Edmund, 175

NAACP v. *Button*, 59*n*
Nader, Ralph, 121
NARAL, 103*n*, 154
National Abortion Rights Action
        League (NARAL), 103*n*,
        154–55

National Association for the
    Advancement of Colored
    People (NAACP), 3, 59*n*,
    102*n*, 103*n*, 134
  Legal Defense Fund, 225
  Marshall's historic role at, 220
National Association of
    Manufacturers, 39
National Black Leadership
    Roundtable, 107
National Coalition to Ban
    Handguns, 149
National Consumers League, 67*n*
National Education Association, 102
National Federation of Business and
    Professional Women's Clubs,
    107
National Gay and Lesbian Task
    Force, 77
National Labor Relations Act, 87
National Organization for Women,
    69, 72, 98, 176*n*, 218*n*
National Resources Defense
    Council, 74
National Security Agency (NSA),
    200*n*
National Wildlife Federation, 102
Nature of the Judicial Process, The
    (Cardozo), 1
Neas, Ralph, 102*n*
New Deal liberals, judicial self-
    restraint and, 41–49, 51–53,
    53, 55–56, 57, 58, 59, 61–62,
    65, 72, 159, 223
New Progressives, 92–114, 135*n*
  Clinton administration and,
    110–25, 158
  emergence of, 93–95, 223
  the judiciary and, 96–125, 152*n*,
    212, 218, 223, 224, 225, 226–27
  as more liberal than traditional
    Democratic electorate, 94, 96
  party unity and, 94–95
  policy focus of, 94–95, 97–99
  in the Republican era, 101–14

  senators cultivated by, 184
  skilled professionals, comprised
    of, 95
New Republic, 41
New Right, 137–58, 223
  combining of secular and
    religious movements in, 141,
    142–43
  the judiciary and, 126, 140, 141,
    144–58, 202, 225–26, 227
    Alito nomination, 217–19, 227
    Bork confirmation battle, 108,
    151–52
    Breyer nomination, 121
    Clinton federal court
    appointments, 113–14,
    157–58
    "ideological litmus test," 149
    O'Connor confirmation, 149–50
    Souter confirmation and, 108
    Thomas confirmation and,
    78–79, 109–10
  the New South and, 137–43
  senators cultivated by, 184
  social legislation and, *see* social
    issues and legislation, New
    Right and
New Yorker, The, 219
New York Times, 88, 184
Nixon, Richard M.
  attraction of disaffected white
    Democrats to, 31
  Blackmun nomination, 133
  Burger nomination, 68, 131
  Carswell nomination, 132–33
  civil rights and, 128, 130, 134–35
  coalition of voters assembled by,
    126–28, 130, 133–34
  economic policy, 130, 136, 137
  federal courts as scapegoat for,
    131–36
    Warren Court, 10, 26, 126, 127,
    129, 136
  Haynsworth nomination, 131–32,
    185–87

presidential election of 1968, 89, 126, 127–29
    Warren Court as issue in, 10, 24, 26, 126, 127, 129
presidential election of 1972, 95, 96, 135
Watergate, 95n, 97, 136
North American Free Trade Agreement (NAFTA), 111
Norton, Eleanor Holmes, 114, 115n
Novak, Robert, 171n, 195
Nunn, Sam, 188n

O'Brien, David, 158
obscenity, Supreme Court decisions on, 27, 30
O'Connor, Justice Sandra Day, 82, 148n, 149–50, 154, 155n, 196–97
    retirement of, 195, 196, 210, 218
O'Daniel, Pappy ("Pass the Biscuits"), 11–12
Oklahoma City federal courthouse bombing, 111
Olin Foundation, John M., 201
Olsen, Ted, 202n
Omnibus Crime Bill, 111
Owen, Judge Priscilla, 208–9, 210

Pacific Legal Foundation, 75
Packwood, Bob, 155
Panetta, Leon, 134, 190
Parker, John J., 3
patriotic symbols, Republican manipulation of, 126, 142, 143
patronage, 88, 92, 98
    federal judiciary and, 98, 112–13, 148, 171n, 202
    New Progressives' disdain for, 97
People for the American Way, 102, 103
Perot, H. Ross, 156
Persian Gulf War, 152
PEW Research surveys, 199

Phillips, Kevin, 127–28, 136
Pickering, Judge Charles, 207n
Planned Parenthood, 72, 103n, 149
Planned Parenthood v. *Casey*, 148n, 152n, 154n–55n
Pointer v. *Texas*, 52n–53n
political-question doctrine, 54–55, 56–57, 65
pornography, 119, 137, 142
    Senate Commerce Committee hearings on "porn rock," 178–79
    Warren Court obscenity decisions, 27, 30
Powell, Justice Lewis Franklin, Jr., 151n
    Roe v. *Wade* and, 71n
prayer in school, 141, 142, 144, 147, 154
presidency, mass media's effect on the, 177
presidential elections
    1952, 89
    1964, 25n, 87, 127
    1968, 10, 24, 26–27, 89, 92, 93, 126, 127–29
    1972, 95, 96, 135
    1976, 96, 101n, 136
    1980, 90, 101, 136, 141
    1984, 90, 141–42, 145
    1988, 90, 91, 107, 143, 152
    1992, 96, 110, 143n, 155–56
    2000, 82, 193, 197–98, 203
President's Committee on Federal Judicial Selection, 148–49, 153
primary elections, 191
privacy, constitutional right to, 53, 117
    Bork and, 106
    Griswold v. *Connecticut*, 60, 106
    Roberts and, 213
private property, judiciary's protection of, 33, 36–38, 43, 47
    see also business interests

progressives, 38–39
  basic beliefs of, 42
  judicial activism, opposition to,
    39–41, 42–49
  New Deal liberals, *see* New Deal
    liberals, judicial restraint and
  New Progressives, *see* New
    Progressives
  the Senate at midcentury and,
    167–71
Protestant evangelicals, *see*
    evangelicals, Protestant
Proxmire, William, 175
Pryor, David, 173–74
Pryor, Judge David, 207*n*
Pryor, William, 207*n*
public-interest law
  conservatives and, 74–75, 225
  Fortas and, 13
  innovative remedies and, 63–64

Quayle, Dan, 156
Quinn, John, 111–12

Rauh, Joseph, 102*n*
Reagan, Ronald, 75
  economic policy, 101–2, 136–37,
    142, 145, 146, 153, 154
  the judiciary and, 144–52, 225
    Bork nomination, *see* Bork,
      Robert
    federal judges, appointment of,
      102–4, 148–49, 153–54, 202
    O'Connor nomination, 149–50
    Rehnquist elevation to chief
      justice, 4, 150–51
    Scalia nomination, 150, 151
  presidential election of 1980, 101,
    136, 141
  presidential election of 1984, 90,
    141–42, 145
recess appointments, 206
Regents of University of California v.
  Bakke, 74

Rehnquist, Chief Justice William, 82,
    115, 123, 211
  confirmation as chief justice, 4,
    150–51
  illness and death of, 210–11,
    212–13
  Roe v. *Wade* and, 71*n*
Rehnquist Court
  Bush v. *Gore*, 82–83
  judicial activism of, 81–83
Reid, Harry, 208–9
religious schools, tax-exempt status
    of, 140, 146–47
Reno, Janet, 111
Republican National Convention of
    1992, 156
Republican party, 126–58
  Bork nomination and, 9, 78
  Breyer nomination and, 121
  Clinton appointments to the
    federal courts and, 113–14,
    123
  coalition of voters first assembled
    by Nixon, 126–28, 130,
    133–34, 136
  economic and tax policy serving
    the wealthy, 102, 126, 136–37,
    142, 145, 146, 153, 154
  family values and patriotism
    message, 126, 142
  Fortas nomination as chief justice
    and, 19, 20
  Harriet Miers nomination and, 5,
    195, 197, 214–17, 223, 226, 228
  New Deal legacy and entitlement
    programs, 86–87
  New Right, *see* New Right
  1958 congressional elections, 175
  in the South, *see* South, the,
    Republican party in
  Supreme Court scapegoated by,
    31–32, 126, 131–35, 149–52
  *see also individual presidents and
    senators*
Richmond School Board, 151*n*

ripeness, 69*n*
Robb, Charles, 188*n*
Roberts, Chief Justice John, 195, 211–13, 223–24, 225, 226*n*, 227
Robertson, Pat, 79, 140, 155–56
Robinson v. *California*, 53*n*
Roe v. *Wade*, 68–71, 106, 107, 121, 144, 152*n*, 154, 155*n*, 225, 227
Justice Ginsburg on, 80*n*, 117, 118
Roosevelt, Franklin D., 92
Court-packing controversy, 3, 47, 48, 87, 88
Democratic party and New Deal legacy, 85–89
election of, 46, 47
Supreme Court appointments, 47, 88
see also New Deal liberals
Rove, Karl, 195, 196, 208, 215
Rudman, Warren, 108, 109, 174
Russell, Richard, 19, 20–22, 29, 164, 165, 175, 183
Rutledge, Justice Wiley, 88

Sacco and Vanzetti, 88
SANE/FREEZE, 107
Santorum, Rick, 203
Scaife Foundation, 201
Scalia, Justice Antonin, 82, 150, 151, 154
Schlafly, Phyllis, 79*n*, 203*n*
School District of Abington v. *Schemp*, 139
Securities and Exchange Commission (SEC), 13, 88
segregation, *see* desegregation
Senate, U.S., 159–93
appointment of senators by the state legislatures, 4*n*, 160*n*, 171*n*
apprenticeship system, 163, 169, 179–80
Appropriations Committee, 20
areas of expertise of senators, 164

Armed Services Committee, 20, 180
campaign costs and contributions, 178, 183
Commerce Committee, 178
committee system, 164, 166, 179, 181–82
compared to the House of Representatives, 160–62
confirmation of judicial appointments, *see* Senate confirmation of judicial appointments
conservatism of, at midcentury, 165–66, 167, 183
courtesy, convention of, 165, 182
delay as strategy in, 23, 157, 160
Democratic Steering Committee, 20
filibusters and the cloture rule, 20–21, 25*n*, 27, 164*n*, 175, 192–93, 224
George W. Bush's judicial appointment and, 204–10, 218, 219*n*
the "nuclear option," 207, 208, 210, 224–25
folkways of, 162–67, 182–83
erosion of, 174, 178–82, 223
nonconformity, price of, 167–71, 180
Foreign Relations Committee, 180
free debate in, 161, 162, 179
as hierarchical institution, 159, 163, 166–67, 181, 183
"holds" in, 157
independence of individual senators, 161, 162, 181, 183, 190–93, 223
as inner-directed chamber, 159, 163, 166, 183
institutional patriotism of, 165, 174, 182
Lyndon Johnson's election to, 11–12

Senate, U.S. (*continued*)
  Lyndon Johnson's understanding
    of, 17–22, 29, 31
  Joint Committee on Non-Essential
    Expenditures, 169–70
  Judiciary Committee, 98, 103, 116
    George W. Bush's
      appointments to federal
      courts and, 203–10
    confirmation hearings for
      Supreme Court justices, *see*
      Senate confirmation of
      judicial appointments,
      Judiciary Committee
      hearings
  leadership powers, 161, 162, 223
  lobbying directed at, 176
  mass media and, 166, 176–79, 181,
    183, 184–85, 221, 229
    folkways of the Senate and,
      163, 164
    local news outlets, 177*n*–78*n*
  at midcentury, 160–73
  national prominence of individual
    senators, 162, 176, 178–79,
    181, 183, 184, 186
  1958 congressional elections, and
    change in membership of,
    175
  nonbinding resolutions, 180
  nonconformists, treatment of,
    167–71, 172, 180, 183
  partisanship in, increased, 190–93,
    194, 200–11, 216, 224
  reciprocity, spirit of, 164–65
  Republican control of, 3, 101, 102,
    122, 198*n*, 200, 204
  staff of senators, growth in, 181
  "the Gang of 14," 209–10, 218, 219,
    224–25
  transformation of, 159–93
  2002 congressional elections, 204
  2004 congressional elections, 206
  unanimous-consent agreements,
    164*n*–65*n*, 209*n*

Senate confirmation of judicial
    appointments
  changes in model Senate behavior
    and, 29–30, 32, 159–60, 179
  democratization of, 216–17,
    220–29
  history of the confirmation
    process to the Supreme
    Court, *see* history of the
    confirmation process to the
    Supreme Court
  increased importance of a
    senator's voting record,
    104–5, 133*n*, 185–86, 187–89
  Judiciary Committee hearings, 15,
    22–27, 30, 108, 109, 119–20,
    123, 132, 150*n*, 157, 186, 213,
    214–15, 216, 219
  media coverage and, 156–57, 183,
    186
  modern politics of, 182–93,
    194–95, 197, 200–19, 227–29
  recess appointments, 22*n*–23*n*
  reform, calls for, 229
  voice votes, 3, 4, 11, 15
  see also names of individuals
separation of powers, 22, 24, 28, 45,
    214, 216
September 11, 2001, 199–200
Shapiro, Martin, 51–52
Shefter, Martin, 142
Shelby, Richard, 187–88
Sheldon, Reverend Louis, 79*n*
Sierra Club, 176*n*
Silberman, Judge Laurence, 201
"silent majority," Nixon's, 128, 130
Simon, Paul, 108
Sinclair, Barbara, 176
Sinking Fund Cases, 45
Sixth Amendment, 52
60 Minutes, 75
slavery, 37
Smith, William French, 150*n*
Snider, Dee, 178
social issues and legislation

judicial activism of the Warren Court, *see* Warren Court, judicial activism of
judicial restraint of New Deal liberals, judicial restraint, the New Deal liberals and
New Progressives and, 94–95, 97–99, 100*n*
New Right and, 126, 137–38, 141, 142, 144, 145, 146–48, 149–50, 153–54, 156
see also individual issues, e.g. abortion; family values; prayer in school
social revolution of 1960s, 130
Social Security Act of 1935, 87
Souter, Justice David, 82, 108–9, 148*n*, 155*n*, 156
South, the
Christian academies in, 139–40, 146–47
Democratic party in, *see* Democratic party, in the South
racial integration and, 24, 134–35, 138–39
Republican party in, 25*n*, 101, 188, 191
the New Right and, 137–43, 158
Nixon's "southern strategy," 126, 127–29, 133–35
Specter, Arlen, 104*n*–105*n*, 179–80, 190, 209, 215
Spock, Dr. Benjamin, 10
standing-to-sue doctrine, 30–31, 34, 59–61, 65
Bork on expanded, 76
state abortion laws and, 69
Starr, Kenneth, 201, 211
state criminal proceedings, Warren Court and, *see* criminal law and rights of the accused, Warren Court and
state legislatures, reapportionment of, 54, 56–57

states' rights, 37
States' Rights party, 25*n*
Stennis, John, 21
Stephanopoulos, George, 114
Stevens, Justice John Paul, 82
Stevenson, Adlai, 14
Stevenson, Coke, 12
Stewart, Justice Potter, 23*n*
Roe v. *Wade* and, 70
Stone, Chief Justice Harlan Fiske, 1, 22, 23, 67*n*, 88, 221
Strauss, David, 82–83
strict constructionists, 10, 80, 127
see also judicial restraint
Subversive Activities Control Board, 19
Sununu, John, 109
Supreme Court
Jewish justices, 1, 3, 118
judicial activism, *see* judicial activism
presidential appointments to, *see names of individual presidents and appointees*
Roosevelt Court-packing controversy, 3, 47, 48, 87, 88
Senate confirmation of justices to, *see* history of the confirmation process to the Supreme Court; Senate confirmation of judicial appointments
strict constructionists, *see* strict constructionists
see also individual decisions

Taft, William Howard, 221
Takings Clause, 81
Taney, Chief Justice Roger, 36–37
tax policy of Republicans favoring upper-income Americans, 102, 126, 145, 146
televangelists, 140, 141, 226
television, *see* mass media

Thomas, Justice Clarence, 82, 156, 188
  confirmation battle, 4, 5, 78–80, 109–10, 157, 182*n*, 188*n*–89*n*, 219*n*
  credentials of, 109
Thompson, Larry, 202*n*
Thornberry, Justice Homer, 21–22
Thurmond, Strom, 25–27, 30, 134–35, 168*n*
Tilden, Samuel, 197*n*
Tocqueville, Alexis de, 160
Tower, John, 180
Tribe, Laurence, 61, 114
Truman, Harry S., 89
Tushnet, Mark, 192
Tydings, Joseph, 133*n*

unions, 91–92
  see also labor
United Mine Workers, 77
United Mine Workers v. *Johnson Controls,* 74
United States Catholic Conference, 72, 74
United States v. *Carolene Products, 67n*
University of Chicago Law School, 201

vagueness, void for, 71
Vietnam War, 9–10, 14–15, 16, 17, 94
  antiwar movement, 93, 96*n*
Voting Rights Act of 1965, 18

Wallace, George, 89, 90, 128–29
war on terror, 199–200
Warren, Chief Justice Earl, 23*n*
  appointment as chief justice, 50
  credentials of, 50*n*, 221
  Miranda opinion, 63
  retirement as chief justice, 10, 17, 18, 23–24, 28, 58, 68, 131
  see also Warren Court
Warren Court, 50–67, 80, 194, 225
  Fortas confirmation hearings, as issue in, 24–27, 28, 30

judicial activism of, 10, 15, 30, 33, 34, 50–66, 83–84
  criticism of, 51–52, 61–62
  legacy of, 80–84
  judicial remedies and, 62–64
  Nixon's scapegoating of, 10, 24, 26, 126, 127, 129, 136
  opinion-writing technique, 62–63
Washington Post, 15
Watergate, 95*n*, 97, 136
Watt, James, 75*n*
Webster v. *Reproductive Health Services,* 154–55, 156
Weissberg, Robert, 90
welfare state, 94, 122
  New Deal legacy, 86–87
  Nixon's economic policy, 130
  Reagan economic policy and, 153
  Republican campaigns and, 128
Westmoreland, General William, 75
Weyrich, Paul, 140
White, Justice Edward, 22, 23, 114
Whitewater Land Development Company, 121, 123, 201
Whittaker, Justice Charles, 222
Whittaker, Judith, 149
Wilder, Douglas, 155
Wilkinson, Judge J. Harvie, 52
Wilson, Woodrow, 190, 221, 222*n*
Wolfson, Louis, 28*n*, 131, 185
Women's Equity Action League, 72
women's groups and judicial confirmations, 107
Women's Legal Defense and Education Fund, 102
Women's Legal Defense Fund, 72, 98
women's movement, 72

Yale Law Review, 12
Yale University, 12–13
Yaloff, David, 150*n*
Yarborough, Ralph, 133*n*
Yeakel, Lynn, 190